JAN DEFIANTLY BURST OUT, "I DON'T THINK OUR SON KILLED himself. I think s_____ _____ ___ __ _____ ____ and then made it look

The words  low Mark would sco_____tive imagination, but _____

Finally he as_____

"Because I remember when Tim was a boy how he hated guns."

Again he studied her, "What reason would someone have for killing him, Jan? Tim wasn't exactly a tough guy who made enemies."

"Don't you read the newspapers, Mark? This is the marijuana-growing capital of the state!"

He nodded, an unexpected compassion in his eyes. "Even if Tim were involved with drugs, that doesn't mean he was murdered."

"But there's something else, something I didn't find out until I started poking around here." Jan combed a shaking hand through her hair.

"Did you tell anyone you suspect it *wasn't* suicide?" Mark's tone suddenly sharpened.

"No. I didn't think that would be a good idea yet." She hesitated. "Although I suppose what I was thinking may have been obvious from the questions I asked."

Mark's gaze flicked back the way they had come on the trail, then ahead, like a hunter suddenly wary that he might be prey as well as predator. He clamped a hand on her writst, and she resisted an unwanted urge to melt into the shelter of his arm.

"Why do you ask if I told anyone?"

His gaze returned to meet hers. "Because I also have doubts Tim killed himself. I also think he may have been murdered."

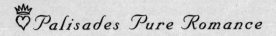
♛♡ *Palisades Pure Romance*

SEARCHING FOR

Stardust

Lorena McCourtney

Palisades is a division of Multnomah Publishers, Inc.

SEARCHING FOR STARDUST
published by Palisades
a division of Multnomah Publishers, Inc.

© 1999 by Lorena McCourtney
International Standard Book Number: 1-57673-414-5

Design by Andrea Gjeldum
Cover illustration by Aleta Jenks

Scripture quotations are from:
The Holy Bible, New International Version (NIV) © 1973, 1984 by
International Bible Society, used by permission
of Zondervan Publishing House

Palisades is a trademark of Multnomah Publishers, Inc., and is registered in
the U.S. Patent and Trademark Office.

Printed in the United States of America

For information:
MULTNOMAH PUBLISHERS, INC.•P.O. BOX 1720•SISTERS, OR 97759

Library of Congress Cataloging-in-Publication Data:
McCourtney, Lorena.
    Searching for stardust / Lorena McCourtney.
        p. cm.
    ISBN 1-57673-414-5 (alk. paper)
    I. Title.
    PS3563.C3449S43   1999
    813'.54—dc21   99-21997
                                                                CIP

    99 00 01 02 03 04 05—10 9 8 7 6 5 4 3 2 1

1

JAN YANKED ON THE HANDLE OF THE UMBRELLA, RIPPING IT free from the tangle of thorned blackberry bushes guarding the steep trail. She raised it over her head, but the umbrella was useless now, rain drizzling through a dozen puncture holes and a ragged tear in the taut, blue fabric. She let the tip droop to the ground and uneasily surveyed the rocky trail ahead.

They'd told her she'd have to walk, but she'd never expected anything like this. Fifty feet ahead, where a rickety footbridge crossed a ragged ravine, misty spray rose from unseen waters roaring down the mountainside. Beyond the bridge, the trail disappeared into a maze of trees with their tops lost in the foggy mist, giving an eerie feeling of world's end just above her.

Hastily she turned to look back the way she had come, seeking a reassuring glimpse of her car below. Yet from here she could see nothing of the sleek, silver Mercedes, only the battered front end of the hulking truck parked in the mud hole where the road ended.

She glanced at her watch. Almost four o'clock. Back home in the manicured yard encircling her Portland house, daylight lingered past six on these late March days. But here on this rain-shrouded southern Oregon mountainside, early darkness lurked in the canopy of heavy branches overhead, waiting to trap her on the trail. An earthy scent of moldering leaves and damp forest, fir and pine and madrone, hung in the air. Perhaps she should turn back, return and make a fresh start in the morning.

Perhaps she should turn back and *not* return, abandon all this as foolish and pointless. She had no idea how far it was to the cabin, no idea what hostile reception she might encounter. Did this isolated trail actually lead *anywhere*?

Perhaps the couple in the secondhand store, who'd looked like ragged holdovers from some seventies hippie's commune, had deliberately given her false information. Maybe they were even now laughing gleefully about sending the city woman with her fancy car and stylish boots and expensive suede jacket on some wild goose chase in the woods.

Yet, even as she stood there undecided, fresh questions joined those that had haunted her for the past three months. Had Tim once walked this very trail, crossed this precarious bridge, felt cousins of these raw raindrops on his lanky frame? She closed her eyes, desperately seeking some remnant of his presence, but all she could feel was the cold drizzle on her upturned face.

Firmly giving herself a mental shake, she snapped the useless umbrella shut. No, she wasn't turning back. She'd come this far, both physically and emotionally, and she wasn't giving up now.

She looked down only once as she crossed the shaky bridge, saw an explosion of tumbling white water through the cracks, and then grimly clutched the metal cable that served as a handrail until she reached solid ground ahead. Beyond the next twist in the trail, around a rocky outcropping, the roar of the creek oddly faded, leaving only the uneven patter of rain punctuated by the heavier plop of drops falling from the wet branches. And something else...

Her neck and shoulder muscles tensed as she strained to hear the faint rumble. The sound became louder as she listened, and then its identity was unmistakable: a vehicle winding up the narrow canyon road below where she'd parked her car. She'd seen no nearby houses, no roads turning off, so it had to be coming here. And now she felt trapped, caught between the unknown ahead and the unknown behind. Perhaps suspecting the couple in the store merely of laughing at her was dangerously naive. They'd directed her to this remote trail, where she was now alone and isolated and vulnerable.

If she hurried, she might be able to reach the cabin before whoever was in the car caught up with her...

She rejected that desperate idea. Even if she could outrun someone stalking her, the cabin and its inhabitants were not necessarily a haven of safety.

Carefully, she left the trail and went up a slope strewn with loose rocks where her tracks couldn't be seen. She was panting by the time she hid behind a screen of brush on the rocky outcropping overlooking the trail, her clothes damp from rain and perspiration, her usual sleek blond hairdo a tangle of wet strands and twigs.

The moments passed with glacial slowness. Cold rain dribbled down her neck. A deer peered at her with liquid dark eyes, then fled in elegant, stiff-legged leaps. A muscle in her leg cramped, and she cautiously changed position to relieve it. From here the growl and crash of the creek was again audible, and she strained to catch some giveaway sound of human activity over it.

No sounds, but—there he was! A broad-shouldered figure in khaki pants and heavy boots, the hood of a clear plastic rain jacket loosely draped over his head. He was obviously better prepared for the weather than she was. She scrunched down behind the brush to make herself smaller. Yet there was something oddly familiar about that determined stride…

A moment later she knew why. In disbelief she watched as he paused almost directly below her, the familiar dark hair revealed when he pushed back the hood.

He studied the trail and hillside warily as if he sensed an unseen presence, and a peculiar and totally unexpected pang flooded through her. How many times had she told herself she didn't miss him, didn't need him, didn't want him, didn't love him? Yet if that were really true, why did she have to keep repeating it to herself, why did she feel this inexplicable yearning now as she watched him?

He turned, as she had, to look back toward the cars below, his edginess almost palpable. A few months ago she'd spotted him at the mall and ducked out of sight. Another time when an encounter was unavoidable, she'd simply nodded coolly to him. Times when he'd called her since the divorce, she'd determinedly held herself remote from him. Yet three months ago, wrapped in mutual anguish, she'd silently clung to him, desperately grateful for the strength of his presence.

Now he flipped the hood over his head and started up the trail again, and a peculiar panic that he'd soon be out of sight made her cry out, "Mark!"

He didn't jump nervously at the sound of her voice, but he turned in momentary confusion before he identified it as coming from above. He stepped back, neck craned to look up at her as she wriggled out from behind the brush. "You okay?" His tone was filled more with concern than surprise.

Belatedly, she realized her presence on the isolated trail probably wasn't as much of a shock to him as his presence was to her. He'd no doubt recognized her Mercedes back there in the mud hole.

Sliding down the side of the outcropping was more precarious than the upward climb, and he caught her as she skidded through the last few feet of loose rocks. She automatically clutched his outstretched arms but let go as soon as she regained her balance. For some strange reason, she didn't trust herself not to wrap her arms around him. Instead, not giving him time to question why she was hiding alongside the isolated trail, she leaped to the offensive.

"What are you doing here? Why aren't you at Linhurst?"

"Spring break. No classes this week."

Spring break. She'd lost track of such events after Tim dropped out of school two years ago. But *timing* wasn't the big question, of course. "*Why* are you here?"

"Why are *you* here?" Mark folded his arms across his chest. He wasn't tan—given a winter lived where the old joke was that Oregonians don't tan, they rust—but he still bore a rugged aura of the outdoors. She wondered fleetingly how he'd maintained that aura even when he was working fourteen-hour days in his legal practice. Or, she reminded herself, *telling* her he was working fourteen hours.

Irrelevant, she chided herself sharply. Meaningless as the till-death-do-us-part words they had once uttered.

And now she realized that even though their questions used identical words, the results were as different as Beethoven's *Fifth* played by a child plunking piano keys and a concert pianist giving a command performance. He may have changed occupations and lifestyle, but he hadn't lost the slash-to-the-bone technique that had made a reporter observe during one of his high-profile trials, *"Could you tell a lie or dodge the truth with Mark Hilliard's laser blue eyes nailing you to the witness stand?"* And then to add in sly reference to the questionable character of some of his better-known clients, *"Maybe that's why he seldom puts the clients he's defending on the stand to question them."*

Jan met his gaze. "I was told that a man called Red Dog might know something about Tim's death." She expected Mark to pounce on her for coming here alone, but instead he simply said, "What do you hope to learn from him?"

She started to backtrack, to hide behind the masquerade of a mother's simple need to find closure after a son's death, but instead she defiantly burst out with the truth, not caring if it sounded melodramatic or paranoid. "I want to find out what really happened to Tim! Because I don't think he killed himself. I don't think he sat down and put a gun to his head and pulled the trigger. I think someone deliberately shot him at close range and then made it look like suicide. I think he was *murdered.*"

The words hung like suspended raindrops. This was the first time she'd let them escape the grief-torn landscape of her mind and said them aloud to anyone. Now she expected Mark to scornfully suggest she had an overactive imagination, but he simply studied her thoughtfully.

She also studied him. The years between his transformation from teenage rogue to high-powered attorney to professor in a small Christian college hadn't eroded his ageless good looks. His jaw was still clean cut and angular, his skin youthfully taut over strong cheekbones, his hair still the black of some Native American ancestor far back on his mother's side, his masculine appeal still potent. But no matter how attractive he might be, she'd never actually allow herself to be attracted to him again.

Finally he asked in a tone markedly more controlled than her passionate outburst, "Why do you think that?"

"Because I remember that when Tim was a boy and the two of you went hunting, how he hated guns and never wanted to go again." She didn't go into how disappointed Mark had been with that nonmacho attitude and the fact that Tim turned vegetarian not long after the trip. "I just can't imagine him using a gun for anything. Especially to...kill himself."

"The report said the gun belonged to him," Mark countered with his old lawyer logic.

"Someone else still could have pulled the trigger!"

Again he studied her, and she wondered what he was thinking. Was he seeing her through the eyes of the lawyer he had once been, weighing her credibility, dissecting each word, preparing a ruthless counterattack? Or was he seeing her through the eyes of an ex-husband? Noting the tiny lines at the corners of her eyes and mouth, and the hair that wasn't the rich brown it had been on their wedding day. She had started using golden highlights when the brown turned mousy, and now her hair was all the sophisticated blond her hairdresser called "champagne dawn." Was he also noting that she'd lost a dozen pounds since Tim's death, pounds her already too slender figure didn't need to lose?

Angrily she discarded those thoughts. She didn't care how Mark saw her, she reminded herself. She did care that he apparently thought her suspicions were irrational figments of her despair. Yet arguing that Tim hadn't killed himself because she believed he hated guns was not a particularly strong line of reasoning, she had to admit. Defensively she added, "And there are other things, too. He called me from down here a few times, and once I thought he sounded afraid."

"Afraid of what?"

"I don't know. He didn't actually say he was afraid. It was just something I sensed, something in his voice."

"But what reason would someone have for killing him? Tim wasn't exactly your confrontational type tough guy who went around making enemies."

Mark's logic about Tim's death and the type of person Tim was—kind, caring, gentle, a boy who preferred tending his collection of exotic plants to guns and hunting—suddenly angered her.

"No, he wasn't tough or confrontational, and he didn't belong in an environment like this! Don't you read the newspapers, Mark? This is the marijuana-growing capital of the state! Is your head buried so far in your Bible that you don't know that there have been a half dozen drug-related murders in this area in recent years? This isn't some innocent wonderland just because there are wildflowers and deer and waterfalls instead of crack houses and gang wars."

Something in his eyes told Jan that her harsh words didn't simply bounce off him, and she felt a momentary shaft of guilt for striking out at the faith he'd found since their divorce. She knew her real anger was with her own feelings of despair and helplessness over Tim's death. She half expected him to lash back at her, but, unlike the Mark of bygone years, he held his temper—and his tongue. "I'm sorry," she muttered into the silence.

He nodded, letting her explosion pass, an unexpected compassion in his eyes. "Even if Tim was involved with drugs, that doesn't necessarily mean he was murdered."

"But there's something else, something I didn't find out until I started poking around here, asking for information about Tim from anyone who'd talk to me." Jan combed a shaking hand through the wet, shapeless strands of her hair. "Usually, all I'd get were unfriendly shrugs or negative headshakes—"

"I know."

She paused, briefly curious about that sympathetic response, but she didn't detour to question it. "But occasionally someone would leak a minuscule bit of information or bring up the name of someone I should talk to, and finally one rough-looking guy gave me a little smirk and said, 'You mean ol' Talkin' Tim?'"

"Talkin' Tim?" Mark's eyes narrowed in suspicion. "Tim was never much of a talker. What did he mean by that?" Then his head snapped up so sharply that his dark hair flung raindrops in her face, and she knew he had made the same connection she had.

"You think the guy meant talking as in *informer?* That maybe Tim went to the authorities about some criminal activity—"

"And was murdered for it. Murdered because he talked." She paused, considering. "Or perhaps murdered because he'd let someone know he was *going* to talk."

"This guy suggested you come out here and see Red Dog?"

Jan shook her head. "No. When I asked what Talkin' Tim meant, he got an odd look on his face, as if he thought maybe he'd already said too much, and walked off. But this afternoon I approached a couple in a second-hand store and gave them my usual story about wanting to talk to someone who'd known Tim, wanting to find closure after his death—"

"Did you ever tell anyone that you suspect it *wasn't* suicide?" Mark's tone suddenly sharpened, like the freshly honed blade of a knife.

"No. I didn't think that would be a good idea yet." She hesitated. "Although I suppose what I was thinking may have been obvious from the questions I asked."

Mark's gaze flicked back the way they had come on the trail, then ahead, like a hunter suddenly wary that he might be prey as well as predator. He clamped a hand on her arm so he could shove her behind him if he spotted danger from any direction, and she recognized it as an instinctively protective gesture.

She resisted an unwanted urge to melt into the shelter of his arm and settled instead for not jerking away from the protection he offered. "Why do you ask if I told anyone?"

His gaze returned to meet hers. "Because I also have doubts Tim killed himself. I also think he may have been murdered."

The knowledge that she wasn't alone in her suspicions felt like a door opening on an icy room filled with dangerous shadows. Because if sharp, shrewd, competent Mark thought it too, perhaps it was true. *Murder.*

Once upon a time their thoughts had been so meshed, so linked that they could finish each other's sentences; each knew what the other was thinking from a mere meeting of glances across a room. Back then, when they were so much in love, when they shared such ambitious, glowing dreams, their thoughts spooned together as sweetly as their bodies curved together in sleep at night. But for so long now, even before the hostile divorce five years ago, they had seemed to leap automatically to opposite sides of any question, any issue.

And now…now their thoughts were linked again, and that lost love rose in a bittersweet cloud—

No! She shook her head. She would not let old feelings rise up to confuse her. "That's why you're here? To investigate Tim's death?"

"Yes. From the moment I first heard it, that official 'death by self-inflicted gunshot wound' didn't ring true to me. By the time Tim was a teenager, I seldom knew what he was thinking. We were almost strangers. But I don't recall him ever being self-destructive. I want to know what really happened."

"His mental state may have been affected by drugs," Jan suggested reluctantly. For a long time she hadn't wanted to admit Tim was even involved in the drug culture, but he was, of course. "The report said there were traces of marijuana and methamphetamines in his system."

Mark nodded. "But I want to know the full truth. And if someone murdered him, I want to know who."

"Do you think the investigation of his death was perhaps not as thorough as it could have been?" The thought tore at her insides.

"I certainly don't think the authorities would deliberately call it suicide to avoid the bother of a murder investigation simply because Tim was part of the drug culture. But murders have been disguised as suicides before, and the authorities may have been fooled."

"And maybe we're both wrong, and he really did kill himself."

"Yes. But I intend to find out."

"How did you happen to come out to this trail?" She turned to glance back at the rain-shrouded pathway.

"Same way you did. By asking questions."

"If you've also been in the area talking to people, I wonder why we haven't run into each other before this?"

"I just arrived yesterday afternoon."

Wryly she acknowledged his superior investigative abilities. He'd acquired a lead to Red Dog in less than twenty-four hours; it had taken her almost four days.

Mark's gaze swept the canyon below where treetops poked through the misty fog like islands of dark spikes. Then his eyes snapped back to hers as if he'd just reached a decision. "I'll take you back to your car and help you get turned around so you don't get stuck in the mud. Then I'll hike on up to the cabin."

"You can't send me back to the car as if this were

some college field trip and I were one of your students! I'm going too."

"Jan, if someone realizes we suspect murder, we could both be in danger, especially if we get too close to the person who pulled the trigger." He clamped his hands on her shoulders. "This is no time to play some amateur detective game—"

"*Game?* You think anything about Tim's death is a *game* to me?"

A muscle in his jaw ticked. "I'm sorry. I didn't mean that the way it sounded. I know how you feel. I just think it would be better if I go alone. I can let you know this evening what I find out. Where are you staying?"

Jan wasn't even tempted to retreat to the warmth and security of her motel room. She shook off his hands. "I came here to investigate for myself, and I intend to do it."

He eyed her smooth-soled boots, more suitable for mall shopping than trail hiking, and her bare head. Vaguely, she realized she must have dropped the umbrella behind the brush where she'd hidden.

His voice softened. "Jan, you're already soaking wet. I just don't want you getting sick from exposure or slipping and hurting yourself on the rocks or taking unnecessary chances with whatever weirdos or outlaws may be up there at the cabin—"

She heard honest concern in his voice, but she lifted her head with a jerk, ignoring the hair plastered shapelessly to her scalp and the squish of her wet boots. "Your concern for my welfare is admirable, but I've managed to take care of myself for quite some time now, and I can do it here."

His heavy brows tightened in obvious frustration at her stubbornness. But what she said was quite true; she *had* managed to take care of herself quite well. Top listing agent at Morganton Real Estate two years in a row. Second-highest agent in sales last year, headed toward the top spot this year. Speaker on alternative methods of financing at a recent seminar. Award winner for a sales video she'd produced last fall. She'd also managed to keep up payments on the expensive Portland house and paid half cash for that Mercedes sitting down there in the mud hole.

She hadn't managed to take care of herself quite so well emotionally, and sometimes her life felt empty and pointless—but she had no intention of admitting *that* to him.

After a long moment staring into her defiant gaze, he made no comment about her hostile claim of self-sufficiency. He simply turned on his heel and started up the trail, leaving her to follow or retreat as she chose.

2

MARK STALKED UP THE TRAIL FOR SEVERAL HUNDRED YARDS before worry about Jan overrode his anger with her stubbornness. The outcroppings of jagged rocks and twists in the trail cut off sight of her behind him, which made him distinctly uneasy in these isolated surroundings. A concern she probably wouldn't appreciate, he thought wryly, given their rocky past. He stopped to lean against a boulder and made a pretense of removing his boot and shaking something out of it. He waited until she silently passed him, then quickly slipped the boot back on his foot and stepped in behind her. Now he'd have no trouble keeping her in sight.

He studied her back as she strode ahead of him, spine so straight, set of head and shoulders so fiercely determined. She was close enough that he could reach out and touch her, but emotionally, he felt the bottomless chasm separating them. So many times he had wondered if that chasm could somehow be bridged, prayed that it might, even tried tentative steps toward building a foundation for a bridge.

But she was having no part of it. Could he blame her? After what he'd done to their marriage, how he'd betrayed her? And then, after that first arrogant, misguided attempt he'd made to get her back, it was no wonder she'd looked warily and suspiciously on his later attempts to start a new relationship, even deliberately avoided him. He'd spotted her a few times…once when she surreptitiously dodged him in the mall, another time when she drove out of a gas station to evade him. And she'd let his messages on her answering machine go unanswered.

She was brilliantly successful in her real estate career. He had heard she'd dated an architect and then a doctor. She'd determinedly built a life without him. Had he any right, simply because he still loved her, to try to invade that life? That was what had kept him from pursuing her as ardently as he'd have liked—the thought that perhaps he had no right even to hope they might get back together.

Yet, was it mere coincidence that they'd chosen this same time to come to the area of Tim's death to investigate? That they'd ended up, this same day and hour, walking this misty trail? Or was the Lord's hand working here? Could he have thrown them together, not only to join forces in learning the truth about their son but also as a gateway to building a new love?

Guide me Lord. Help me find out what really happened to Tim. Show me how to do your will with my love for Jan. Let me know how to show her your love and salvation.

Jan stopped so abruptly that he almost crashed into her. Over her shoulder he spotted a dull glimmer of something ahead.

"That must be the cabin," she whispered.

He took the lead and she followed. A hundred feet farther on, he also stopped abruptly where they were still hidden by the trees. The cabin, a haphazard structure of rusty metal roofing and unpainted plywood and board slabs with the bark still clinging, stood in a ragged clearing. A narrow, leaning structure that was almost a caricature of an outhouse huddled nearby. A tumbledown fence of chicken wire surrounded weeds in what might have been a garden plot at one time. Smoke rose from a leaning stovepipe.

Mark stared, trying to picture his son in this place. But he couldn't. No matter how hard he tried. Any more than he could picture Tim dead.

O God, help us...

Had Tim lived under these primitive conditions? Jan wondered in dismay as they watched the cabin, a spiral of smoke the only sign of life. She thought of Tim's big, airy bedroom back at her Portland home...its private bath, entertainment center with TV and VCR and CD player, his electronic games, motorcycle posters, and workout equipment. Had he really preferred living like *this?*

"May I make a suggestion?" Mark's voice was so low she strained to hear him.

"Yes, of course."

"I think we should take it slow and easy here. Present ourselves to this Red Dog simply as grieving parents and not give him or anyone else in the cabin reason to think we suspect murder."

"We are grieving parents." She took a shaky breath. "Do you ever feel more than grief, Mark? Do you ever feel...guilt? Guilt that maybe this wouldn't have happened if we'd been better parents? Guilt that maybe Tim wouldn't have been in this forsaken place to take a bullet if we'd managed to keep our marriage together?"

Mark didn't try to comfort her or make a case for their innocence. He simply nodded. "All the time. I feel we brought him into the world…and then we…*I*…failed him."

For a moment all the old bewilderment rose like a choking flood in Jan's throat. Where had it all gone wrong? Their love and marriage, their beautiful baby… She shook her head, feeling the same, old, impotent helplessness that had struck when Tim left home, the pain that had slashed deep into her soul when he died. "Until Tim left home, I never had a clue that anything was wrong in his life. His school grades weren't good, but he never got into trouble. I thought everything was fine. And then one evening I came home and he was just…gone."

She tensed, knowing she was wide open for criticism or accusation about paying too much attention to her work and too little to Tim, a recurring theme of guilt for her, but Mark was lost in thought.

He sighed deeply. "I think about how, if I'd found the Lord earlier in life, I could've reached out sooner to Tim with my faith, and it might have changed the whole path of his life. My failure to open his eyes and heart to the Lord is one of the biggest regrets of my life."

Mark's faith. This, too, was a puzzle and bewilderment to her. He had no family background in faith. Where had it come from? She doubted his father, tough, hard-drinking, logging-legend Oscar Hilliard, had ever been in a church before his own funeral. Mark himself was better known in their younger days for his exuberant ability to outrun a police car in his souped-up pickup than for any pious spiritual inclinations, and during their marriage they'd only attended church when it seemed professionally worthwhile.

If asked at any time before he accepted Christ, she would have said Mark was the last person in the world she'd ever have expected to "get religion." On the surface he did indeed appear to have changed, and sometimes she wondered if the lack of a spiritual element in her own life was part of the emptiness she often felt. In fact, earlier on she had felt a curiosity, even a tentative pull toward the faith Mark had embraced, but Tim's death had cut off any vague leanings in that direction.

"Regrets that we didn't take him to Sunday school can't change anything now." She lived with a mountain of regrets and guilt, but Mark's words about the focus of his regret merely angered her. She dismissed them with a sharp jerk of her hand. "What matters now is learning the truth about his death."

He grabbed her arm, and she saw a flare of anger in his own eyes, but before he could say anything, a sound made them both glance toward the cabin. The plank door inched open, board squeaking against board although no movement showed within the dark crack.

"I was told to make plenty of noise when I arrived. If Red Dog thinks someone is trying to sneak up on him, he's been known to blast a shotgun welcome." Mark stepped into the open, lifting his arm in a friendly wave. "Hello! Anybody home?"

Jan slipped up beside him, curling her hand around his other arm to further emphasize that they were just a harmless, friendly couple.

The board door opened wider and a skinny, wiry man stepped into the shadowed opening. Jan could make out long, brick red hair, a sharp nose, and a shaggy red beard. He was dressed in faded bib overalls and a once white T-shirt, with the unlikely addition of what appeared to be new and expensive Nikes on his feet. He was no sitcom version of a good-natured hillbilly, however. Jan could almost feel hair-trigger nerves crackling across the clearing. She suddenly suspected he knew all about the questions she and Mark had been asking around town, and apprehension snapped like a pit bull at her nerves. Other people had been unfriendly, even openly resentful of her questions, but never before had she encountered nerves poised on explosion. So *why* was he so nervous?

"There's a No Trespassing sign at the bottom of the trail!" The man gestured them back the way they had come.

Jan had seen the weathered board with the warning slashed across it in red paint, but she had decided to ignore it, as Mark apparently had also.

"Yes, we saw it," Mark called back genially. His arm tightened on Jan's hand, and he pulled her toward the cabin. "And we don't mean to intrude, but we're Tim Hilliard's parents, and someone told us a man named Red Dog who lived up here had known him quite well. Losing Tim…he was our only child, you know…has been very difficult for us, and we just wanted to talk to someone who'd been a good friend to him these last couple of years."

By the time Mark finished his chatty speech, they were within a half dozen feet of the cabin. The man's vigilant stance didn't change, and no smile parted that red beard, but Jan didn't see a shotgun aimed at them although that didn't mean there wasn't one just out of sight behind the door. Up close, Jan realized he was considerably younger than the red beard made him look from a distance, probably not more than a few years past Tim's nineteen. She could also see his eyes now, a murky, river-dark shade of green.

"What d'ya want to talk about?" His gaze narrowed, darting from Mark to her and back again.

"You are Red Dog?" Mark asked. The red beard dipped fractionally in reluctant affirmative. "And this is where Tim's suicide occurred?"

Jan noted that Mark carefully made no pause before the word *suicide,* did nothing that might suggest their skepticism.

"Yeah. I was gone for a few days. When I come home, Tim was right there." He pointed a bony finger at the weathered wooden steps at his feet. "Dead. So I went back to town and called the cops."

The rain, which had let up for a few minutes, suddenly opened into a hammering deluge of icy drops mixed with hail. The wind slanted the cutting mixture into the doorway. Red Dog took a step backward, clearly ready to slam the door.

Mark drew her close. "May we come in?"

Jan would prefer just to stand there and let rain and hail hammer her. The last thing she wanted was to cross those steps where Tim had died. But when Red Dog didn't slam the door in their faces, Mark responded as if the bearded man had offered an invitation and headed for the opening. His arm clamped down even tighter, supporting her as dizziness weakened her knees when she had to step over the dark blotch stained deep into the top step. When they were inside, Red Dog clanged a metal latch behind them, and somehow it felt to Jan like the ominous closing of a trap.

She stood there dripping on the bare wooden floor, looking around cautiously, her stomach churning in spite of the pleasant scents of wood smoke and coffee and simmering stew. The rainy late afternoon light filtering through two grimy windows dimly revealed a homemade wooden table, mismatched chairs, a sagging sofa, and a wood-burning stove that apparently served for both heat and cooking. The room was, in fact, uncomfortably hot and moist. Drying clothes hung from a makeshift clothesline strung across the open rafters of the ceiling. Above was a loft with blankets dangling from an unmade bed. A holster hung from a nail beside the primitive ladder to the loft, the dark handle of a pistol protruding. Mark had died from the bullet of a .38 caliber pistol.

"This here's Bonnie," Red Dog said.

Jan jerked, automatically clutching Mark's arm tighter. Until that moment, she hadn't noticed the dark-haired girl standing behind a makeshift kitchen counter. Unlike Red Dog, a deeper inspection showed the young woman to be older than Jan's momentary first impression of a big-eyed child. She was pretty in spite of a face that was too thin, her long hair in braids tied with fur-and-buckskin thongs. She wore a black turtleneck under a loose denim shirt plus feather earrings. Yet a first impression of Native American ancestry was belied by her very blue eyes and pale skin.

Red Dog twitched a thumb toward the girl. "She didn't move in until after Tim killed himself." The explanation was apparently an effort to deter them from asking the girl questions.

Why? Jan glanced at Bonnie. Did the girl know something he didn't want them to know? Jan clenched her hands to restrain herself from hurling incriminating questions at Red Dog. *It wasn't suicide, was it? Do you know who killed him? Were you standing here when it happened? Or did you do it?*

As if he knew what she was thinking, Red Dog suddenly became busy filling the stove with more wood, his movements quick and jerky as a nervous squirrel. The firebox roared when he opened it, sending out a puff of smoke.

"Would you folks like to sit down? Have some coffee?" Bonnie motioned between the sagging sofa and an aluminum pot on the stove. She had a pleasant voice, soft, almost musical. "Take off your jackets?"

Mark whipped off his rain jacket. "That'd be great."

Jan didn't want coffee, but she recognized that Mark was still trying to put this on the level of a friendly, nonthreatening visit. Here in the small cabin, the vibration of Red Dog's nerves felt like the warning rattles of a snake she had encountered as a child, and she had the uneasy feeling that any unexpected movement on their part could make him strike just as fast.

Red Dog dropped to a wooden chair by the stove, one heel tapping the floor with a jittery rhythm. Reluctantly, Jan nodded yes to the coffee.

"Black, please." With equal reluctance she slipped out of her suede jacket.

Bonnie poured coffee and silently handed the plastic mugs to them. Jan perched on the edge of the old sofa with hers. The heat and dampness from the drying clothes was beginning to make her own feel steamy, and her wool pants clung damply to her legs. Mark carried his coffee to a window fogged with beads of steamy moisture. He elbowed a patch clear to peer outside. A square of plywood crudely patched a broken pane.

"Beautiful country," he offered. "Tim always liked trees and flowers. He grew a small jungle of exotic plants when he lived at home."

"Yeah, Tim could grow stuff all right." Red Dog grinned. Jan thought she detected a sly snicker in the comment, as if he knew some joke they didn't.

"He gave me a bouquet of some pretty purple flowers he grew himself one time," Bonnie said. "Pansies, I think they were."

"So you knew him, too?" Jan asked at the same time that Red Dog threw the girl a venomous glare.

Bonnie glanced at Red Dog, then shrugged her narrow shoulders and flipped a dark braid back over her shoulder. "Not really." She busied herself lighting an old-fashioned lantern on the table, the flicker of the flame throwing leaping shadow-monsters on the walls.

Jan made a mental note that if they didn't learn anything from Red Dog to try to get the girl alone. She sensed the girl had some connection with or affection for Tim. Red Dog stood again, his gaze skittering between them, and Jan had the sudden intuition that he was as much afraid as hostile toward them. Which didn't, she decided uneasily, make him any less dangerous.

Mark sipped the coffee as if it were his favorite espresso and he had all the time in the world to savor it, then moved to sit down next to her. "We had become strangers with Tim during the past couple of years after he left home. Could you tell us about him?"

Red Dog muttered the answer Jan could have predicted. "Not much to tell."

"Did he like hunting, do a lot of it here?"

"Can't hunt deer but for just a few weeks in the fall," Red Dog stated with a virtuous air that Jan doubted matched his actions. She'd bet anything that stew simmering on the stove had fresh venison in it. She noted another gun in a rack beside the door. "Besides, Tim didn't eat meat."

"What became of Tim's gun?" The lantern light brought out the strong line of Mark's jaw and the dark gleam in his hair. Strangely, it reminded Jan of a time so long ago when she was pregnant with Tim and they'd had so little money that she tried to cut Mark's hair herself. It had gotten shorter and shorter as she frantically tried to make the sides come out even, truly a ghastly haircut, and she cried and he comforted and teased her until laughter and love took over…

"The pistol? The cops took it."

Jan wiped away the useless memories. "It surprises me that Tim even owned a gun," she said cautiously. "Back home, he always hated guns."

"Everybody has a gun around here. Lots of survivalists in these mountains. Some of 'em think we're going to have to fight it out with the government one of these days. Always telling us what to do, taking away our rights, pushing us around."

Jan sensed this was a hot subject with Red Dog, one he'd happily expand on, but Mark expertly swung the conversation back on target.

"Had Tim lived here in the cabin with you for long?"

"A few months."

Red Dog was cagey. Jan pressed her lips together. Noncommittal. As if he didn't intend to be pinned down about anything.

"Did Tim talk in his sleep?" Mark went on conversationally. "We heard someone call him Talkin' Tim and thought maybe it was because he talked in his sleep." He shrugged. "He wasn't very talkative to us back home."

Jan blinked at that spur-of-the-moment invention on Mark's part, so far from their real suspicion about the reason for the Talkin' Tim name, but Red Dog laughed, the sound unexpectedly close to a real belly laugh. "Yeah, he talked in his sleep, all right, but that wasn't why we called him Talkin' Tim."

"Oh? Why was he called that?"

Red Dog hesitated, then gave a what-does-it-matter-now shrug. "Ol' Tim, he used to go down by the creek at night and talk to the plants, tell them how tall and pretty they were, have a real conversation with 'em. Sometimes he'd even sing to them."

Offhandedly, as if they were discussing growing cantaloupe or beans in a family garden, Mark said, "Marijuana plants, you mean?"

Another hesitation, another shrug. "Yeah. Sure. Marijuana. And Tim was good at growin' pot. The best. He'd talk to those plants, and I swear they listened and grew just for him."

Red Dog nodded as he spoke, his tone now holding a belligerent pride in Tim's talents, and Jan hovered on the edge of a hysterical burst of laughter. Tim had talked to his plants back home when he was a boy. She never placed any credence in it, but they grew with astonishing exuberance, and she encouraged his interest in his greenhouse jungle that bloomed with exotic, almost unreal-looking flowers. And then he came here and transferred his plant-growing talents to *marijuana,* and they called him Talkin' Tim because he was so good at it.

Jan's loose-jointed thoughts had been detoured, but Mark's hadn't, and he backtracked to Red Dog's first admission. "But you say that Tim did talk in his sleep?"

"Oh, yeah, did he ever. Nightmares, I guess. Weird stuff. Always screaming that something was gonna get him."

Jan leaned forward, her attention no longer slipping into the past. "He was afraid of someone?"

Red Dog tensed, stringy muscles cording his arms above clenched fists. "Not who. *What,*" he insisted. "He talked about seeing dragons and flying lizards. Weird stuff like that. It was them he was scared of. He said that was why he liked to talk to the plants at night because the dragons and lizards weren't out there. Although sometimes the voices were."

"Voices?" Mark repeated in that casual, tell-me-more tone that he'd always used so effectively as a lawyer.

"The voice of someone he was afraid of?" Mark's elbow jabbed her in the ribs, warning her to stay away from this, but she ignored him. They were never going to find out anything if they didn't dig below surface chitchat. "Maybe the voice of someone he was afraid might kill him?"

"No! I told you! It was these weird dragons and flying lizards he was scared of—"

"Imaginary dragons and flying lizards don't put a bullet in a young man's head," she said softly.

"He killed himself!"

"Did he?"

The room went silent, except for the patter of rain-drops on the metal roof, the soft hiss and bubble of stew. And ragged breathing. And the pound of her heart filling the entire room. Moisture and heat and fear.

Her suspicions were out in the open now, hanging there like waiting trapdoors.

Red Dog's skin paled against the frame of red beard and hair, his fists clenching spasmodically. And Jan knew she should have listened to Mark's warnings, should have heeded her own intuition about Red Dog's ready-to-explode nerves. But it was too late now—

"That's why you're really snooping around here, isn't it? Because you don't think Tim killed himself." Red Dog's river-green eyes flared wildly. "You think somebody murdered him. You think *I* murdered him! And you're figurin' on runnin' to the cops!"

"We'll just see about that," Red Dog snarled.

Jan's heart was about to burst from her chest. *I'm not ready to die, Lord! Don't let Mark's death be on my conscience too!*

3

RED DOG LUNGED TOWARD THE LADDER, SMASHING INTO Bonnie and sending her careening backward into the pile of firewood. Jan froze. He was going for the gun in the holster!

"Red Dog, don't—!" Bonnie looked terrified.

Mark jumped to his feet and charged toward Red Dog, no heed for his own safety as he put his body between Jan and the bearded man.

"No!" Fear for Mark lurched Jan to her feet.

He grabbed Red Dog by the shoulders, spinning him around, and they crashed to the floor together. The holstered gun fell with them. The two men wrestled around the kitchen counter. Mark was heavier and stronger but Red Dog was fast and wiry. A flailing foot spun the gun toward Jan, and in spite of her aversion to guns, she snatched it up, afraid Bonnie might get to it first. But Bonnie was crouched behind the wood box, unmoving, watching the men with a horrified expression.

Another flailing foot splintered the bottom rung of the ladder, and Jan fumbled with the holster. Perhaps, if she could get the gun out, she could somehow help Mark.

But Mark didn't need help. A moment later he pushed Red Dog to his feet, one arm holding the bearded man's arm twisted behind him.

"Okay, what's going on here?" Mark demanded. Both men were breathing hard.

"Hey, man, what d'yuh think you're doing?" Red Dog grimaced. "I wasn't going for the gun."

"No? What were you doing then?" Mark didn't release the twisted arm, but he let up enough to take the pained look off Red Dog's face.

Red Dog hesitated, eyeing the gun in Jan's hands in a way that suggested to her he wasn't necessarily telling the truth about the gun. If Mark hadn't acted so swiftly, the situation might have turned out much differently. Finally Red Dog muttered sullenly, "Bonnie, get that book from up there under the bed."

A *book?* Jan wondered, bewilderment adding to her confusion and fear. She knew Bonnie had originally thought Red Dog was going for the gun too.

Bonnie jumped to follow Red Dog's orders, lithely climbing the ladder in spite of the broken rung. A moment later she scrambled down, glanced at the two men, hesitated, then handed a narrow volume to Jan.

"What's this?" Mark inclined his head toward the book.

"It was Tim's. *That's* what I was going after." Red Dog managed to sound self-righteous within the snarl, as if Mark had unfairly wronged him. He jerked his arm, and this time Mark let him go but remained close, ready to overpower him again if need be.

It was a journal or ledger of some kind, Jan realized; the cover, cheap cloth edged with imitation brown leather. She set the gun on the sofa behind her, glad to be rid of it, so she could look at the journal. No name identified the journal's owner, but she instantly recognized Tim's handwriting on the first page, the loose-jointed, sprawling letters that matched his lanky frame.

There was no date, just a dash separating the word *Sunday* from a description of a hike he'd taken and a rare type of wildflower he'd found. Only the scientific name of the flower, *Trillium rivale,* meticulously printed, was easily legible among the scrawled words, as if this flower was more important than anything about himself.

"Read the last few pages," Red Dog commanded.

Still keeping a wary eye on Red Dog, Mark stepped across the room to look at the journal with Jan. Reluctantly, wishing she could pore over every word, Jan turned to the end pages. Along the way she saw the writing gradually changing, becoming smaller and more cramped, and near the end the letters crammed together like rows of toothpicks, all the same size, an *e* indistinguishable from an *l*. Here there was no punctuation, often no spacing between the words. It was as if Tim's frantic thoughts had crowded in on him too fast to separate into words, so fast that they overwhelmed him.

Jan's heart ached as in the last pages she deciphered words about nights when he couldn't sleep or was afraid to sleep, days of despair and hopelessness and black feelings of worthlessness, jeering voices that often harangued him, eerily specific descriptions of the monsters that came to him in the night. It was a word graph of a deteriorating mental condition, a downward plunge into chaos. The journal ended with a repetition of two words, whether his own thoughts or a deadly command of the voices, she didn't know: *"doitdoitdoitdoitdoit."*

"Oh, M-Mark…" Pain, hot and suffocating, swept over her at the clear revelation of Tim's deteriorating mental condition.

"He killed himself. He really did kill himself."

Jan sagged against Mark as his hoarse whisper echoed her own stark, inescapable conclusion. His arms went around her, supporting her, and they clung together as they had at the funeral, shutting out the other mourners then, shutting out Red Dog and Bonnie now. Yet the support was more than the strength of his physical comfort. Jan felt a joining on a far deeper level, her emotions reaching back into the love they had once shared, the love that had been so alive and vital, the love that had created this son now speaking to them from this strange journal.

"Right," Red Dog interrupted, still self-righteous. "He killed himself. So don't be tryin' to pin nothin' on me."

Jan shook her head. Her throat ached, a physical pain, as if a ruthless arm held her in a death grip, but another pain stabbed even deeper into her soul. Tim's pain, Tim's despair and confusion, the utter aloneness of his words as his mind splintered and collapsed. She felt the black pit of his depression, heard the voices raging in his head. Oh, Tim, Tim, Tim…Tim dying here, so lost and alone.

Suddenly she realized how she was clinging to Mark. She didn't want to cling to him, didn't want to remember the power of his embrace, how it gave her the feeling of…coming home. *No!* She thrust herself away from him, then turned to Red Dog.

"Why didn't you *help* him?" She let her anger with him override her confused feelings toward Mark. She shook the journal at Red Dog. "You must have seen what was happening to him! Why didn't you take him to someone? Why didn't you get help for him?"

"I did tell him he was actin' nuttier'n a fruitcake," Red Dog said defensively. "I knew he had some bad trips on meth, but I never knew how far off the deep end he was until I read this stuff."

Jan looked up at Mark. Tim had needed help, desperately needed help, and this was what he'd gotten. Red Dog telling him he was "nuttier'n a fruitcake." Yet even as she blasted the silent accusation, she saw a raw truth that went beyond anything Red Dog had done. She and Mark had failed Tim so completely that he wouldn't even turn to them in his most desperate time of need. He'd preferred a final exit to coming to them. That truth made her knees sag again, but this time she turned away from Mark and slumped to the sofa.

Mark's face looked as pale and stricken as she felt, but he pulled himself together quickly enough to see a gaping hole in Red Dog's neat, not-my-fault, wrap-up of the situation.

"So if it did happen exactly as the authorities said, why are you afraid of us?" Mark challenged bluntly. "If you're so innocent, why does our being here make you so nervous and jumpy?"

"I'm not scared of you," Red Dog blustered, but his fidgety gaze didn't meet Mark's. "But *she's*—" his head jerked toward Jan—"been running all over asking questions, puttin' it in peoples' heads that Tim might of been murdered. Then she shows up here, and *you're* with her. And if the two of you, law-abiding, tax-paying, church-going Mr. and Mrs. Upright Citizen, start yelling murder, the cops are gonna listen. They'll start another investigation. And then I'll be the one they try to fry."

"Why?"

Red Dog hesitated as if he were going to stonewall, but then he shrugged. "Tim really lost it here a couple weeks before Christmas. He went around shooting at those 'voices' and took out a couple of windows." He nodded toward the plywood patch nailed over a broken pane. "So I told him to just pick up and get out. Then after he was gone, I found some money I had was missing. When I tracked him down at a place over on Hangman Creek, he claimed he didn't know anything about it, but I warned him if he didn't get it back to me real quick that he'd be sorry. *Dead* sorry. There were plenty of people there who heard me threaten him." He hesitated and then added reluctantly, "I guess I probably threatened a few of them too, if they got in my way. Sometimes my temper kind of…roars out of control. So if the two of you raise a big ruckus and the cops start checking and latch on to all that…"

"The journal makes his suicidal state of mind plain enough. Didn't the authorities use it in their determination that he'd committed suicide?"

"I never showed it to 'em. There's some…uh…stuff in there, names and deals and stuff, that I figured they didn't need to know."

"So he brought the money back here when you weren't home and then sat down on the front steps and killed himself?" Mark crossed his arms against his chest and lifted his eyebrows.

"He came back and killed himself, and then I found I'd been wrong about the money being missing. I'd moved it a couple times for safekeeping and just forgot where I'd hid it last. Tim had never taken it after all." Red Dog blinked, then covered his small surge of emotion with a savage kick at the stack of firewood. "I should of known he wouldn't. Tim was a good guy, not a low-down thief."

Jan's head felt murky, clouded by these bizarre standards of honor. Being good at raising illegal marijuana was commendable; taking money from a friend was punishable by violence.

"But if the authorities started accusing you, you do have the journal to show them." Mark apparently was still unconvinced that his and Jan's suspicions were the only source of Red Dog's nervousness.

"I know it's Tim's journal. *You* know it's Tim's journal. I know it proves Tim killed himself. So do you. But the cops, who knows about cops? They start thinking murder, some hotshot wants to make a name for himself by nailing a nasty ol' drug-dealing murderer, the journal 'accidentally' disappears, and I'm a sittin' duck. Tim didn't have any other enemies." Red Dog hesitated again, red eyebrows pulled together in a scowl. "Not that I was his enemy, because I wasn't. But it would look bad to the cops."

"In a way, it looks as if we were all his enemies." Jan bowed her head and clutched the journal to her chest, desperately wishing she could undo the past, somehow go back and start all over again. Unexpectedly she felt a touch on her arm.

"He loved you, he really did," Bonnie said, her voice low but urgent, her blue eyes luminous with concern. "Sometimes he talked about how he was going to get clean and go home and make a whole new start. But his head was just so messed up with pot and meth—"

"I think it's time you left." Red Dog motioned

toward the door. Jan didn't protest. She tucked the journal under her arm. Red Dog eyed it warily. "You figuring on going to the cops with that?"

Jan and Mark exchanged wordless glances. "No," Mark said gruffly. "We just want it because it was Tim's."

Red Dog suddenly snatched the journal away from Jan. He flipped through it, tearing out pages here and there, then thrust them into the stove. They disappeared in an instant roar of flame. He handed what was left of the fire-censored journal back to Jan, his green eyes triumphant, as if he figured he'd outsmarted them after all.

Mark wrapped his arm around Jan's shoulders as she edged across the stained steps again. He didn't remove his arm as they headed toward the opening in the trees, the trail barely visible in the foggy mist and near darkness, her slender back within the curve of his arm, her hip pressed tight against his. In spite of the rain, her hair still held a faint fragrance of some delicately flower-scented shampoo. It all felt so good, so right. Except that under these agonizing circumstances, could anything really be "right"?

Yet he didn't release his grip, and she didn't pull away. Perhaps that was only because she was numbly unaware of the contact, but he felt a brief surge of hope. Was there yet a chance for them, in spite of all his past mistakes, all this pain that now engulfed them?

At the edge of the woods, she paused and looked back at the dim glow from the window of the cabin. "He really did kill himself, didn't he?" she asked softly.

"There's no doubt about it now. I think about that old saying, 'Be careful what you wish for. You may get it.'"

He understood her meaning immediately. For them it was, "Be careful what you want to know, because you may find out." And they had found out.

"Would it have been better if our suspicions had been confirmed, and he had been murdered?" He asked the question as much of himself as of her.

She shook her head, hair brushing his cheek as she dipped her head, her voice muffled against the collar of her jacket. "There's no way anything could make any of this *better*."

"But there's almost a feeling of…of letdown…" His voice trailed off because he wasn't certain himself exactly what he meant.

"Yes." She tilted her head back to look up at him, the gray-green of her eyes lost in the darkening shadows, but understanding and agreement in her voice. "I came here all fired up with the idea that I'd find out who killed him. Bringing the guilty person to justice was something I could still *do* for Tim. Angry mother as avenging angel, bringing justice down on the wicked. Maybe, subconsciously, I thought if it were murder then someone else would be to blame. But now the only person I find to point an accusing finger at is myself. I'm to blame for Tim's death, not some murderer with a gun."

She'd put into words exactly what he meant about "letdown." He, too, had desperately wanted to *do* something for his son by finding a murderer. And his own finger pointed at himself instead.

"Oh, Jan, hon…" He turned her to him and wrapped both arms around her, his jaw against her temple. Mist dampened her hair, but the moisture at the corner of her eye was tears. He sought what comfort he could think of to offer her. "I did research on schizophrenia for a case one time, and Tim's hallucinations and voices sound much like that."

"And we failed him so badly that he wouldn't even come home to us for help when he desperately needed it."

"The person most desperately in need of help doesn't always know he needs it." Oh, how true that had been about himself! Desperately in need of a Savior, yet living most of his life without ever knowing it.

He'd tried to talk to Tim about his newfound faith before Tim left home, but by then they were almost strangers. Even more important, perhaps, was that Tim was also aware of some of his father's wrongdoings. So it was no surprise that Tim had put so little stock in anything his father had to say, and his only response to Mark's talk about Christ and salvation was a vague, "Well, I'll think about it."

"If we're going to point accusing fingers, I make an even better target," he added. But somehow he doubted Jan even heard, so deep was she in her own remorse and guilt.

A glazed look of despair spread over her face. "Now I wonder if his mental state was deteriorating even before he left home. And I was too wrapped up in networking and getting listings and making deals to notice."

"Tim was never one to share with anyone what he was thinking or feeling—"

"And what does that say about me as a mother?"

"Don't do this to yourself, Jan."

"I remember once when he was younger—oh,

everyone at the office thought it was so cute!—I was so busy that to get my attention, Tim finally called the receptionist and made an official appointment with me so he could talk about my coming to a class party."

"And you went, didn't you?"

"Yes, but he shouldn't have had to make an *appointment* with me."

Mark shook his head. "Don't do this to yourself, Jan."

"What am I supposed to do? Go on as if nothing happened? Pretend none of it was my fault? Sell more houses? Make more money? Join a club? Get a hobby? Look for a new husband?"

"You could open your heart to the Lord."

She broke away from his embrace. "Will that bring Tim back? Is God going to perform a miracle? Will I look up and Tim will be standing at the door, strong and healthy and smiling?" She answered her own question with a fierce shake of her head. "No. No miracles."

"I believe God gives us a daily miracle, considering how minuscule we are in the midst of all he's created, that the Lord still knows and loves each one of us, that he's concerned about our daily lives."

"Then why didn't he save our son?"

Her grief was so strong, it was almost a physical force. He longed to touch her, to offer her the comfort of his embrace, the strength of his faith. But he couldn't. Not yet. So he gave her what he could: the truth.

"Jan, I believe God knew Tim, knew his heart and his struggles, and that God is as brokenhearted by this as we are. I believe he wanted to reach Tim, to save him, but that Tim wouldn't listen, wouldn't open himself to the love that was there for him. Not from God, and not from us." He fought back tears. "I believe God cared about Tim. More, even, than we did."

"Do you?" Her expression was one of weary wondering...even of yearning. He had the sense that she wanted to believe, and his heart raced. *Jesus, please...*

But then she held out a hand, palm up. "It's starting to rain again," she said, cutting off both him and the brief spark of interest he was sure he'd seen in her.

She tucked the journal under her jacket and started down the trail, pace fast and determined. She didn't look back. He followed, touching her only once, to keep her from losing balance when her heel skidded toward a gaping hole in the wet footbridge.

Her rejection of *him* frustrated him. He wanted her in his life, in his arms! Yet deeper than that frustration was a sadness that she also rejected the Lord, that she was so closed to all the Lord offered. He ached that she was shutting herself off from the most important element of this life—and the life beyond.

Yet he knew where she was coming from. He'd been there. He remembered his own uncaring, even cynical attitude toward anything spiritual in his earlier days. God had had no part of their lives or marriage, and now her only view of God was that he'd stolen their son from them. And he had to admit that it had taken some struggle and prayer to get past his own hurt and resentment toward God about Tim.

At the parking area she plunged unheedingly through the mud toward the silvery blur of her Mercedes, barely visible in the darkness. She unlocked the door, and even though he doubted she wanted polite gestures from him, he reached around and opened it for her. He also held the door open, stopping her from closing it and shutting him out.

"There's a restaurant in the motel where I'm staying. Nothing fancy but decent food. Would you like to have dinner there?"

"No, I don't think so. Thanks anyway."

"Jan, you shouldn't go without eating—"

"I'll pick up a sandwich and take it to my room." She paused, and he could just imagine her telling him that her eating habits were none of his business now, but instead, in a tone more weary than hostile, she added, "I just want to shower and crawl into bed and spend the evening reading through Tim's journal."

"I understand."

"I'll send the journal over to you after I get home. I know you want to read it too."

"You're leaving in the morning?"

"Probably."

He tried once more. "Perhaps we could have breakfast together first?"

"Mark, I don't see any point in struggling through some phony show of social niceties. I've never been sophisticated enough to go the divorced-couple-as-best-friends route."

"I wasn't asking out of a misguided attempt to play a modern civilized divorced couple like actors on some TV sitcom! I just thought…"

He paused. He hadn't thought out the invitations ahead of time. He only knew he desperately wanted to keep her from slamming the door and driving away from him.

"I just thought it might be good for both of us if we spent a little time together."

It was too dark to see if angry retorts simmered in her expression, but he couldn't blame her if anger was her reaction. He mentally prepared himself for her reply: *Spend time together? What a lovely idea. Too bad you didn't think of that when we were married, when you were too busy defending your wealthy, sleazy clients from justice…or cheating on me…to spend time with me.*

Instead she said gently, "I don't think so, Mark," which was somehow more final than any sarcastic retort. "But I'm grateful that you were here today, that we found out the truth together."

She closed the door, and he backed away and didn't try to stop her again. He knew the sins he'd committed were forgiven now, that Jesus had taken them to the cross. He could do his best to make up for past wrongs by living a better life, trying to do more good and less harm. He could share his faith and do his best for the young people he encountered at Linhurst. But the legacy of the past remained: Tim was dead and Jan was no longer his wife.

The Lord forgave sin on an eternal scale, but the earthly consequences of his wrong choices, like prison for a guilty man, marched grimly onward. And the most maddening part of it all was he knew he deserved it. What a fool he'd been.

Jan needed no help getting the Mercedes turned around in the mud hole. He slogged over to his own modest Honda, and by the time his headlights cut a tunnel in the canyon darkness, all sight and sound of her had vanished.

Back at his motel room, he thumbed through his Bible, sampling verses here and there as he sometimes did when he felt restless or discouraged. He reflected on what he had said to Jan. Yes, he did believe that God's love and care was a daily miracle. The Lord had created a world of land and sea, mountains and deserts and creatures; created a universe of planets and stars and unseen wonders scientists were still discovering out there. Yet in the midst of all that awesome creation, he still cared deeply about each human he'd placed on this earth; he still cared about Mark Hilliard. Jesus had died for Mark Hilliard, something else that was still a miracle to him. Just as he had also died for Jan, and it saddened him that her heart and mind were so closed to that truth.

He settled into the book of Mark, as he often did. He'd been so astonished when he first discovered the name Mark in the New Testament, as if it were somehow a special message to him, and he'd always felt a special kinship with the words written in that book. He especially liked the words about Jesus in the fourth chapter: *"Who is this? Even the wind and the waves obey him!"* It reminded him that even when things seemed to be spiraling out of control, the Lord always *was* in charge.

He didn't feel as restless after the time spent in the Word and in prayer. He was grateful that the Lord had taken away the uncertainty about the circumstances of Tim's death. Yet in spite of that, a full sense of closure escaped him; everything still felt up in the air, unraveled and unfinished. Perhaps because, like Jan, the now inescapable fact of suicide also dragged him deeper into the pit of guilt. *Oh, Lord, why did I waste years chasing after foolish things, letting my ego and selfish desires run my life, instead of being a good father to Tim and a good husband to Jan?* For a while after the divorce he'd gone even further, lived life with hurricane force, intent on reveling in his "freedom." Attractive women used astonishing and ego-flattering ploys to meet him; a slick local magazine put him on its cover. His career, with a high-profile, murder-for-hire case, vaulted upward. A reporter dubbed him the High Wizard of Technicalities because he oftentimes dug up obscure legal points to get his clients off.

Yet in less than a year, the bubbles in this champagne life began to fizzle. A vague, undefined dissatisfaction set in. He had scrutinized this the way he would an annoying legal problem, examined all the details and angles as if they were a set of statistics, and briskly concluded that his dissatisfaction was because Jan and Tim were missing from his life.

With his usual arrogance and all the subtlety of a judge issuing a sentence, he'd set about correcting that situation. He informed Jan that he'd changed, the divorce had been a mistake, and he wanted to remarry her. He embellished this with a barrage of flowers and gifts and eventually made a grand entrance at the house flourishing tickets for a second-honeymoon luxury cruise.

Jan's response as he stood at her door, where his unopened gifts and wilting flowers were stacked, was as swift and sharp as a flashing scalpel. "Three months after the divorce, this might have worked. Maybe even six months. But the thing is, now I don't *care* if you've changed…although I don't really think you have. But now it doesn't matter because somewhere along the way

I changed. I used to love you. I don't love you anymore."
And she'd tossed the tickets on top of an unopened box
of expensive lingerie he'd sent and stalked away.

He was insulted and angry. He launched into
another brief, totally unsatisfactory fling with fast living.
He won another case that proved clever legal maneuver-
ing could triumph over justice. He hammered his body
into even more impressive shape at his health club. On
the outside his life glittered and sparkled, but inside it
was as hollow as the interior of a cheap chocolate rabbit.
Yet it was a case from a half-dozen years earlier returning to haunt him that finally stopped him in his tracks
and started him on the path that eventually led him to
the Lord. And a *real* change in himself and his life.

He grabbed the remote control and clicked until he
found a nature program on TV. He determinedly tried to
watch it, but after a half hour of lions, he gave up. He
yanked the few clothes he'd brought with him off the
hangers in the closet and jammed them in the suitcase.
He knew he couldn't sleep, so he may as well use the
time to make the long drive home. Belatedly he realized
he hadn't followed his own advice to Jan about eating,
but he wasn't hungry.

He was in the bathroom gathering his shaving gear
when the ring of the phone startled him. He stepped out
of the bathroom but merely looked at the jangling
instrument. Who could be calling him? He'd only left
this number with a few people.

But Jan knew where he was staying—

He sprinted across the room, cracking his shin on
the nightstand in his sudden haste. "Hello?"

"Mark, I've found something in Tim's journal."

On the rare occasions she'd contacted him since the divorce, she always formally identified herself, as if she assumed the breakup had somehow nullified his ability to recognize her voice. But this time she offered no cool, polite preliminaries, and an excitement he hadn't heard in years simmered in her voice.

"Can you come over right away?"

4

THERE, ANOTHER MENTION OF HER!

Jan marked the page with a scrap torn from the scratch pad in her purse, excitement rippling through her. The excitement wasn't a full-blown joy. She was still too wounded by Tim's death even to approach joy, but now this incredible possibility had opened the door on a wild new hope.

She clutched the precious journal to her chest as she shoved back the heavy drape at the window and peered down at the parking lot. Mark was just getting out of his Honda. Odd, she thought, how her heart unexpectedly reacted with a thump as she watched him jog toward the motel entrance. For a strange moment she felt seventeen years old again, and he was arriving at the house in his shined-up pickup to take her to a movie, body lean and athletic, hair a silver black gleam under the streetlight. Lots of guys just honked at the curb for their girls, but Mark, in spite of his wild-streak reputation, always came to the door....

She dropped the drape, banishing the memory, and a few moments later he knocked on the door. When she opened it, he instantly asked, "Is something wrong?"

She touched her hair, only then realizing how bedraggled she must look. She'd intended to shower and wash her hair, but she started reading Tim's journal as soon as she returned to the motel room and hadn't been able to put it down. She also realized her face must look pale and washed out, makeup faded by the rain. Not, she thought wryly, the way any woman wants her ex-husband to see her, especially when she knew he'd dated some of the most glamorous and sophisticated women in Portland. Yet all she detected in his gaze was concern, not criticism of her appearance.

"No, everything's fine. I just wanted you to see—" She hesitated, the thought only now occurring to her that perhaps he wouldn't be nearly as thrilled and excited by this as she was. She stepped back. "Please, come in."

He stepped inside, started to take off his tan Windbreaker, then looked at her questioningly, as if uncertain if she had in mind a visit that would last long enough to call for removal of the jacket.

"You can just drape it around the back of the chair." She motioned to one of the two chairs drawn up to a round table in a corner of the room.

The room was quintessentially motel—a blurry seascape print on the wall, an oversized lamp on the table, the domineering eye of the television set, and bland colors. Yet to Jan, its very ordinariness somehow emphasized Mark's masculine vitality, his dark hair glistening with a few drops of rain, shirt cuffs turned back over strong-boned wrists. As always, he seemed to take control of a room the moment he entered it, just as he'd taken control of her heart from almost the first time she saw him and held it for so many years.

He wanted her back; she knew he did. And even though she didn't want to feel it, fought against feeling it, the potent attraction he'd always held for her was still there. He still stirred her, still aroused longings she preferred not to investigate too far. She remembered the desperate fear she'd felt for him at the cabin when she thought Red Dog was going for the gun.

A bit primly, not wanting him to know how she was reacting to him, she sat in the other chair, the journal still clasped against her chest.

"Did you have anything to eat?" He raked his hand through his wet hair.

She dismissed the question with an impatient jerk of her head. "I guess I forgot. This is more important. First, that girl Bonnie knew Tim considerably better than she let on. I can't tell timing because Tim apparently wrote in the journal very erratically, and he didn't date anything, but she was his girlfriend through about the first half of the journal."

Mark lifted a dark eyebrow. "Another reason suspicions might land on Red Dog if questions were raised about Tim's death since she's apparently his girl now."

Jan nodded. "But then Tim starts mentioning another girl. He calls her Stardust, and says her eyes are the color of wild blue lupine."

Jan found the comparison sweetly enchanting, so typical of Tim to connect the color of a girl's eyes with one of the flowers he loved. Meadows of wild lupine were common in Oregon, the spiky blue flowers unfettered by human fences.

Mark smiled. "That sounds like Tim."

"I think she may have been someone very special to him."

Jan spread the journal on the table. She opened it to the first page on which the girl's name was mentioned. "He writes here about how she cut her hand on a rock. Although at this point he already seems to know her fairly well. Perhaps he mentioned her in the pages just before this that Red Dog tore out."

"Our not-so-helpful censor," Mark commented wryly.

She showed him several other references to Stardust, one where Tim said she'd cooked some really good lasagna, another where she was trying to keep alive a baby quail she'd found. Then Jan skipped forward to the important page. With her fingertip she underlined the words, which at this point were beginning to run together but were still fairly legible.

"'Stardust says she thinks she's pregnant.'" Mark paused to decipher the odd writing and separate the joined words. "'I told her I thought there was a test or kit or something you could get at the drugstore to tell for sure.'"

Jan had reacted to that statement as if it were a lightning bolt to the heart, but Mark just sat there, a faint furrow above his dark brows. "Don't you see what this means?" she cried. "We may be grandparents!"

Mark, ever the skeptical lawyer despite the change in his profession, saw flaws in her swift conclusion. "This doesn't necessarily mean this girl was pregnant with Tim's baby. Given the rather casual and changing relationships among the people he knew, maybe she's just telling him she may be pregnant with *somebody's* child."

"Then read this!" Jan grabbed the journal and flipped forward to another page. Here the writing was becoming even more difficult to read, the size of the letters beginning to shrink to dehydrated squiggles.

Mark started where Jan's trembling finger pointed. "'Stardust went to the—'"

"Clinic, I think it says," she filled in.

Mark nodded. "'Stardust went to the clinic and they said she had to quit…smoking pot.' Is that right?"

"Yes, I think that's what it says. And then he's wondering if 'all the stuff' he's done with drugs will affect the baby." She waited expectantly, but Mark just sat there, brow still lightly furrowed. Jan jumped to her feet. "Mark, don't you see? That proves it! It's Tim's baby too! That's why he's worried that something he's taken might affect it. He wouldn't worry about that if it *weren't* his baby! Which I think shows an admirable sense of responsibility."

"And then he killed himself." Mark's tone was heavy, not accusing but pointing out inescapable fact: Tim had abandoned this child, if it was his, abandoned his responsibilities in the most basic and final way possible, a way that could never be reversed.

"Was that because we were both too busy making money and building our careers to teach him the responsibilities of being a parent? Maybe this is a second chance for us to make up for the past!" Her heart soared with the possibility. "Because this means that something I thought could never happen after Tim died may yet happen…maybe has already happened!"

She paused, considering that what was true for her was not true for him. "You can marry again, start a new family and wind up with a whole houseful of grandchildren, so maybe this doesn't matter all that much to you. But this is my only chance, Mark, my one and only chance for a grandchild!"

Tim had arrived much earlier than they planned to have children, less than a year after their wedding. They wanted more children, but, under the financial pressure of getting Mark through college and law school, with Jan working nights so she could be at home with the baby during the day while Mark was in classes and working his own job, they carefully put off having more children.

Then, even before the time arrived when it would be financially responsible to expand their family, the possibility had been snatched away from them. A tumor and unavoidable hysterectomy had cut off all chance of more children for Jan.

"Jan, whether you believe it or not, this means every bit as much to me as it does to you. This baby is a living part of Tim, all that's left—"

"A special gift from God!" she cried with a sense of wonder.

He looked surprised at her fervent exclamation, and, in truth, it surprised her too. Her times at church, where she'd always felt like an uncomfortable outsider, had been few and far between; her relationship with God was basically nonexistent. Yet she'd never thought of herself as some etched-in-stone atheist, and at the moment this really did feel like a miraculous gift from a higher power. A grandchild!

For a moment, from the thoughtful look on his face, she thought he was going to latch on to her statement and launch into some minisermon, but instead he simply nodded agreement. "Does the journal give any clue about what became of their relationship or where she might be?"

"I haven't gotten all through the journal yet." Jan smiled a little self-consciously. "I got so excited when I realized Tim might have a baby that I rushed to call you right away."

"I'm glad you did." He pulled the chair she'd vacated over closer to his. "Sit down. Let's see what we can find in the rest of the journal."

Together they scrutinized the pages, helping each other decipher the cramped scrawls and strings of joined words and confusing leaps in time and from subject to subject. In one sentence Tim wrote about a dream he'd had; in the next he voiced fury about some destructive logging going on nearby. Timing was impossible to determine. Sometimes it sounded as if perhaps weeks went by in between entries, but at others it appeared he had written in the journal several times in one day. Sometimes the comments were down-to-earth normal about the weather or a trip to town, but another time he described in minute detail the iridescent green scales on the evil dragon/lizard lurking outside his window.

They found several more mentions of Stardust, but only one was relevant to her pregnancy, and that only in a roundabout way because Jan inferred from a comment about Stardust being "sick to her stomach again" that she was having morning sickness. Then, after two missing pages, she was never mentioned again.

"So, what does that mean?" Jan asked slowly when they reached that terrible final line of "doitdoitdoitdoit." She felt frustrated and let down, taken to the top of a mountain of hope, then hurled into emptiness. "Did they break up?"

Mark drummed his fingers on his thigh. "He doesn't mention any arguments or disagreements between them."

"No, but earlier I never saw mention of any argu-ments with Bonnie, either. After a few pages she just wasn't mentioned anymore." Jan pressed her fingertips against her temples. "Poor Tim. His life was just so...mixed up."

"So what's our next step?"

"I don't know what you're going to do, but I'm going to search for Stardust!"

He reached over and jiggled her shoulder lightly, as if to waken her. "Of course we're going to search for Stardust. That wasn't what I meant. I meant, where do we start? I suspect Stardust isn't a real name any more than Red Dog is."

Jan fingered a tattered corner of a page in the journal. Touching the journal, even painful as the words were to read, gave her a small sense of connection with Tim. His fingers had touched these pages just as hers now did.

"It would help if he'd described her beyond the lupine blue eyes," she admitted. "We have no idea how old she is, whether she's tall or short, slender or husky, blonde or brunette or redhead."

"We don't know if she's still pregnant or has already had the baby. Or if she's still in this area. She may have picked up and left."

A sinking feeling of despair settled around Jan. When she first read the words that convinced her they had a grandchild on the way, or perhaps one already born, she had felt as if the baby was so close that at any moment she'd be holding it in her arms! But now a deadening sense of hopelessness overtook her. Mark was silent too.

"Could we go to the authorities for help?" she asked finally.

"I don't think we can expect any help from them. Stardust isn't a wanted criminal, at least so far as we know," he added, as if it were an uneasy second thought. "She also isn't really a missing person."

"She is to us. Although I don't suppose that matters. If only we hadn't wasted so much time; we should have rushed down here right after Tim's death!"

"Yes."

She ran a hand through her still bedraggled hair. "Maybe it's a mistake to try to find her ourselves. 'Playing amateur detective,' you called it earlier. Perhaps it would be more effective to hire someone experienced in these matters."

Mark nodded. "Perhaps. But our amateur detective work hasn't done too badly so far, and we are right here on the spot. I'd rather not waste time locating and getting an investigator on the job. If we're unsuccessful we can consider hiring someone later, but right now I'd rather try to find her ourselves."

She leaned forward, eyes searching his face. "You mean that, Mark? It means enough to you that you'll stay here and search for her with me?"

"It means more than you can possibly know." His voice was husky with intensity. "And we are going to find her."

Now she could believe it. With Mark on the job, it could happen. She smiled tremulously. "I wonder if it's a boy or girl. I wonder if it looks like Tim when he was born, with a headful of wild, dark hair. And such wise blue eyes...I remember thinking he was telling me he knew all about being a baby, but what did I know about being a mother?"

"We'll find out," Mark vowed. "We'll find out everything there is to know about Tim's child."

"I think talking to Red Dog and Bonnie again might be a good starting point. I'll bet Bonnie knows something about the girlfriend who came after her." Even though Jan had pretended haughty disinterest, she had kept track of who gossip said Mark was seeing.

"Yes. Good idea. I also think we should check birth records at the county courthouse. If the baby has already been born, Stardust may have listed Tim as the father. From a birth certificate, we can find out her real name and perhaps other information that may help locate her. We can also talk with the clinic she went to. There's probably only one in a town this size. I strongly doubt, even if they can identify her from the limited information we have, that they'll officially tell us anything because of confidentiality regulations. But we might find someone sympathetic who'll slip us some helpful information on the side."

"Mark, that's a wonderful idea!" And if anyone could wheedle information out of someone, she was certain it would be Mark.

"But if we're really going to brainstorm this, I'm going to have to have food to keep me going," he announced. "How about you?"

"You didn't eat after you got back to town?" When he shook his head she couldn't resist chastising him lightly. "And here you were preaching at *me* about eating."

"Actually, I was feeling pretty down. When you called, I was throwing things in a suitcase, getting ready to make a night drive home."

"Then I'm glad I didn't wait ten minutes later to call."

"So am I."

He reached across the table and covered her hand with his, his look filled with such tenderness, even longing, that for a wild moment she thought he was going to take her in his arms and kiss her. Her reaction as she looked into his eyes confused and dismayed her because she was not at all certain she would resist him. And giving in to the confusing passions that suddenly flickered through her was unthinkable! But perhaps he sensed her confusion because all he did was squeeze her hand lightly and then reach for his jacket.

She pushed away the strange mixture of relief and disappointment that he hadn't carried through on the kiss and concentrated on his announcement about the need for food. "I'm not sure if there's anything open here this late."

"I doubt if I'm going to find takeout escargot or coq au vin, but when I drove over I saw a teenage burger hangout that looked as if it was going strong. Still like everything but mustard on your burger?"

She nodded, surprised that he'd remembered.

"And coffee with cream, no sugar?"

She nodded again. "Except that this late in the evening I have to stick to decaf now, or I'm awake until three o'clock in the morning."

He smiled wryly. "Me, too. Old age setting in, I guess."

She smiled too. "We're entitled. After all, we may be grandparents."

Although he looked anything but old enough to be a grandparent, standing there broad-shouldered and slim-hipped in a jacket and khaki pants.

The door closed behind him, and she rushed to the

window and lifted a corner of the drape so she could watch him cross the parking lot to his car. After several moments he still hadn't appeared. Then she spotted him crossing the street, walking to the burger stand with that familiar, determined stride.

They'd walked everywhere when they were first married, too short on money to buy gas for anything but the most essential purposes. Back then, it had seemed as if an abundance of money would solve everything. Now she knew how little it actually solved.

About as much as sneaking peeks at your ex-husband through the window.

At the thought, she hastily let the curtain drop, feeling the heat rush into her cheeks. With a sigh she went to the bathroom to run a brush through her hair and apply a swish of mascara and dab of lipstick. *Foolish,* she chided herself, *a weak imitation of the full armor of makeup I apply before leaving for the office every morning.* And foolish for a much more important reason. What did it matter how she looked? She wasn't trying to make herself *desirable* to him, for heaven's sake. They'd merely agreed to do a job together: find Stardust.

Yet, as she eyed her reflection critically in the wall-wide mirror, she thought she looked better than she had in weeks. But she also saw that the improvement had nothing to do with makeup or hair. It was the fresh glow of life in her face, a sparkle of hope in eyes that had long been dulled by pain and despair.

She was back at the table studying the journal again when Mark returned. She was reasonably certain he'd noted that she'd done a minor repair job on herself, but he didn't comment.

"Food." He held up a sack fragrant with scents of burgers and fries and hot coffee. "And something even more important." A triumphant grin split his face. "A clue about Stardust!"

5

"TELL ME!"

"Food first," Mark proclaimed.

He spread paper napkins on the table, put a hefty cheeseburger on each, and angled a tray of fries between them. She opened the containers of coffee and added packets of creamer to both, then, with perfect memory, a half packet of sugar to his. She sat down at the table, lifted the cheeseburger, then set it down.

"I'm sorry. I suppose you say grace before you eat now."

He was surprised and pleased with this conciliatory attitude, and as he offered thanks for the food and asked for a blessing on their search, he also added silent thanks for what seemed a small crack in Jan's armor against both God and himself.

When he finished, she dutifully took a small bite, as if calculating how little she could get by with eating before he'd tell her anything. And she needed to eat! She'd always been slender, but now her figure was so willowy that she looked as if it might bend to the ground like some drooping branch. Yet she was still so very lovely. Even at Tim's funeral, the devastation of tears and lines of anguish carved on her face couldn't destroy the elegant loveliness into which the kitten-cute good looks of her teenage years had matured.

But now, after a first bite, she surprised him by exclaiming, "Hey, this is really good!"

She peered at the drippy sandwich as if she'd forgotten that food really could taste good. But he knew that it was not the burger stand's cook who deserved credit. It was hope nibbling into the despair that had engulfed her for months, hope that revived her taste buds as well as her spirit. And the hamburgers were good, hot and juicy. He'd jogged all the way back to the motel so they wouldn't get cold.

"I suppose I *could* tell you what I found out while we're eating."

"Unless you'd like a quick dousing with hot coffee," she warned with unexpected spirit, "I think you'd better do just that."

He finished chewing the bite in his mouth and set the cheeseburger back on the napkin. "Okay, the place was full of teenagers loading up on junk food—"

"Look who's talking," she murmured as he dipped a french fry in a puddle of ketchup.

"So I had to wait for my order. I figured while I was standing around I might as well ask these kids if anyone knew a girl named Stardust. At first all I got were wary, suspicious looks, as if they figured I were some undercover cop trying to worm my way into their confidence for some covert reason."

Jan nodded. "I know the look. I got it enough times. So then you…what? Won them over with your dazzling charm and magnetic charisma?"

Her smile and teasing words lifted his heart, and he smiled back. "I wish my charm and charisma were that powerful." *Especially on you.* "But no, I just gave them the straight facts, that we wanted to find Stardust because we thought she might be the mother of our grandchild, and we wanted to make sure both she and the baby were okay. Everyone just stood around, not saying anything, and I was about to decide I'd get better results if I just offered to pay for information. But finally this one kid stepped up and said he thought maybe she'd gone to the local high school for a while two or three years ago."

He saw a quick shadow cross Jan's expressive face and knew what she was thinking. Such a flimsy clue!

"There's more," he said hastily. Was he dragging this out, he wondered guiltily, just so he could be with her a little longer? "Then he said that later, after he hadn't seen the girl at school for a while, he and his father went hunting in the woods out east of here. They thought they were on government land, but some guy came running out screaming that they were on his property and to get off. So they hotfooted it out of there. The guy looked mean and mad enough to use them for target practice, this kid said. And then when they passed a shacky old house on the way back to their pickup, he was pretty sure he saw her riding a horse bareback near an old log barn."

"So how do we find this place?"

"He drew me a map." Mark pulled the folded napkin out of his pocket and handed it to her. "We can drive out there tomorrow."

She frowned as she studied the sketch done with ballpoint pen, and Mark had to admit that *map* perhaps overstated the squiggly lines. But he was pleased to see that she hadn't stopped eating, and the burger was almost gone.

"Did he know more of a name for her than Stardust?"

"Unfortunately, no."

"How about a description?"

"He thought she was probably a sophomore when she was in school, so that would make her about the same age as Tim, eighteen or nineteen now. Long hair, blondish, he thought. Medium size. Quiet, kind of a fade-into-the-woodwork girl. He couldn't remember the color of her eyes, and no one else could remember her at all."

Jan nodded slowly. "Tim would like a quiet girl who rode a horse bareback." She paused thoughtfully. "Do you suppose there's any point checking with the school?"

"Couldn't hurt."

She tapped her upper lip with her forefinger, the way she always did when she was deep in thought, and he wished he'd had more substantial information to offer her.

"I know this clue doesn't exactly light up like a neon sign pointing the way," he added, "but it's more than we had before."

"Yes, and we also have a list of other possibilities. Talking to Red Dog and Bonnie again. Looking up records at the courthouse. Talking to the clinic and school." She smiled with more spirit than he expected, a flash of the old verve in her eyes. The same way she'd looked just before she took him up on his dare to follow him far up in an overhanging tree and jump into a swimming hole back when they were teenagers. "How long can you stay?"

"Classes at Linhurst start again next Monday, but I'll take more time off if we need it. How about you?"

She didn't even hesitate, though he knew it meant

lost time at the real estate office, which translated to potential lost sales. "Whatever it takes. For the first time since Tim's death, I feel as if I can stop looking back and start looking forward."

He dared another touch, closing his hand over hers, and she didn't pull away. "We'll find her."

He finished his hamburger and the fries while she sipped her coffee. Reluctantly, unable to think of any reason to linger longer, he said, "We'll take my car in the morning, okay? There's not much damage the rough roads around here can do to it."

She nodded and handed him his jacket from where he'd tossed it on the bed when he returned with the hamburgers. She followed him to the door. He stepped onto the balcony walkway. Moisture from the day's rain still lingered in the soft spring air, but stars sprinkled the sky now. A fragrance of pine from the grove of trees behind the motel scented the air, and frogs croaked lustily somewhere in the distance. He felt awkward, like their long ago first date when he hadn't known if he dared kiss her or not. He hadn't tried it then, he recalled wryly, and he didn't now.

"If that breakfast invitation is still open?"

He glanced back at her standing in the doorway, her slim figure haloed by light from the room. He thought she smiled when she saw his surprise, but with her face in shadow because the bulb over the door was burned out, he couldn't be sure. "Yes, it is!"

"I'll meet you in the restaurant at your motel. Seven-thirty?"

"Great! See you then." And he strode down the

walkway feeling as jaunty as a kid with a frog in his pocket. *Thank you, Lord! Maybe it's not too late after all.*

Mark braked at the stop sign branded with bullet holes. Farther back they'd passed a few farmhouses with white-face cattle grazing behind barbed-wire fences, even a neat vineyard, but here fir and pine and shiny-leafed madrone crowded right up to the edge of the gravel road. Sunshine flashed on the back of a sleek black crow perched at the top of a dead snag, and even its raucous caw sounded faintly musical on this fresh-washed morning.

Normally, the spring sunshine would have lifted Mark's spirits, but he knew it wasn't a change in weather that made him feel the way he did right now, united with Jan in this search for their grandchild.

"Do we turn here?" He braked and peered at the unmarked roads leading in different directions from the crossroad.

Jan rotated the napkin a quarter turn as she tried to orient the tangled lines of the map with the gravel and dirt roads. "Left, I think, although this could be a different crossroad than the one marked here. Do you want to take a look?"

Mark automatically glanced in the rearview mirror, but he suspected they could safely have a picnic in the middle of the road before another vehicle came along. Jan handed him the napkin/map, and he also turned it from side to side trying to make sense of it. They'd already made one wrong turn and had to backtrack from a dead end.

"I know that kid at the burger stand was trying to be helpful, but his map-drawing skills could definitely use some fine-tuning."

"Although the artistically placed ketchup stains do lend a nice decorative touch."

Mark glanced up, pleased to hear the companionable laughter in her voice. Their shared breakfast had also been congenial although by some unspoken agreement they'd kept the conversation impersonal.

"But the mustard blobs are just a bit too much, don't you think?" he asked with a critical tilt of his head.

"Oh, yes. Definitely artistic overkill."

They smiled at each other, and he scratched at a yellow stain on the napkin with his thumbnail. "I think you're right. We turn left here. You know what this reminds me of?"

"What?"

"Remember that scavenger hunt we went on back in high school? Somebody's birthday party, I think it was, and we chased all over the countryside trying to find all the weird stuff on the list—"

He broke off suddenly, groaning within himself. What was wrong with him? Now she probably thought he was being insensitive comparing that frivolous scavenger hunt of long ago with today's serious search for their grandchild! He glanced at her, intending to apologize, but he saw her eyes light up.

"I remember! And we were supposed to bring in an Elvis Presley record of 'Heartbreak Hotel,' so we were out in your aunt's garage with a flashlight, going through boxes and boxes of her old records—"

He grinned. "And I managed to back into that cactus plant she'd put in the garage to keep it from freezing, and I yelped so loud that one of the neighbors called the cops."

Their eyes met in the midst of the laughter, and hers were warm and bright. Mark wanted so much to lean over and kiss her. He touched her shoulder, and, as if reading his intentions all too accurately, she suddenly became very busy straightening a twisted strap on her purse. He simply squeezed her shoulder and drove on. He was disappointed, but it still felt as if something unexpectedly warm and sweet had happened between them, something with tantalizing potential.

After a couple of miles, with her finger stabbed into the napkin to mark a point on the map, Jan said, "I think the house should be on the right at a fork in the road just up ahead."

Yes, there was the fork, but that was definitely no "shacky old house" behind a rustic rail fence. Mark braked, and they both stared. The big A-frame house had a shake roof not yet aged by weather, plus a red-wood deck and a satellite dish in the yard. The sound of some unseen power equipment roared from somewhere in back.

Her mouth dropped open. "This can't be the place."

"But there's the old log barn, just like the kid said." Mark pointed to a dilapidated barn and collapsed corral partly visible behind the trees.

"Let's see if these people know anything, then." Jan sounded hopeful, but not highly optimistic, which was exactly how Mark felt.

They found a man with a noisy weed-eater ripping through a thigh-high stand of grass and weeds out behind the house. When they got out of the car and approached him, he turned off the engine and pulled down a protective face mask.

"Get away from the city. Go back to nature. Live off the land," the silver-haired but fit-looking older man grumbled good-naturedly. "Raise your own food, enjoy the simple life. Nobody tells us Californians who come up here with more money than brains that weeds and deer want your garden, and your wife isn't about to eat the pet steer she raised from a big-eyed calf." He waved toward a smug-looking black steer placidly chewing its cud behind a fence.

They laughed and chatted for a few minutes, while the man detailed the woes of a city man living the rural life. Finally he got around to asking amiably, "Well, as they say around here, what can I do you for?"

Mark explained about Stardust and why they were looking for her. Not unexpectedly, the man shook his head regretfully.

"We never met the people who lived on the place before we bought it and don't know anything about them. Except that there was an old house here when we bought the place, and it burned down a few days later under rather suspicious circumstances. We were shaken up about it at the time, but it was probably a good thing because we built this new place instead of trying to fix up the old one."

"Do you know the name of the people who lived here?" Mark's gaze roamed toward the old barn and corral. "At this point, we don't even know Stardust's last name."

The man shook his head again. "They were renters,

and I don't even know where you'd locate the former owner. I understand he had a few run-ins with the law and took off for whereabouts unknown after we paid him off. I'm sorry." Sympathy was clear in the man's eyes. "I know how we'd feel if we had no contact with one of our grandchildren."

"May I leave my name and number with you in case you hear anything?" Jan pulled a business card from her purse. The man agreed, and Jan circled her home phone number and handed it to him.

"Okay, we struck out this time," she said after they were back in the car. He knew how disappointed she was, but her mouth was set in determination rather than the despair he feared. "What's next on our agenda?"

"How about the school and the clinic?"

"Sounds good."

Driving back to town, Mark impulsively pulled into the driveway of an old trailer he hadn't noticed on the way out. A man whose face looked too young to have the gray braid straggling down his back glanced up from where he was puttering with an ancient rototiller. Mark would've preferred that Jan stay in the car, but she was right beside him when he approached the rough-looking guy.

The man dropped a wrench and picked up a screwdriver. He gave them a disinterested glance. "Yeah?" The word sounded more like a challenge than a welcome.

Mark gave him a miniversion of their story. "So the girl we're looking for may have lived in the old house up the road a ways, the one that burned down a couple of years ago. We were just wondering if perhaps you knew the people."

The guy poked the screwdriver into the internal workings of the rototiller and didn't look up again. "Nope."

"Maybe some of your friends knew them," Jan suggested.

"Maybe."

"Have you ever even heard of a girl named Stardust? Or our son, Tim Hilliard?" Mark asked, feeling frustrated.

"Or maybe someone named Red Dog?" Jan added.

The probing screwdriver paused long enough to hint that the name Red Dog was perhaps familiar, but the spoken answer was the same as before. "Nope."

"I'll leave you my card," Jan said again. Mr. Man-of-Few-Words didn't lift a hand toward the card when Jan held it out, and she set it on the battered rototiller. "I'd appreciate hearing from anyone who knows anything about the family or Stardust. They can call my home number collect."

"We don't want to cause trouble for anyone." He placed his hand on Jan's shoulder. "We just want to find our grandchild."

No reaction or response.

As they returned to the Honda, the rototiller, which Mark would've sworn was lifeless as a pet rock, unexpectedly roared. When he looked back, he saw the rotating blades churn through a white spot on the ground. Jan's card. He started to tell her, then remained silent. Actually, he was relieved the card had been destroyed. He felt distinctly uneasy with the idea of having home information about Jan spread all over the countryside where anyone could latch on to it. Living alone in that big house... Who knew what unsavory characters might turn up on her doorstep?

Driving back toward town, they passed a subdivision of five-acre tracts with big, new homes and then, only a mile away, an old bus apparently occupied by a large family, given the evidence of a clothesline filled with clothes in graduated sizes. Mark was again struck by the unlikely mix of inhabitants in this area. People like Red Dog and Tim, heavy into the drug culture with their hidden marijuana plots and meth labs; prosperous newcomers intent on getting away from fast-paced city lifestyles but often bringing much of it with them; conservative old-timers, perhaps baffled by both.

Mark pulled in beside the old bus, suspecting that these people were more likely to have known Stardust or Tim than the people in the big houses. A bearded guy poked his head out from under an old truck and called a friendly greeting. He turned out not to know anything definite, but he thought he may have worked with Tim on a temporary job pruning grape vines in the vineyard down the road. He was considerably more cooperative and talkative than Man-of-Few-Words, but even so, when Jan started to hand him her business card, Mark stepped in and gave the man one of his own cards instead.

Jan looked mildly annoyed as they walked back to the car. "Why did you do that?"

"I just don't think it's a good idea for you to give out too much personal information about yourself. Considering the kind of people Tim and Stardust were involved with, it might not be a good idea to have one or more of them drop in unexpectedly when you're home alone. Let's let them get in touch with me first."

Jan frowned but she didn't argue.

Because the last man had mentioned the vineyard, Mark also stopped there. Another blank. The owners were new, transplanted Californians, and they hadn't hired any temporary help since buying the vineyard. They'd never heard of either Tim or Stardust. Mark left his card anyway.

It was past one o'clock by the time they got back to town, and they decided to grab a quick lunch before tackling the clinic and school. Mark suggested the restaurant at the motel again.

"Oh, let's do the burger stand," Jan countered. "Maybe we'll run into some more helpful teenagers." She smiled. "Besides, their burgers and fries were really good."

"Junk food," Mark warned.

Jan tilted her head with an unexpectedly contemplative expression as she gazed off toward the mountains. "Maybe what I need in my life is fewer power lunches and more junk food," she suggested lightly, then added with a smile, "Metaphorically speaking."

Mark wasn't sure what she meant, but her expression held none of the cold, distant hostility of the past several years, and he decided he approved, whatever it meant.

"Burgers it is. Shall we go all the way and have shakes and onion rings too?"

"Let's."

Unfortunately, there were no young people at the burger stand; the only other customers were a touristy looking older couple. But when the red-haired young woman handed them their order, she said tentatively, "Aren't you the guy who was in here last night asking about a girl named Stardust?"

"Yes, that was me."

"I was thinking about that, and I remembered something." She tilted her head as if to ask if he were still interested, and he nodded encouragingly. "Last fall or winter sometime, I don't remember exactly when, a couple came in and they stuck in my mind for two reasons. One was, the guy was upset with her because she ordered a hot dog, and he was telling her that all meat, especially hot dogs, has terrible stuff in it, and he sounded, well, you know, kind of like a fanatic or something."

Mark and Jan looked at each other, and even though "fanatic" wasn't a word they wanted to hear about their son, he saw excitement spark in her eyes. Yes, that could definitely be Tim!

"And the other reason I remember them is because he called her Stardust, and I thought, wouldn't it be wonderful to be called something different and romantic and dreamy like that. My name is Mary, and my nickname is just as ordinary." She looked sideways and wrinkled her nose as she lifted a slightly frizzed handful of carrot red hair. "With this hair, one guess as to what that nickname is."

"Do you remember what he looked like?" Mark asked.

Mary shook her head. "No. But I remember her because of the pretty name, and she was pretty too. Small and dark-haired, with a way of tossing her head that said no one was going to boss *her* around. Then she told him he could just eat all the rabbit food he wanted, but she wasn't going to. And she went ahead and got a hot dog, and he got, I don't know, french fries or onion rings, I think, something like that."

"Do you remember what color her eyes were?" Jan leaned forward. "Our son described Stardust as having eyes the color of wild blue lupine."

The young woman looked rather wistful, as if she wished someone would describe her eyes that sweetly, but she shook her head. "No, I don't remember her eyes."

The waitress had to wait on two women with a handful of small children then, and Mark and Jan decided to continue the questions later. Mark carried their lunch outside to a wooden table.

"Small and dark-haired is certainly a different description than the medium-sized and blondish I got last night." He swung a leg over the bench of the picnic table, sitting beside Jan rather than across from her. "Now I don't know what to think."

"This young woman sounds quite sure of her description," Jan said thoughtfully. "Perhaps the boy you talked to last night just didn't remember the girl at school all that clearly. Or maybe she had her hair bleached blonde when he knew her."

"But this one also doesn't sound like a fade-into-the-woodwork kind of girl. Apparently she wasn't about to let Tim—if it was Tim—tell her what to do, and she didn't back down from an argument in public."

Jan nodded. "Maybe there's more than one Stardust. Sometimes a nickname gets popular. I remember there were two girls called Kitten when we were in high school. And names themselves run in cycles. Maybe it's a real name for both girls because eighteen or nineteen years ago there was a run on Stardust for some reason."

"In any case, it does confuse things, having two descriptions."

"But it makes me think Tim really must have been in love with her. No one else seems to remember the color of her eyes, but they really made an impression on him."

"Could be." Mark remembered all the times since the divorce when he'd thought of Jan's big gray-green eyes. How he'd once tried to decide on a color name for them and came up with sea-willow green. Perhaps he and Tim had shared traits he'd never recognized, he thought regretfully.

"You're not getting discouraged already, are you?" The onion ring stopped halfway to her mouth.

"Perhaps a bit discouraged." He smiled. "But definitely not defeated. 'Hard pressed on every side, but not crushed; perplexed, but not in despair.'"

"A Bible quotation, no doubt?" Her return smile made the question teasing, not hostile, though her expression was faintly bemused, as if hearing anything spiritual from him still seemed strange to her.

"Something Paul said in a letter to the church in Corinth, to be exact. Paul is a pretty interesting guy, actually, with a good many worthwhile things to say."

She didn't turn chilly but the smile faded. "I don't really think I need a sermon or Bible lesson right now, if you don't mind."

Actually, a good many Bible lessons were exactly

what she needed, he thought, but he knew pressing the point now would only antagonize her.

"Back to our conflicting descriptions of Stardust, then."

She nodded. "I think we have to work on the one solid description we know is accurate because it came directly from Tim. His description of her eyes as lupine blue."

After eating their lunch, they went back inside and talked to the waitress again. Except for the ages of the couple—perhaps nineteen or twenty, she really wasn't sure—and the fact that the girl wore big, jangly earrings—she'd already given them all the information she had. She couldn't remember seeing either the guy or the girl again and had no idea if they lived in the area or were passing through. She also couldn't think of anyone who might have further information.

"We certainly appreciate the information you have given us." This time he wrote his name and number on a napkin because he was out of business cards. He'd handed out a lot of them before he and Jan started working together.

They decided it would save time if they split up to tackle the school and clinic. He gave Jan her choice, and she chose the school. He learned where the town's lone clinic was located simply by stepping back into the burger stand and inquiring of the red-haired young woman. They drove back to the motel to pick up Jan's car and agreed to meet at the restaurant again for dinner and to exchange findings.

The clinic did not have an impressive array of doctors. The sign in front of the modest frame building listed exactly one M.D., one nurse-practitioner, and one dentist. Inside, older people, a pregnant girl, several women with small children, a long-haired guy with his leg in a cast, and a woman in a neck brace crowded the reception room.

Mark took a seat and settled down for a long wait. He knew there was no chance of coaxing information from the woman at the reception desk while she was coping with phone, computer, and an obvious excess of patients. In the meantime, he studied the patients and speculated whether any of them looked like potential sources of information.

Yet even as he thought that, he knew how misguided categorizing people by appearance could be. Sometimes the most respectable-looking people were in to shifty dealings, the most glamorous had the dirtiest little secrets, the most innocent-looking committed the most despicable crimes. He should know, he thought wryly. He'd had some of them as clients when he was an attorney.

On impulse he chose the least-likely looking person in the room, a gray-haired older woman with heavy nylons sagging around her ankles. Rather than just moving over to ask her questions, he went to the magazine rack, picked up an old copy of *People* magazine, and casually took a seat beside her instead of returning to the one he'd had.

"Beautiful day, especially after all that rain yesterday," he offered conversationally.

"The Lord makes them all, but I must say I usually like his sunny days better than the rainy ones." She gave him a smile that lit her weathered face with a gentle radiance.

"Have you lived around here a long time?"

"If you consider forty years a long time." This time her smile had an unexpected glint of mischief. "Although at my age, looking back, forty years isn't all that long. And it's nothing, of course, compared to the eternity I'm looking forward to spending with the Lord."

"Me, too," he said sincerely, liking her and glad he'd chosen to talk to her even though there was no chance she'd know anything about people such as Tim and Stardust.

She looked at him more closely. "You sick, come to see the doctor? He doesn't look like he's old enough to hardly be out of high school, but he knows what he's doing."

"For a long time my soul was sick, but Jesus took care of that." Mark knew she'd know what he meant, and her approving nod said she did. "I'm here for another reason."

Briefly he repeated his story. "I came here hoping Stardust may have come to the clinic sometime, but I have my doubts if they'll give me any information even if she had."

He expected a few words of sympathy at best, but she astonished him by saying, "I never knew any girl named Stardust with lupine-blue eyes, but I might of known your Tim. There was a bunch of what we used to call hippies, maybe there's some other name for them now, living several miles past my place out on Ladyluck Road. Ladyluck was the name of an old mine out there, closed down years ago, of course, though my husband used to pan a few flakes out of the creek up there." She shook her head, as if to rid herself of the digression.

"Anyway, they tried to pass themselves off as a 'retreat,' or something like that, but everyone knew what they did mostly was grow marijuana up there. And a lot of other bad stuff went on, too, from what I heard. But sometimes a nice young man named Tim came down and worked in my garden for me. Tall, skinny boy, all legs. But I had a stroke and had to move to town a couple years ago—" She grimaced and poked at her right arm, which he now realized lay stiff and useless against her side. "So I don't know if he or any of that bunch are still up there."

A nice boy, "all legs," who worked in her garden. Yes, that could be Tim! He had an excited feeling that, like slowly rising building blocks, these bits of information were eventually going to take shape as an identifiable structure.

She told him her name was Ina Anderson and gave him directions to Ladyluck Road and the "retreat" up the road. He was halfway inclined to abandon any further efforts at the clinic, thinking he'd drive over to the school and share this information with Jan immediately rather than wait for dinner. But a sense that he'd best not leave any stone unturned kept him in the office until long after Mrs. Anderson had seen the doctor and hobbled out.

It was after five o'clock before the reception room finally emptied, and he approached the middle-aged woman behind the oblong window. He repeated his story once more. She was friendly and sympathetic but said she couldn't possibly give out any confidential information about a patient. But when he turned to leave she added in a low, hurried voice, "But I've been working

here more than three years, and I don't remember anyone named Stardust ever coming in. And I think I would
remember because my daughter got in with some
strange cult down in L.A. and decided to call herself
Starlight. So if this girl did come in, it must have been
under a different name, her real name, probably, if she
was a welfare patient. But I couldn't give you any information, even if you knew that name."

"I understand. And thanks for that much." If they
had the correct name, there were ways information
might possibly be obtained from the clinic, perhaps even
legally. But they didn't have the name, and at the
moment he was still hoping for something quicker and
less complicated than the slow legal route. More and
more he was getting the feeling, as so many of his old
legal papers used to proclaim, that time was "of the
essence."

He went back to his motel room, showered, and
changed clothes. Jan was waiting at a corner table when
he went down to the restaurant, looking fragile but lovely
in an ivory turtleneck sweater and black pants. Her
expression when she looked up at him from a menu was
so openly hopeful that he instantly knew her own investigative efforts at the school had not been successful.

He slid into the chair across from her. "Nothing?"

She shook her head regretfully. "Nothing."

"Because they couldn't, or wouldn't, tell you anything?"

"Couldn't, I think, because they really seemed to be
trying to help. They let me talk to the woman who
teaches all the freshman and sophomore English classes,
and if Stardust went to school there, she'd have had to

take one of them. But neither she nor anyone else could remember any girl called Stardust, either blondish and medium-sized or petite and dark-haired. If we could just find out her real name…" She shook her head, and he saw a glisten of tears in her expressive gray-green eyes. But she also shook off the moment of discouragement and tilted her head as she looked at him. "But you look as if you're just bursting with some big secret."

Seeing the waitress approaching, he quickly scanned the menu. When Jan ordered a seafood salad with ranch dressing, he did the same. He asked for iced tea, and she seconded that.

"Unfortunately, I don't have some marvelous secret," he admitted, sorry to disappoint her. He suspected what Jan saw in him was his secret happiness at being with her again. *What would she say, Father, if I told her that?* The thought almost made him smile, but he held it back. "But I did get another vague possibility." He explained what the elderly woman at the clinic had told him.

"Ladyluck Road," Jan mused. "I like that. We could use some luck. It's a good omen."

Mark had never had much belief in luck or omens even before he accepted Christ. What he had believed in was his own strength and drive and determination, his own sharp wits and cocky ability to surmount any hurdle, conquer any obstacle, break any boundary. Self-reliance and self-sufficiency had been his passwords.

He knew better now.

"I'll put my faith in the Lord, not luck," he said quietly.

Help her understand, Lord. Help her to see. Open a door for me to share your heart with her…

But Jan didn't reply. She just sat there, staring out the window, leaving Mark with the distinct feeling that he—and God—were being determinedly ignored.

6

JAN GLANCED AT HIM AS THEIR SALADS WERE SERVED, AND FOR a moment he thought she was going to question or challenge his statement on faith versus luck, but she didn't. Was it a good sign that she was giving what he said serious thought? He smiled and pushed her lightly for a response.

"No reaction?"

"I sometimes think about God and faith and spiritual matters." She sounded reluctant to make the admission. "But if some things in life aren't just plain old luck, don't we have to blame God for all the bad as well as give him credit for the good?"

"Meaning that we can blame him for Tim's death?"

"Tim's death. The collapse of our marriage." She sighed. "Wars. Disease. Famine. Floods. Hurricanes. The usual list of disasters."

"There's another biblical quotation—"

Jan rolled her eyes and groaned, but she also surprised him with an unexpected smile. "Somehow I can't quite get accustomed to you as a man who spouts Bible verses."

"Spouts?" His eyes narrowed. "*Spouts?* You make me sound like an overheated teakettle shooting off steam."

"Or maybe a rusty old hot water heater spouting more water than Old Faithful…" She flushed, obviously embarrassed that she'd brought up that long-ago mini-disaster, but then their eyes met and she burst out laughing.

He groaned and laughed too. "Me and my big plans for a romantic weekend."

"It was romantic, for a while," she consoled. "Candlelight, fire in the fireplace, dancing barefoot…"

Mark had wanted to do something special for Jan, to give her a little break from work and an energetic eighteen-month-old, so when a friend offered them the use of his rustic mountain cabin for a weekend, and the friend's wife said she'd take care of Tim, they jumped at the chance.

And, as Jan said, it had been romantic for a while. The cabin was more rustic than they anticipated, rustic to the point of tumbledown, actually, but they roasted hot dogs in the fireplace and danced to scratchy music from an ancient eight-track player.

"And then I had my big inspiration about turning that old bathtub into a romantic hot tub for two." He shook his head.

"I never did understand exactly what happened with the water heater," Jan admitted.

"There was so little water pressure that it looked as if it would take a month to fill the tub to the top, so I went outside and wrenched the valve all the way open. But the increased pressure was just too much for the seams on the old water heater." And boom! The explosion came like a giant water-filled balloon breaking, water spouting and spurting everywhere. "And then I rushed back outside to turn off the valve, but it broke when I was trying to get it closed, and the water just kept coming."

Jan started laughing again. "I've never seen so much water. I thought we were going to float away like Noah in his ark. I saw us swooshing down the mountain."

He grinned, remembering a certain bit of lacy lingerie. "And, as I remember, you weren't exactly dressed for travel."

And this time her flush was a full-blown blush.

By the time he'd found another valve at the well to get the water completely shut off, they, the cabin, and everything in it were drenched, and romance was definitely a casualty of the flood. They'd spent a nonromantic night mopping and draining and drying and cleaning up, and the next day getting a plumber to install a new water heater.

"What's that old saying about the best-laid plans of mice and men going astray?" he suggested wryly. "Include the hot tub plans of an overenthusiastic husband trying to play romantic lover."

Jan swallowed at his mention of that intimate part of their married life. She took a sip of water, although whether to distract herself or him he was uncertain. By the time she put down the glass, she seemed in full control of herself again. "Well, we got rather sidetracked there—"

He touched her hand. "It feels good to laugh with you again, Jan."

She looked pensive for a moment, then shook her head as if clearing away cobwebs. "Let's see," she said briskly. "Where were we? You were about to enlighten me with some appropriate Bible quotation about luck, I believe." She held up a graceful hand with a Band-Aid around the little finger. "And explain to me that if it wasn't just bad luck that I found this big, painful hangnail on my finger this morning, what was it?"

He reached across the table, brought her hand to his

lips, and kissed the exposed tip of the finger. "All better now?" He smiled, still holding her hand.

She stiffened at his unexpected touch, and he heard the quick intake of her breath. She inspected the kissed finger when he finally let it go. "We'll see."

He turned serious. "Okay, I don't remember the exact words, but the verse I was going to mention is in Matthew, something to the effect that the rain falls on both the righteous and unrighteous. We only have to look around to see that calamity—or hangnails—can happen to anyone. But the things that happen because of mistakes we make as sinful human beings can't be blamed on God. Instead, we can be grateful that he offered us a cover for those sins, Jesus' death on the cross."

Jan was silent for a moment, fingering her silverware. "Okay, I'll think about that," she finally said, and it sounded so much like the skeptical response Tim had once given him that for a moment he felt a wash of despair. But again she smiled unexpectedly. "But you can pray for me, if you'd like. Maybe that'll do the trick."

"I'll pray for you," he agreed, and he did, silently adding the words at the end of the blessing. Although not for the first time, of course.

Jan picked up her fork, signaling an end to the discussion. "Now let's eat, okay? Other people have come and gone, and we haven't even started on our salads yet."

He nodded, spooned ranch dressing onto his salad and brought up another idea that had occurred to him after leaving the clinic.

"How about posting flyers around town? It probably wouldn't take more than a day or two to get something printed. Although I'm undecided what we should put on a flyer. We don't even have a definite description of Stardust to offer."

"We could just give Tim's and Stardust's names and say that if anyone had known either, we'd like to talk to them. But writing up something by hand might be a better idea than a printed poster or flyer," she added thoughtfully. "I think the people Tim and Stardust associated with might be suspicious or put off by anything too formal, anything that looked too much like some authoritarian wanted poster."

Mark nodded, appreciating her quick insight into a lifestyle that was so foreign to her. "You're right. We wouldn't want anyone to be reluctant to contact us because of fear they might wind up having to deal with the authorities in some incriminating official investigation."

"Yes. I don't care who they are or what they've done, if they'll just help us find Stardust." She dropped her fine-boned wrist to the edge of the table, as if the fork were suddenly too heavy for it. "Talking about it this way seems to suggest that deep down we're already acknowledging failure, that we know we'll be leaving here without finding Stardust or learning anything definite, and all we can do is hope someone may contact us later."

"Well, we certainly haven't reached that point yet," he declared firmly. "I'm still hopeful that we'll walk in somewhere and Stardust will be there, either pregnant or with the baby already in her arms. And that she'll be delighted to see us."

Jan's slim body straightened in the chair, a forkful of shrimp paused halfway to her mouth. "It never occurred to me that she might *not* be delighted to see us. But that's possible, isn't it?" A hint of panic fluttered in her voice. "If she and Tim fought and split up, it's possible she won't want anything to do with us."

Mark groaned inwardly when he saw the discouraging possibility cut lines around Jan's mouth and cloud her eyes. Now he'd inadvertently given her something new to worry about. Then she brought up an even more devastating possibility that somehow had never occurred to him.

"What if after Tim died, or maybe even before if they broke up, Stardust decided she didn't want a child," she said slowly. "What if we don't have a grand-child...because she had an abortion?"

"Oh, surely not—" Yet abortions were performed all the time, thousands of them. His own apprehension closed his throat on a bite of shrimp, and he went into a sudden explosion of coughing.

A waitress rushed over, but he waved her away and managed to gasp, "I'm okay." He took a sip of iced tea and after another minute was more or less back to normal.

"*Are* you okay?"

He nodded. "I simply hadn't ever thought of that." Now he had to wonder why he hadn't. Given his years in the criminal justice system, he was hardly a naive innocent about the appalling things people did out of selfishness or greed or casual disregard for anyone but themselves.

Unexpectedly, by the time his small choking crisis was over, the stricken look on Jan's face had smoothed. "If I had any doubts about your sincerity in all this, I believe that little episode convinced me. The possibility of losing our grandchild to an abortion really upsets you, doesn't it?"

"Of course it upsets me!" Then her first line hit him. "You've had doubts about my sincerity in wanting to find Stardust and our grandchild?"

Her slim throat moved in a guilty swallow. "Well, not exactly *doubts*…I mean, I've appreciated your diligence since we've been working together to find her."

"But why would I do all this if I wasn't sincere…?"

When her gaze wavered off-kilter, an appalling thought struck him. "Did you think I was just using this search for Stardust as a way to—" He hesitated and then decided he may as well be blunt. After all, given his track record of atrocious behavior in the last months of their marriage, she had a right to such suspicions. "To inveigle my way into your bed? To liven up spring break with a quick fling?"

A faint color rose to her cheeks. "It occurred to me you might like to take advantage of the situation if you could. I get the impression that you still find me…well, not unattractive."

"Not…" He shook his head. "Jan, I won't lie to you, I find you far more than just 'not unattractive.'" The color in her cheeks deepened, but he pressed on. "But no matter how much I may want to be with you, to hold or touch you, I won't."

Her gaze came to meet his, and what he saw there made his heart pound. *Jesus, make me strong, for Jan's sake as well as mine.* He drew a breath and went on. "Sweetheart, I told you not long after our divorce that I'd changed. I claimed it when I pursued you and showed up at your door with cruise tickets for a second honeymoon—"

She opened her mouth to protest, but he held up a hand, stopping her. "You were absolutely right, I *hadn't* changed then. That was before I'd found the Lord, and I was still the same old arrogant, do-it-if-it-feels-good, manipulative me. But I really *have* changed now. I've given up the practice of going around trying to scheme or seduce my way into a bed where I don't belong."

She blinked at his frankness, then sat up straight, her fingers folded together on her lap. "Well, I'm glad to hear that."

"But I'll say it again. Saying that I find you 'not unattractive' is the understatement of the year! Jan, you are, as you have always been, the most attractive, most appealing, most desirable woman I have ever known. I know you may find that hard to believe, given my past wrongdoings, but it's true."

She swallowed. "That's very…flattering."

"And I have to admit that what you suspected about wanting to share your bed is a thought that…hasn't been entirely absent from my mind." His grin held a certain chagrin. "But I don't want to be with you for some fling!" His voice went husky. "I miss you, Jan, in every way it's possible for a man to miss his wife. But there isn't an ulterior motive behind why I've stayed to search for Stardust with you. I want to find her and our grandchild as much as you do. Another family and a houseful of grandkids, as you suggested earlier, isn't even a remote option for me. This is also the only grandchild I'll ever have. And I intend to do everything in my power to find this baby."

She nodded, tears suddenly bright in her eyes.

"As for the abortion, well, I don't think we should grab on to worries ahead of time. There's a far greater possibility Stardust *hasn't* had an abortion and *will* be delighted to see us when we locate her. The Lord has already done so much for us here. He's provided us with Tim's journal, which let us learn Stardust and the baby exist. I also think the fact that we came here at the same time, that we met on that trail, is more of his doing," he added almost recklessly. "A verse in 1 Peter says, 'Cast all your anxiety on him because he cares for you.' And that's exactly what I think we should do, trust in the Lord, in his guidance and care, and not get sucked into worry about remote possibilities."

Jan smiled, a smile that wobbled a bit, but still a smile. "Still spouting those Scripture quotations, I see."

"Which doesn't mean I'm not still stumbling and making mistakes. As the familiar old saying goes, Christians aren't perfect, just forgiven."

Her expression, a little blank, reminded him that that was undoubtedly not a familiar old saying to her. And he also had to remember what she'd once told him, that she didn't really care whether or not he'd changed because it was too late; she didn't love him anymore. It was a powerfully sobering thought.

Mark picked up his fallen napkin and set it on the table. Their meals were still unfinished, but he felt as if he'd had enough to eat. Jan, too, was now angling her silverware across the plate.

"Look, would you like to take a walk or drive or something?" he asked. "Maybe we'll feel like having coffee or dessert later."

A walk sounded good to Jan. She hadn't brought a jacket, however, and the evening had turned cool. They took the Mercedes back to her motel, and he waited outside while she ran upstairs for a jacket. When she returned, he tucked her hand under his arm.

"So, where shall we walk?" He smiled. "It's a big choice, you know. We can walk down the west side of the street and come back on the east, or walk down the east and come back on the west."

"I don't feel up to making decisions right now. You decide and I'll follow." She resisted the temptation to rest her head against his shoulder.

He chose the west, and they strolled along, stopping once to look at a lighted display of properties for sale in a real estate office, another time to study an eclectic collection of old tools and household utensils in the window of an antique store. She didn't really feel like talking, and apparently that was fine with Mark.

Do we look like an old married couple? she mused as she studied their dim reflection in a window, arms linked. *Maybe.* She took in Mark's reflection…there was no denying it, he was certainly physically attractive. Lean, with a long-legged, solid-shouldered build. The kind of shoulders a woman could lean on. Good-looking, clean-cut features…no, more than that. Handsome. Definitely handsome. And that mouth…so strong, and yet with an upturn of good humor, giving the impression of a ready smile. An assured stance, a hint of mature virility—a man who'd stood the test of time and come out strong.

A trick of the street lighting silvered his dark hair, giving a clue of how he'd look in years to come. One look would tell any woman, here was a wonderful man to grow old with...

No doubt about it; if she were seeing him for the first time, she'd turn around for a second look! And she'd want to know more...

Sadness washed over her. And that was the problem. She *did* know more. More than she'd ever cared to know...how he betrayed her, the heartbreak he caused her.

She swallowed around the sudden tightness in her throat. She didn't want to risk that kind of devastation again! And yet...

His touch, his voice, his looks, all the old physical appeal still stirred her, and the changes she was seeing in who he was and how he lived intrigued her. His steadier, less volatile temperament, his abandonment of his high-powered legal career, his sincere regret for his wrongdo-ings...even his commitment to the faith she still didn't understand impressed her.

Her emotions twisted and floundered. Something that felt all too much like love unexpectedly burgeoned within her, and she instantly clamped down on the unwanted feeling, shoved it through the paper shredder of her mind.

Yet even that couldn't take away a certain confusing regret that he hadn't tried to go further than just *think* about renewing the physical intimacy that had once been such a powerful force between them.

Although she certainly would have rejected any such gesture anyway.

She suddenly realized Mark had turned away from the display window and was studying her.

"You look as if you're having some big argument with yourself," he observed, much too accurately for her comfort.

She managed a smile. "And why would I argue with myself when I have a perfectly good ex-husband to argue with?"

A crowd of teenagers congregated around the burger stand, but when Mark gave her a questioning glance, Jan shook her head. She wanted to find Stardust. The possibility of never knowing her grandchild made a hollow emptiness inside her. But for the moment, she didn't feel like prying and digging for scraps of information. She was weary of trying to put two and two together and coming up with a question mark. Tomorrow she'd jump back into the investigation, attack it the way she did a difficult selling or financing problem, but tonight she simply wanted to stroll in the peaceful evening with Mark.

They were holding hands as they strolled now, and his felt solid and warm, like a secure anchor in a sea of uncertainty. Self-consciously, thinking of her too intimate thoughts about him only moments earlier, she transferred her hands to the pockets of her jacket. She knew the small gesture did not go unnoticed, but he didn't comment, simply linked arms with her again. And it would seem prissy and rude to object to that, she decided.

"The weather is supposed to be sunshiny and nice

again tomorrow, according to a report I heard on the car radio," he said.

She appreciated his understanding in turning the conversation to trivial, everyday matters just now. He apparently understood that for the moment she wasn't up to deep discussions. A little dreamily she said, "I think I'll set out some petunias when I get home, and maybe marigolds on the west side of the house where it gets so hot in summer."

"Alfredo still takes care of the yard, doesn't he?"

"Yes, but I think I'll set out the petunias and marigolds myself."

He glanced at her but didn't comment on the oddity of that although she noted to herself that it *was* odd. Not since the early days of their marriage, when she had a profusion of hanging plants and overflowing window boxes, had she done any gardening. In fact, it had always amazed her how talented Tim was at growing things. But something, maybe the fertile scent of spring in the air, a time of new life and renewal, gave her an urge to get out and start digging and planting. Or maybe, she thought with an inner smile, it was just a grandma thing.

"We had a community garden on a vacant lot at Linhurst last year. I know as much about gardening as I do about rocket launching, but I put in some cucumber plants, those long, skinny kind I like. And then some of my students played a joke on me and substituted brussels sprout plants."

"You hate brussels sprouts!"

"Right. But when I finally caught on, which unfortunately took quite a while, considering my lack of gardening expertise and plant identification, I didn't tell the students. I just waited until it was time to harvest my crop and invited them all to a barbecue at my place." He chuckled. "They were expecting steak, and I served brussels sprouts. Lots and *lots* of brussels sprouts. Which they turned out to be no more enthusiastic about than I am."

Jan laughed delightedly. "Did you have a brussels sprouts rebellion?"

"Mostly just some grinning students who realized they'd been had. And eventually I did bring out hot dogs and hamburgers, so all was well."

Jan realized she felt a certain envy. There was something so warm and happy-family about his relationship with the students. She thought of her own huge house, silent and empty. Of course it was marvelous for entertaining clients and business associates, she reminded herself. And a friend once pointed out that she had so much space she'd never have to throw anything away in her entire life. It also didn't have to be silent. There was a fantastic sound system; she could fill the house with anything from Pavarotti to Reba McEntire with the flick of a switch.

They had reached the sidewalk's blunt end at a grove of dark pines. They crossed the street, which was also the highway that passed through town, and headed back toward the motel. Instead of going to the restaurant for dessert, they stopped at the brightly lit grocery store, one of only two in town, and bought chocolate-and-nut dipped ice cream bars.

Jan had served an elegant frozen creation from a specialty shop at her last dinner party, resplendent with silvery sparkles and imported chocolate. It hadn't tasted nearly as good as this, she decided as she let a smooth chunk of ice cream melt in her mouth. Although this wouldn't be so good, she suspected, without the scent of spring in the air, the stars overhead, the croak of frogs…and Mark beside her. Somehow they were holding hands again, and this time she didn't pull hers away.

At the motel, he walked her to the steps leading to her second-floor room. She thought he might kiss her, but he merely brushed a strand of hair back from her temple and tucked it behind her ear.

"Do you know you're more beautiful now than you were back in high school? And you won a Spring Queen crown back then."

She knew she should simply murmur a graceful thanks for the compliment, but she couldn't help lightly saying, because he had to have noticed, "Blond hair and all?"

"Color it purple with puce stripes, and you'd still be beautiful."

She couldn't help laughing at the extravagance of that flattery. "And what do you know about puce?"

"Not much. But I know what I like." His eyes roaming her face told her what that was. "See you at breakfast?"

"Bright and early."

The next morning over Mexican omelets, they debated whether to try the "retreat" on Ladyluck Road or go back out to Red Dog's cabin. Jan suggested a morning expedition to Ladyluck followed by an afternoon hike up the trail to the cabin, and Mark agreed.

Ladyluck Road, to Jan's surprise, turned out to be easy to find and well marked. But the "hippie retreat" of the past had definitely changed. A half dozen neat greenhouses lined the road, and at the gate an impressive sign arched over the driveway read: Ladyluck Farm and Herb Gardens. Farther back was a big warehouse building plus several houses and trailers. The only thing that was as Jan expected was the long braid of the man who stepped out of the warehouse when they drove into the yard.

"Quite an operation you have here." Mark's surprise was obvious. "We were expecting—"

He broke off without saying what they'd expected, and the lean, long-haired guy in patched overalls grinned.

"Dirty hippies, junk cars, the smell of pot in the air?" Candidly he added, "That used to be us, but after seeing enough of our friends go down on drugs, we wised up, kicked out the druggies, and went legit. Now we're the biggest herb-producing farm in this part of the state. We ship our products all over the country." The pride in his voice was obvious.

With a wry grin Mark said, "The people we want to talk to you about may have been some of the ones you kicked out."

Again he went through their story about Tim and Stardust and a possible grandchild. An unexpectedly pleasant scent lingered about the herb grower as he listened carefully, the tangy fragrance of some dried herb he'd apparently been packaging in the warehouse. Jan sniffed, trying to identify it. Basil, perhaps? Or thyme?

"Yeah, I remember Tim. Hard worker when he

wasn't spaced out on something. I think he left before we got around to kicking him out. Took up with a guy called Red Dog. But you probably know that because it was Red Dog's place where Tim was found dead."

"What about Stardust?" Jan asked. "We don't have a description of her, except that Tim's journal said she had lupine-blue eyes."

The braid wagged in a negative shake, sending off another wave of the herb scent. "I don't remember ever hearing of her. Bonnie was Tim's girlfriend here. I'd hoped she'd help him straighten out, but it didn't happen."

"Can you think of anyone else who might know anything helpful?" Mark asked.

"Red Dog, of course. Or I think Tim lived with some people out on Hangman Creek for a while, though I don't know any names. Tim was a likable guy, even though I heard he got—" He paused, apparently to amend whatever words he'd started to use to describe Tim's aberrant mental condition. "—kind of different along toward the end there."

Once more Mark left his name and address.

On the drive back to town, Jan struggled with a down-spiraling discouragement until a new thought suddenly occurred to her. "Is it possible that Bonnie is Stardust? That for some reason she started using a different name, or maybe Tim just decided to call her that? The description that girl at the burger stand gave sounds a little like her, small and dark-haired, and her eyes are blue."

"I hadn't thought of that, but I suppose it's a possibility," Mark agreed, though she could see the idea didn't hit him with the same excitement it had her. "Although we certainly didn't see any baby, and she didn't look pregnant."

"But it's possible she's only—" She'd been thinking in terms of a baby already born or due soon, but that could be all wrong. She hurriedly calculated backward. "She could be less than four months along and not showing yet. Maybe we were that close, just inches away from our grandchild and didn't know it!" Jan felt a pang, an ache, as if she'd let something indescribably precious slip through her fingers.

"But wouldn't she have told us?"

"Not necessarily. Maybe she figured it would make Red Dog angry. Maybe he'd warned or threatened her not to tell anyone."

"But if it was something Red Dog didn't want us to know, wouldn't he have torn the part about a possible pregnancy out of the journal too?" Mark argued.

That sounded logical, but— "Maybe Bonnie is letting Red Dog think it's his baby."

"I don't know, hon." Mark shook his head. "Bonnie and Stardust being the same girl… It's possible, I suppose, but it just doesn't strike me as very probable."

For a moment Jan's thoughts were brought up short when Mark used the small, casual endearment *hon*. Did she like it? Resent it? She wasn't certain. She jerked her attention back to his doubt about this new possibility she'd suggested. "Just circumstantial evidence?"

"I don't think it's even strong enough to be considered circumstantial."

"But it is a possibility."

"Maybe."

Mark might be doubtful, but it *was* a possibility. And, Jan vowed with a growing sense of excitement, she was going to confront Bonnie with it this very afternoon.

7

MARK KNEW EVEN BEFORE THEY CROSSED THE CLEARING around the cabin. He couldn't pinpoint exactly what was different. It was more a feeling than anything openly visible, a lingering air of emptiness, an aura of abandonment. On the door he saw proof of what he felt.

"It's padlocked!" Jan gasped.

The lock laced through the hasp gleamed shiny and new against the weathered wood.

"They may have just gone somewhere for the day," Mark suggested. But he didn't believe the hopeful words even as he said them. The lock had a look of finality and permanence. He cupped his hands around his eyes to peer through a murky window, and what he saw confirmed his suspicions. "They're gone. Moved out."

"But that old truck is still down where we parked," Jan argued.

"Apparently they had some other transportation."

Jan had to see for herself. He dragged a chunk of firewood to the window for her to stand on so she could also peer inside. Together they studied the bare mattress in the loft. Empty shelves, empty clothesline, empty gun rack by the door. The pistol and holster were gone from the nail on the ladder, the aluminum coffeepot gone from the stove. All that remained were the shabby furniture and some discarded magazines carelessly scattered on the floor.

"We should have come here first, before they had a chance to get away!"

In hindsight, he agreed. "It's possible they moved out the very night we were here."

He saw her bewilderment as she stepped down from the wobbly chunk of wood. "But why? After seeing the journal, we know Tim killed himself. We weren't accusing Red Dog after that. We promised we weren't going to the authorities."

"They may not have believed us. They may have figured we were going to make trouble for them anyway. Or maybe they'd already planned to move on and just made an instant decision to go. Red Dog didn't strike me as the hallmark of stability."

"Maybe we can find them! Maybe they haven't left the area. Maybe they just moved somewhere else nearby. Closer to town, perhaps. Somewhere that isn't so isolated."

Mark nodded. "We can look."

Yet even as he said the words, he knew the search was basically over. They could stubbornly go through the motions, doggedly keep trying. But they weren't going to find Red Dog and Bonnie. Neither were they going to find Stardust and their grandchild. Yet he couldn't bring himself to say those disheartening words to Jan just yet.

They did go through the motions. They drove to the courthouse in a neighboring town and checked local birth records for any mention of Tim's name as father. Nothing. They drove more rural roads, talked to more people about Red Dog and Bonnie as well as Tim and Stardust, left Mark's name and address and phone number in more hands. Jan carried Tim's journal with them everywhere, as if it were some talisman that could connect them with him, and she always added that lone bit of definite information they had—that Stardust's eyes were the color of wild blue lupine.

The rain returned, and they spent a dreary afternoon making up handwritten posters and tacking them up on bulletin boards at the grocery stores and a feed store and several other places around town. Afterward, they had an early dinner at a Chinese restaurant, although Jan rearranged more food than she ate.

On the drive back to her motel Mark suggested, "Would you like to do something this evening? I saw a movie theater when we drove in to check the courthouse records."

"Thanks, no. I think I'll just shower and go to bed early. Perhaps read through some of Tim's journal again."

He wanted to tell her not to torture herself that way, that they'd already extracted every possible clue from the journal. But he knew she would read and reread it until every painful word was burned into her memory.

At the parking lot, where the wet asphalt paving gleamed darkly under the overhead lights, he asked lightly, "Breakfast?"

Jan hesitated, and he thought she was going to say no to that also, but finally she nodded. They hadn't talked about giving up on the search yet, but Mark wasn't surprised when she added quietly, "But it will have to be early. I'm going home tomorrow. There's nothing more we can do here. All we can do now is hope."

"And pray."

"Have you been praying?"

"Yes. Of course."

"Has it done any good?"

Jesus, help me. Give me the right words to say to share my faith with her. Open her heart to hear them!

"God doesn't always act the moment we ask for something, but he's always there, Jan, loving and caring about us."

"Is he? I wonder. Does he treat his followers any better than those who ignore or reject him? I'm not a committed Christian, and I lost a son. You're a committed Christian, and you lost a son, too. So what difference does being a Christian make?" she challenged bleakly. "Is your heartbreak any less than mine?"

"No, the heartbreak isn't any less, but—"

She cut him off with an impatient gesture, and her voice suddenly unfurled all the bitterness and disappointment accumulated over the days of rising and falling hopes. "Then you can tell your God to bring me my grandchild, and when he does, *then* I'll believe in his love and caring."

Rain hammered the roof of the car and streamed down the windshield, blurring the overhead lights of the parking lot into ragged rivers of silver on the glass. Mark knew he could expound at length on the Lord's love, the ultimate proof of that love in Jesus' sacrifice. He could quote Bible verses by the score. But he also knew he couldn't promise that the Lord would deliver their grandchild to them.

So all he did was offer another quick prayer for help and say gently, "Whether you believe it or not, his love and caring is there, Jan."

She sat there silently, the world around them shut out by the veil of rain outside the car and moisture misting the inside of the windows. In her lap, her forefingers twined together in a forlorn knot. "Once upon a time there was love and caring between us, too," she said softly. "What happened to it? Where did everything go wrong?"

"I was too self-centered. Too ambitious. Too money hungry. Too impatient. Too willing to shut my eyes to the difference between right and wrong in order to get ahead. I had an ego that could leap tall buildings in a single bound."

Unexpectedly she touched a finger to his lips to silence him. "It wasn't just you. I wanted the same things. Money. Status. Possessions. But they didn't seem like unworthy goals at the time, did they?" She sounded almost wistful. "When you were going to school and Tim was a baby, and we were both working so hard and sometimes hardly seeing each other—"

"And we could barely scrape up enough money to buy groceries and gas, and there was never enough for even the tiny luxury of a movie or dinner out."

She leaned back against the seat, her gaze turned upward but unfocused. "I remember thinking what heaven it would be if we could just have a little house of our own instead of that tiny apartment. A house with two bedrooms and a fenced yard for Tim to play in. And a car that wouldn't conk out in the middle of a busy intersection."

"A good steak instead of cheap hamburger. A TV set that didn't turn faces green or have wavy lines running across it. A nice dinner on our anniversary instead of tacos with a coupon. No bill collectors hounding us."

"I remember how we used to joke about it, that we weren't poor, just 'pre-rich.'"

But somehow what had started as a simple desire to better themselves had kept growing and expanding until it was an unrecognizable monster controlling their lives. They had planned, after Mark passed the bar exam, that Jan would stay home with Tim. But his first position had been so low paying and the student loans hung like nooses over their heads that she'd taken a temporary job as receptionist in a real estate office. They'd managed to buy a little house, but after he got in with a more prominent law firm they needed a better car, *two* better cars, and then a house more in keeping with his new status. Soon Jan had worked her way into selling real estate and turned out to be astonishingly good at it. Then a more prestigious firm wanted Mark, and eventually an even bigger, more impressive house seemed essential, along with a demanding and prominent social life. They needed a housekeeper because they were both so busy, a tutor when Tim's grades faltered, an expensive security system to protect all the glittering possessions they acquired.

And somewhere in there they'd become not a couple, united, but two driven, ambitious people going their separate ways, climbing their separate ladders of success. A certain ugly competitiveness even developed between them. Plus a self-righteous feeling on his part, he remembered sadly, that he was entitled to some special rewards as one of the hottest young attorneys in town, rewards no husband should even want, much less feel entitled to.

"And Tim got caught in the middle of it all." Her voice lowered almost to a whisper. "And we failed him."

"But there was one big difference between us." She fixed him with a gaze, and he spelled it out—even though she already knew what it was: "You were always faithful."

"Yes. I was always faithful."

And the fact that he hadn't always been faithful hung between them, irrevocable and unchangeable.

"I'm sorry, Jan," he said huskily. "I can't begin to tell you how sorry I am for what I did."

It wasn't the first time he'd said that to her. But early on, he'd simply been sorry she found out. In his arrogant, self-centered way, he wanted her and his fun on the side too, and losing her was a shock. But since finding the Lord, he was truly heartsick at the simple fact of what he did because it would have been just as wrong even if she never found out.

"Well, water under the bridge now." He'd detected a small catch in her voice earlier, but now the tone was steady and neutral, not even a hint of emotion in it. "We've both moved on."

"Have we moved far enough that we might consider seeing each other again after we get home? The college sometimes has events I think might interest you. Or maybe we could just get together for dinner sometime?" She didn't respond, and he smiled wryly. "I realize this isn't the best time to suggest this, considering the unhappy reminders of my past mistakes that we've just been discussing. But in spite of the frustration and not-so-happy ending of our search here, it's been so good being with you again, Jan. I don't want it to end here."

He reached over and took her hand in his. She didn't withdraw it, but it lay there cold and unresponsive, not turning to clasp his with the warmth that had once been so much a part of her.

"Mark, I've appreciated having you here. We made a more thorough search together than I ever could have done alone. I also know now that you do care as much as I do about finding our grandchild. But memories and a dead son and the tenuous possibility of a grandchild are all we have in common now. There's nothing more."

There was more for him, much more. But a one-sided love was as incomplete as the proverbial one hand clapping. He let the pain wash over him, absorbing it silently because he wouldn't try to inflict some pain or guilt on her for her decision. She didn't owe him anything simply because he'd changed or because he still loved her.

He leaned over and kissed her on the cheek. "But we're still on for breakfast?"

She nodded, but he wasn't surprised when he went down to the restaurant early the next morning and the waitress in the section where they always sat handed him a note. It was from Jan, and it said she'd decided to leave for home even earlier. She also thanked him again for sharing in the search. She hadn't agonized over a closing, searching for some just right expression of impersonal friendliness. It simply ended with her name.

He realized the waitress was looking at him questioningly, waiting to take him to the table he and Jan usually shared. He stuffed the note in his pocket. "I think I'll just skip breakfast this morning."

"Have a nice day, then."

Yeah. A nice day.

JAN ARRIVED HOME JUST BEFORE NOON. AFTER REALIZING SHE was going to be away more than just two or three days, she'd called an elderly neighbor and asked him to pick up her mail and newspapers. She found everything neatly sacked in two plastic bags in the garage.

She unlocked the back door, kicked off her shoes, and stood at the tiled kitchen counter flipping through the pile of accumulated mail. Advertisements, magazines, bills. All her business mail went to the office, and nothing here appeared interesting enough to bother opening in a hurry.

She looked around the large, airy kitchen with a vague feeling of having walked into some stranger's house. The air had a nebulous scent of disuse, as if she'd been gone much longer than ten days. She'd been too busy at the real estate office at the time they had the house built to fuss with details, and an interior decorator took care of everything—white-oak cabinets, the open space above lined with antique teapots selected by the decorator and placed with artistic grace among twining vines of artificial green ivy. Another artificial touch of homey brilliance was gleaming copper-bottomed pans, never used, hanging on the wall. And nearby, spice racks filled with every conceivable spice were also seldom used. An arched doorway opened onto a family room done in warm wood and earth colors, where glass doors opened to a patio surrounded by perfectly trimmed, perfectly fertilized grass and perfect yellow daffodils.

Alfredo had been doing his job well.

All very lovely, and yet…

She smiled wryly, suddenly struck by the incongruity of one lone person with a *family* room. It wasn't just incongruous. It was…sad. Determinedly, she brushed away an unexpected gathering of tears and checked her answering machine for messages. She listened to a parade of business matters, the lone personal call from a woman she'd known when Mark was in law school, now just passing through and calling to say hello.

She turned off the machine in the middle of something about a pending sale. Urgent, the caller insisted, and perhaps it was, but somehow this brand of urgency now seemed vaguely overstated. Urgency was finding her grandchild…and she'd failed.

Tomorrow she'd get back in the swing of things, put aside this feeling of weary melancholy, tackle all the piled-up problems, soothe all the ruffled feelings, sell more houses, maybe even pull a coup and sell that rundown minimall that had been on the market for months.

But today…

Today she was going to start at the beginning of Tim's journal and read it all again. She opened a can of tuna to make a sandwich and carried it and a cup of orange-cinnamon tea to a chair in the family room.

The phone rang a couple of times while she was reading, but she merely glanced at it, took another sip of tea from the cup beside the uneaten sandwich, and let the machine pick up. Yet when it rang a third time, around four o'clock, and she heard Mark's voice leaving a message for her to call him, she snatched up the phone. Had he heard something new about Stardust after she left the motel?

She interrupted a little breathlessly. "Hi, I'm here—"

"I guess I should be flattered that you picked up to answer my call," he said wryly, "when my instinct tells me you're probably ignoring some other calls."

She didn't bother to tell him his instinct was right. "Did something happen after I left?"

"The waitress gave me your note. And then I packed up and came home too."

"Oh." She tried not to feel let down.

"I just called because I wanted to make sure you got home okay."

"Yes, I got home fine. No problems." She hesitated briefly, then asked, "You?" She was only asking to be polite. It had nothing to do with the fact that she didn't want to break the connection with his voice.

"No problems. Everything okay there at the house?"

"Yes. I'd called old Harry to come over and take care of my mail and newspapers. And Alfredo has been here on his regular schedule."

He didn't need to know all that. Okay, so she *was* dragging this out. Next, she'd be going all helpless and telling him she broke a fingernail or the refrigerator was making an odd gurgling noise.

"Old Harry is still around, huh? Still turning down all offers to buy his little place?"

Some people considered Harry Warren's little house a neighborhood eyesore and would like to see it torn down and a more appropriate house erected on the prime bit of property. But Jan admired his stubborn determination to live and die in the home he had shared for over fifty years with his now dead wife. He and the house somehow celebrated a lifetime commitment that was lacking in the lives of most people she knew…including her own.

"Still turning them down." She was about to add that he'd recently had the place reroofed, but then she realized the ridiculousness of prolonging this conversation with meaningless chitchat. She brought it to a brisk conclusion. "You'll let me know if anyone contacts you about Stardust?"

"Yes. Of course." He hesitated, as if he wanted to add something more, but finally all he said was, "Take care of yourself, Jan. It was good being with you for a few days."

"You too."

A week went by. Two. A month. The daffodils withered and the two varieties of lilacs bloomed, the blend of pale lavender and deep purple a living monument to Alfredo's eye for dramatic effect. Jan lost her brief enthusiasm for doing some gardening herself. Petunias and marigolds could wait another season.…

Mark borrowed Tim's journal for a few days, and after he returned it, she took it up to Tim's old room where it seemed to belong and put it away in the drawer of his nightstand. She wouldn't read it anymore. Standing by his old bed with the green and yellow jungle-print spread he'd chosen, she promised herself that someday soon she'd get around to sorting through and getting rid of things.

Mark called several times, once suggesting a musical

event at the college, but she refused, giving him some excuse. Sometimes she thought about what she'd told him she'd think about—how Jesus had died to cover the sins of each and every one of them. Sometimes it also seemed as if God—if there really was a God—was working on her in odd, almost sly little ways. Accidentally tuning her in to a Christian radio talk show about Bible prophecy and current events that she found so intriguing she started listening to it regularly. Making the music and words of a praise song she heard on the same station run through her head with annoying regularity. *Our God is an awesome God...* Going into the yard one evening to cut some flowers for her office desk and being struck by the unique beauty of each one, the incredible attention to each tiny detail of petal and leaf that proclaimed the work of the Creator.

Yet even as she felt some strange, not quite identifiable pull, she resisted it, instead giving herself over to the mundane matters of daily life.

She conscientiously tried to eat regularly and take care of her health. She had some out-of-town clients over for dinner. A man to whom she'd earlier sold a condo asked her out, and nagging herself that she needed more of a social life, she accepted. It was a pleasant enough evening although she learned far more than she ever wanted to about the plumbing business. He didn't ask her out again; however, and she was relieved.

She sold a house and the minimall and received enthusiastic praise from her boss. An earlier client wrote a glowing letter of appreciation for her inventive financing, which had clinched the sale of his property. She got several listings through referrals from previous clients.

Yes, she should definitely make top salesperson this year.

Yet somehow the satisfaction she'd once felt with such triumphs didn't rise to the surface in exhilarating bubbles as it once had. Why not? she wondered one evening as she stood looking at Mt. Hood off to the east through the window of the seldom used living room. The city was in shadow, but sunset still lingered on the mountain, blushing the snow to a faint pink. Why was she feeling like this, all restless and fidgety? The glossy evidence of success was still all around her. The house, the mountain view people always raved about, the Mercedes, the fresh deposit in her bank account. But somehow it all felt like a shell, hollow and empty inside. Or maybe a trap…

She knew the feeling was partly because her sense of failure more than offset any success. Failing Tim, failing his baby. She sometimes wondered if it was also because Mark was absent from the equation of success equals satisfaction. Early on, they'd gleefully shared every success, his or hers. They celebrated his getting a new client or winning any case, even the barking dog one, with hugs and kisses. Their finances in slightly better shape, they celebrated her passing the exam to get her real estate license with dinner and dancing, and splurged on a local Whitney Houston concert when she made her first sale.

Even after their relationship had begun to sour, Mark had been a part of her satisfaction because she could always feel a triumphant "So there!" gratification when she made a sale or received recognition. It proved she was competent and successful…that he couldn't look down on her from his hottest-attorney-in-town heights.

Because by then another subversive element had entered their relationship. Earlier, when they were both struggling so hard just to get Mark through school and survive, she'd felt no deficiency in herself. She didn't compare herself unfavorably to women in his college and law school classes. But later, after he started climbing up in the world, she was painfully aware that she, unlike he and his associates and their wives—and the smart, attractive, educated women who flirted with him as if she were nonexistent—had no education or sophistication.

They had fancy degrees; she had a diploma from a high school in a logging town slowly fading out of existence. They did things such as backpack across Scotland, dance in Paris, bargain in Hong Kong. She went to the Space Needle in Seattle on high school Senior Escape Day. They knew what clothes to wear and when, what to serve at dinners. She was painfully aware of too often being over or under dressed, of serving what was "out" to guests.

So each sale, each glossy *thing* she acquired, proved her competence, her worth. She might not be able to discuss the art in some London museum, but she could buy her clothes at the most exclusive stores, have her hair done at the best salon, and buy the advice and assistance that gave her knowledge on what was "in" and what was "out" at a social gathering.

She could also keep up the payments on this house and buy the Mercedes. She sold houses to Mark's associates or sold their houses for them; they came to *her* because they knew she was good. And now that Mark had dropped out of the legal profession, Jan was reasonably certain she had more assets and a larger income than he did.

She knew something else, too—something that sometimes puzzled, sometimes frustrated her: Mark didn't care. The rewards they worked so hard to acquire no longer mattered to him. He had his faith.

Well...how did I get onto all that?

Exasperated, Jan turned away from the window, where the pink blush had turned to icy blue on the mountaintop. Yet even as she determinedly switched her thoughts to the subject of a client she should contact, something that had never before occurred to her intervened.

Why *didn't* Mark have more assets than he did? She got the house, but she certainly hadn't cleaned him out financially in the divorce. He had almost two high-flying years at his law firm after the divorce before he abruptly abandoned his legal career to go back to school and then start teaching at Linhurst. Shouldn't he have more than he apparently had, which, as far as she knew, was just the middle-aged Honda and a modest house near the college?

Which brought up other unexpected thoughts. Did he clean that house himself? Wash his own clothes? Cook his own meals? Was he dating these days? Seeing someone regularly?

The sudden stab of pain brought on by that last question made her clamp down hard on her wayward thoughts. None of that was any of her business; furthermore, she didn't *care*. Not about his finances, his housekeeping, his meals, or his love life. What she needed to think about at the moment, she decided briskly, was her own dinner, which turned out to be another tuna sandwich because when nothing looked appealing at the supermarket, she always shrugged and threw in a few cans of tuna.

She was eating that sandwich at the breakfast bar in the kitchen, idly thumbing through a brochure put out by another real estate office, when the phone rang. She almost let the machine pick up. If she had to talk to that breathless Sanderson woman again, to whom she'd already shown five houses today, the last one rejected because the door of the master bedroom faced the wrong direction and interfered with the proper *feng shui* of the room—

She shrugged and picked up the cordless phone on the counter. Catering to clients' peculiarities, *feng shui* included, was her job.

"Hello."

"Jan, this is Mark. Stardust is here."

9

Surprise and joy and a dozen questions fluttered like
tossed confetti in Jan's mind, but she didn't take time to
try to scrape them together. She was already scrambling
off the leather-topped stool when she said, "I'll be there
as fast as I can."

"I'll give you directions here to the house—"

"I know the way."

She sensed surprise from his end of the line, but she
also didn't waste time with some evasive explanation.
Because she wouldn't admit the truth to him, of course,
which was that she'd driven by his place a couple of
times, although not recently.

She didn't bother to change from the casual leggings
and sandals she wore—she just rushed out to the garage
and impatiently edged the Mercedes backward as the
automatic garage door rolled smoothly upward on its
tracks.

Yet on the drive across town, stuck behind a slow
moving truck, she wished she had taken just a few
moments to collect her scrambled thoughts. It would
have made more sense to suggest Mark bring Stardust to
the house. She also wished she had taken time to ask just
a *few* questions because curiosity raced rampant in her
mind now. Was the girl Bonnie? Where had she been
while they searched for her so frantically? Was she still
pregnant or had she already had the baby?

Pregnant, Jan decided. Otherwise Mark would have
said, "Stardust and the baby are here."

Unless...Jan frowned as a horrible thought came to her. Unless something had happened to the baby, and Stardust had just come to tell them some terrible truth. Now that she thought about it, Mark had definitely sounded guarded on the phone. Miscarriage, abortion...

No, no, no! She would not borrow trouble. Not because of those Bible verses Mark had once quoted to her, but simply because the thoughts were too unbearable. She edged the Mercedes into the other lane, trying to get around the truck, dodging back just in time to miss a speeding sports car headed her way. Then she clutched the wheel and settled back in the seat. *None of that,* she told herself firmly. *Patience. You've got to take care of yourself. You're an almost-grandma now, and that grandchild needs you!*

It had been over a year since she last sneaked over to peek at Mark's house, but she located it easily. It was a seventies-style ranch house, standard three-bedroom, two-bath model. Even in her haste, her experienced real estate woman's eye automatically noticed that the shake roof was in good condition, the corner lot was extra large, and the landscaping—a Japanese maple and artistically arranged boulders surrounded by low-growing juniper bushes—was nicely low maintenance.

She didn't even get her finger on the doorbell before the front door opened. Mark's tall figure, in after hours garb of jeans and a light blue T-shirt emblazoned with his college's name, filled the doorway. She bounced on tiptoes, impatiently trying to peer around him.

"She's in the bathroom. Jan, before we jump into anything I think we should talk—"

Jan didn't wait to hear what he wanted to talk about.

She saw a fragile figure step out of the hallway and pushed right on past Mark.

"Stardust?" The trembling word caught somewhere in her throat.

The girl, definitely not Bonnie, looked so painfully young and vulnerable. Straight, straggly blond hair falling from a shadow of dark roots, no makeup, pale skin with a sprinkling of freckles across her nose, tattered sandals on her feet.

And definitely pregnant! A slight but unmistakable bulge showed beneath the faded blue tunic and tight-fitting pants she wore. Sweet relief surged through Jan.

She crossed the living room and wrapped her arms around the girl. Stardust's thin body felt even more fragile and vulnerable than she looked, and after a long, heartfelt embrace, Jan forced herself to loosen her crushing grip. She leaned back and looked into the girl's eyes, and they were blue…oh so blue!…with just a hint of violet. Lupine-blue eyes. Jan smiled, feeling a long-lost connection with Tim just holding this girl. Yet also feeling dismay at the faint blue shadows on the translucent skin beneath the girl's eyes.

"Are you okay? Have you seen a doctor? Is the baby okay?" The anxious questions tumbled out, but Jan didn't wait for answers. She turned to Mark without releasing Stardust. "Has she had something to eat?"

"She said she wasn't hungry—"

Jan looked back at Stardust and rolled her eyes. *Men!* And for the first time the girl offered a wisp of a smile. "Scrambled eggs and hot chocolate?"

The girl nodded. Jan took her by the hand and led her to the counter that separated the kitchen and the

modest dining room. She helped her scoot up onto a tall
wooden stool, rather hard and plain compared to the
luxuriously padded leather stools at her own breakfast
bar.

"You just sit there now and take it easy. How did you
get here?"

"I rode a bus to Eugene, but I didn't have enough
money to come all the way. So I hitchhiked from there."

Jan tried not to let her shock at that form of transportation show. There were, she knew, apt to be many
more shocks along the way. Stardust did not look like a
girl who came from a background with carefree cheer-
leading, a frilly bedroom, and a cookie-baking mother.
Briskly she filled a cup with milk, set it in the
microwave, and took a carton of eggs from the refrigerator. Realizing she'd jumped in and taken over Mark's
kitchen without even asking, she stopped and glanced at
him questioningly. He smiled, his hand waving a you're-
doing-fine gesture of approval.

"Stardust called me from a gas station out by the
highway, and I drove over and picked her up," Mark
added in explanation of the girl's arrival here. He took a
carton of hot chocolate mix out of a cupboard and set it
beside the microwave.

"Do you have luggage?" Jan asked.

Stardust pointed to a battered blue suitcase beside
the sofa. The sides were sunken. An old jacket with a
torn sleeve hung over the suitcase. Got to buy that girl
some clothes, Jan thought instantly. Decent shoes. Get
her hair cut. And get some vitamins and minerals into
her. Take her to Dr. Addington. Maybe they could do
Lamaze classes together!

Jan leaned against the counter. "Do you have a name picked out for the baby?"

Stardust looked startled. "No. Not really. I guess it still seems…not quite real," she hesitated, "especially with Tim dead."

"Well, there's plenty of time for thinking about names—" Jan stopped short, uncertain what the size of that tummy bulge indicated. "Isn't there?"

"I guess so. I went to a doctor once about a month ago. But about all he told me was that I'm definitely pregnant."

Again Jan hastily hid her shock. Stardust had seen a doctor *once?* "You'll be under regular prenatal care now."

"Did you see Dr. Nahum at the clinic?" Mark asked the girl. "That was one of the places we went when we were trying to locate you."

"No, I went to a doctor down in California. I've been down there since a little while after Tim died. I had to get away after that happened. It was just so…awful."

"Where in California have you been?" Mark asked.

"At my mom's in Oakland. But she isn't very happy about me being pregnant."

From the girl's downhearted tone, Jan suspected that was an understatement. "We are."

"Anyway, after things didn't work out at Mom's, I came back to Oregon a few days ago. And that was when several people told me Tim's folks had been down from Portland and were looking for me. Then I saw Mr. Hilliard's phone number on a poster at the store." Stardust nodded toward Mark rather warily. "So I decided just to come on up here."

"We can let your mother know you're with us, so

she won't worry," Mark offered.

"Oh, she isn't going to worry." Stardust's small smile had a bitter twist. "She was glad to see me go. And her husband, too."

"He's not your father?"

"No. Actually, I guess he isn't even her husband. She's been married four times, but I don't think she married this one."

Jan's heart ached for the rootless and unstable life Stardust had obviously lived. "Tim's father and I are divorced, as Tim probably told you, but—" she glanced at Mark, then added firmly—"we're still friends, and we both want to do all we can to help you and the baby."

"Yes, that's right," Mark agreed quickly.

Stardust looked down, her thin forefinger scratching at some invisible spot on the counter. "I guess you know Tim and I weren't married."

"We know," Jan said quickly. "It's okay."

She briskly whipped the eggs to a froth and poured them into a hot skillet. The bell on the microwave sounded, and she removed the hot milk and stirred in the chocolate mix. She set the cup in front of Stardust.

"There, that'll do you good. You need the calcium to make a big, strong baby."

Although Jan had to wonder how this frail, none-too-healthy-looking girl could possibly manage a safe pregnancy and birth, somehow she would, Jan vowed fiercely. A safe birth and then a wonderful future for both of them. Jan would make it happen.

Mark, with his usual expertise, smoothly led the conversation back to the subject of the doctor. "The doctor didn't give you a delivery date?"

"He said maybe August or September." Stardust ducked her head again, the straggly blond hair slipping across her thin face. "With everything that happened, I didn't keep track of things like I should of, so he couldn't tell for certain."

"How involved have you been with drugs?" Mark asked bluntly. "Is this something that may affect your pregnancy?"

Jan gave him an annoyed glance. Yes, this was important. But it was a medical thing to discuss with the doctor, not something to jump on Stardust about. If he wasn't careful, he was going to make the poor girl think she wasn't welcome and scare her off. "Mark, I don't think—"

"Oh, that's okay, Mrs. Hilliard. I suppose it's natural you folks would think I might be into drugs. Almost everybody else I knew was. But I wasn't. I was scared of them."

Jan brushed past Mark at the end of the counter and hugged Stardust again. "You don't have to be scared of anything or anybody here," she promised. "We'll take care of you." Looking at Mark over Stardust's shoulder, she had the uneasy feeling he wasn't welcoming the girl quite as wholeheartedly as she was.

She dished up the eggs, added a slice of toast and some orange wedges, and watched the girl eat like a hungry puppy. And Mark had fallen for that scared "I'm not hungry" stuff!

After the girl had eaten, Jan set the dishes in the sink. "Sorry to eat and run, but Stardust looks exhausted. I think it's time I got her home and to bed."

They hadn't discussed this, and Mark looked as if he

were going to protest, but finally he simply frowned lightly and said, "I'll carry the suitcase out to your car."

At the car, Jan solicitously settled Stardust in the passenger's seat and carefully buckled the seat belt around her. "Precious cargo." She smiled and patted the small bulge of the girl's tummy.

Stardust smiled back. Her fingers, the broken nails chipped with a startling poison-purple polish, lightly rubbed the buttery leather of the seat. "I never rode in a Mercedes before."

"Do you feel the baby move yet?"

"Yeah, sometimes. It's a really weird feeling, kind of like Ping-Pong balls sliding around inside me."

Jan wished the baby would move right then so she could feel it—her grandchild!—but it stubbornly remained motionless, and finally she closed the door.

Mark stood at the rear of the car, waiting for her to open the trunk. She caught a tempting fragrance of barbecuing meat floating from the backyard of a neighbor, with it the happy squeals of a child and a drift of bluish smoke. The houses were close together here, unlike Jan's exclusive neighborhood where barriers of expensive trees and shrubs and spiked metal fences made each home an exclusive island.

"What are your plans?" Mark asked as she unlocked the trunk of the car with her key and lifted the lid.

"Just take her home and put her to bed. I'll stay home from work tomorrow and see what needs to be done. I'll try to get her in to see my doctor right away. I still go to Dr. Addington."

"Is he still handling pregnancies now? Lots of general practitioners aren't these days, I understand. The wife of a colleague is pregnant with twins, and I could ask them who—"

"I'm sure Dr. Addington can refer us to someone good if he can't take care of Stardust himself." But she appreciated that he was trying to be helpful even though he still seemed markedly less enthusiastic about Stardust's arrival than she was.

"Look, I don't have any classes until eleven o'clock tomorrow. How about if I come over first thing in the morning? Perhaps I can help out in some way. I want to be part of this too, you know."

The offer surprised and pleased Jan. "Thank you. That would be nice. I think Stardust would appreciate it too. I believe we both got the impression that you have some doubts about her."

"Not exactly doubts." A faint frown line creased Mark's forehead. "Perhaps a few reservations."

"In what way? We knew when we were looking for her that she probably wasn't going to be some squeaky clean girl-next-door or college sorority type. But she seems sweet and polite. Wearing purple polish on her fingers and toes isn't some raging sin."

He looked off toward the south, where the clock tower on Linhurst's library rose above the housetops and trees, his head tilted as if he were a bit perplexed himself about his reservations. "I guess I'm not convinced she's telling the full truth about everything," he said finally. "The drugs, for instance. I doubt she's always been quite as drug free as she wants us to believe."

"Becoming a Christian apparently hasn't changed your suspicion and cynicism about people!"

"That may be true." He smiled faintly. "But being a

Christian has changed what comes *after* my cynicism and suspicions. Now I want to help them find their way with Jesus because without him, we're all lost. And I do want to help Stardust even though I have some reservations about her."

Jan shrugged impatiently. "All I know is that I failed Tim, and I'm not going to fail his child. If Stardust is lying about anything, I'm sure it's only because she's afraid we'll reject her if we know the truth. But I will bring up the possibility of drug use with the doctor so he can deal with it in regards to the baby."

Mark set the suitcase in the trunk of the car, and Jan slammed down the lid. She intended simply to get in the car and be very calm and sensible about this, but suddenly, in spite of Mark's less-than-enthusiastic attitude, the joy and sheer wonder of it all bubbled up inside her.

"We have a grandchild, Mark! We really do! Isn't that incredible? Maybe the way it's happening isn't exactly ideal, not the way we once thought we'd become grandparents. But doesn't it make you just want to shout it to the world and ring bells and turn cartwheels anyway? It does me!"

He grinned. "Yeah, I guess it does. Pretty exciting, isn't it? Grandparents. Although I can't say that you really look like my idea of a grandma."

He took her hands in his and let his gaze drift down her slim figure to the stylish blush of peach polish on her toenails, then back up to her eyes. Jan felt another blush on her cheeks even though she knew his exaggerated appraisal was gently teasing rather than truly suggestive.

"I can't think of anything I've ever looked forward to more than this prospect of being a grandma."

SEARCHING FOR STARDUST   133

"Planning to buy a rocking chair?" he inquired, his hands still holding hers. "And a little-old-lady fringed shawl?"

"I may." She gave him a teasing jab in the chest with her fingers. "And you, Grandpa? Perhaps get one of those reclining chairs that flings you to your feet by launching you like a rocket? Take up cribbage, perhaps?"

He grinned again. "What I'd really like to do is take the little old lady in her fringed shawl dancing."

His smile and the smoky warmth of his eyes did unnerving things to Jan's composure, but she managed to react with a prim, "Well, we'll see."

"Is that a promise?"

"It's a we'll-see promise, not a we'll-do promise."

"Okay, I'll settle for that. How about if I stop by the bakery and pick up croissants for breakfast?"

"Breakfast?" Jan arched an eyebrow. "How did we get to *breakfast?*"

"You said first thing in the morning would be okay for me to come over." He opened the door of the Mercedes and closed it after she slid in, ending further discussion with that take-charge way he'd always had. "And that means breakfast. So I'll see you then."

As soon as Jan eased the car away from the curb, Stardust leaned her head back against the seat and closed her eyes.

"Tired?"

"I walked quite a ways from the bus depot before I got a ride."

"You just rest, then. Sleep if you can."

And a few minutes later, when she glanced at the slight figure buckled into the passenger's seat, the girl's head indeed drooped in sleep. Slumped, the slight bulge of her pregnancy was more noticeable.

The miracle of life, Jan thought with awe. Tim was dead, but a part of him lived on. God's gift. Jan didn't think she could get all wrapped up in religion like Mark was, but the creation of a new human being was such a miracle that it was hard *not* to acknowledge that there was a god behind it all.

And with a blooming sense of wonder, she acknowledged what all this meant. She'd told Mark that if God brought her grandchild to her she'd believe in him and his love and caring. And God had done it!

"Okay, God," she whispered awkwardly, "I give you credit for this. Thank you for the baby. Thank you for bringing Stardust to us. Thank you for everything. I'll do my best to take good care of both of them."

At the house, Stardust stirred when Jan turned the Mercedes into the gated driveway where brass coach lamps topped the brick corner posts. She blinked when she saw the two-story house looming ahead of them, a warm light turned on by the automatic system glowing through the paned windows. Seeing it through Stardust's wide eyes, Jan realized again what an impressive house it was. Pale gray, Tudor style, twin chimneys, double front doors accented with formal shrubs in tall white urns. Of course, what didn't show, she thought ruefully, was the huge mortgage.

"Wow, this is where you live? It's a lot nicer than Mr. Hilliard's place."

"I think you can call him Mark, if you'd like. And I'm Jan." She smiled as she pressed the remote control to open the garage door. "Although I'll be pleased to change that to Grandma as soon as the time comes. I'll take you inside and then come back for your suitcase, okay?"

"I can carry it—"

"Oh no, you won't. From now on, no straining and lifting things for you, little mama," Jan scolded gently. Inside the kitchen she paused. "I thought you might like to have Tim's old room. But there's another bedroom, if being in Tim's room would make you uncomfortable."

"No, Tim's would be great. He used to tell me how nice it was."

"Did you and Tim break up before he died?"

"Did he say we did?"

"I hadn't talked to Tim for some months before his death. The only reason we even know about you was because his friend Red Dog gave us a journal Tim kept, and he talks about you in it. But then it just stops mentioning you, so we didn't know what happened. Except that he thought you were pregnant."

"We didn't exactly break up. But Tim got, well, kind of, you know…"

Jan squeezed an arm around Stardust's thin shoulders. "That's okay. We know about how Tim was, the mental problems and all. That's all behind us. Now we're going to concentrate on you and the baby."

Jan went back to the car to retrieve the suitcase. Upstairs, she led Stardust down the hallway to Tim's room, then excused herself to get fresh towels. When she returned, Stardust was standing in front of his entertainment center, looking awed at the big TV screen and array of electronic equipment.

"I keep telling myself I should get rid of all this, but now I'm glad I didn't because perhaps you can enjoy some of Tim's things. Although there aren't any CDs for the player," she added when she noted Stardust peering at the empty cabinet. "Tim took them when he left."

"They'd be out-of-date by now anyway."

"And the room is rather masculine looking, isn't it?" Jan frowned as she glanced around the big room with its bulky chrome and black workout machine, barbells, and motorcycle posters. She managed a light laugh when her gaze fell on the wild jungle-print bedspread. "And I never quite agreed with Tim's strange taste in bed coverings. But we can do something about all that. Would you like me to unpack your suitcase?"

"No, thanks. I can do it later. All I want is to take a shower and go to bed. I'm really tired."

Jan laughed. "I'm hovering, aren't I? It's just that I can't begin to tell you how excited and happy I am that you're here. When Tim died, I thought all chance that I'd ever have a grandchild was gone. And now you've come, and I'm just so…happy." Except that happy couldn't begin to cover what she was feeling. She resisted an urge to reach out and pat that precious tummy bulge again.

"I'm glad I'm here too."

"I won't wake you in the morning. You just sleep as late as you want. Then later we'll see about clothes and a doctor's appointment and whatever else you need."

"Will Mr. Hilliard…Mark…be here?"

"He said he'd be over in the morning."

Stardust rubbed a finger across the polished footboard of Tim's bed. "I have the feeling he doesn't like me."

Ah, perceptive girl. She knew something wasn't quite right. Jan shook her head firmly. "I'm sure it isn't that he doesn't like you. It's just that Mark used to be a lawyer; and lawyers sometimes have a jaundiced view of the world, I'm afraid."

"What is he now, if he isn't a lawyer anymore?"

"Didn't Tim tell you anything about us?"

"Not really."

Not surprising, Jan thought ruefully. He'd left home to get away from them. He wouldn't go around talking about them as if they were part of some good ol' days past. "Mark became very religious after he and I were divorced, and now he's a professor at a Christian college. I sell real estate."

"I don't remember Tim talking about brothers or sisters."

"No. He was our only child. Actually, we're kind of short on family. Mark and I were both raised in a little logging town south of Mt. Hood. Mark's mother died when he was in junior high, and then his father died when Mark was in college. My father abandoned my mother and me before I ever started school, but I don't recall that we really missed him much.

"For years she worked as a bookkeeper for a logging company to support us. She remarried about fifteen years ago, but she and her husband were both killed in a car accident a couple of years later. Mark and I have some uncles and aunts and cousins scattered around here and there, but no one we're close to." Jan suddenly realized she was standing here babbling about trivial family history, and this poor girl was sagging against the footboard, practically dead on her feet. "Anyway, as I said, we're short on family. So that's another reason you and the baby mean so much to us. And we weren't very good parents to Tim, I'm afraid, so we're definitely aiming to be better grandparents."

"Better parents than mine, I'll bet. My mom's third husband tried to…well, you know, do things he shouldn't. That's why I left and came up to Oregon."

"Oh, hon, I'm so sorry—"

"I guess I'm really tired now."

"You get a shower and some sleep, then. And if you need anything, there's an intercom system." Jan showed her how it worked, which buttons to press. "It's a little temperamental, sometimes works and sometimes doesn't, but I haven't had any use for it in recent years, of course, so I never bothered to get it fixed."

"Is there a maid?"

"No, just me. But if you need anything, you just yell. Even if the intercom doesn't work, I'll hear you and come running."

Running, dancing, cartwheeling, Jan thought joyfully as she closed the bedroom door behind her. Already the house felt as if it were coming alive. She was looking forward to tomorrow more than she had looked forward to anything for a long time. Taking Stardust shopping, changing the room to make it more feminine, talking to her, getting to know her…watching that little bulge grow…! She could hardly wait.

And she realized there was something else to which she was also looking forward: breakfast with Mark.

10

THE DOORBELL CHIMED WHILE JAN WAS JUST FITTING A FILTER into the coffeemaker. She hadn't expected Mark quite so early and self-consciously ran her fingers through her uncombed hair as she crossed the living room. Even after all these years, opening the front door to let him in as a guest still felt odd and awkward. When the house was first built, he had swept her up in his arms to carry her over the threshold and kissed her when he set her down...

For a moment, when he just stood there looking at her, his tousled hair back lit to a dark gleam by the morning sun, she thought perhaps he was remembering the same moment. But all he said, sounding a little apologetic, was, "I hope I don't smell like some football locker room. I came directly from my morning run."

He was in gray sweats and running shoes, his lean face still showing a healthy afterglow of exercise, his grin appealing. All grandpas-to-be should look so good. More than one college coed had a crush on him, she'd bet.

He held up a white sack with a delicately tempting fragrance. "But I brought croissants. Fresh."

"Good. I'm starved." And she was she realized with a certain amazement. For the first time in weeks she was honestly *hungry*. He followed her across the ivory carpet of the living room back to the kitchen, where she pulled a carton of orange juice from the fridge and poured a glass for him.

He wrapped his long legs around a stool and sat at the breakfast bar, taking the same place at the end where he'd always sat when he lived here. If she tried, she could think of unpleasant battles that had erupted in this very spot, angry words hurled like knives and bricks across the ceramic-tiled counter. But at the moment, having him here simply felt surprisingly comfortable.

"Stardust isn't up yet?" he inquired.

"I told her to sleep as late as she wanted. I think she's worn out, and not just from the trip up here. She hasn't had an easy life."

"You had a chance to talk with her a bit more, I take it?"

"Not really. But enough to know that she's been pretty well kicked around most of her life. I gave her Tim's room. I think she appreciated that." Jan took her own glass of orange juice to the breakfast bar and leaned against the counter opposite Mark. "It's so wonderful to have her here. With the baby coming, it's like a part of Tim has come home after all this time. A second chance."

"I presume you intend to invite her to live here until the baby is born?"

"Of course. She has nowhere else to go. And I'd be delighted to have her stay here even if some other place were available for her."

"And then what?"

"I don't know. I guess I haven't thought any further than that," Jan admitted. "But I want to do all I can to see that the baby gets a good start in life and help Stardust get her own life straightened out, too."

"A good start isn't just material things."

Jan nodded. "I know." She took another sip of orange juice, then pressed the cold glass to her cheek. "Maybe that's part of where we went wrong with Tim. But there are certain basic material needs every child, and pregnant girl, has, and I intend to see that Stardust and the baby have what they need."

Mark suddenly swiveled on the stool. "Hey, look who's up with the early birds!"

Stardust stood at the bottom of the carpeted stairs in the same clothes she'd worn the day before, except now she was barefoot and looked even younger and more vulnerable. The bad bleach job was still glaringly obvious, but she'd washed her hair and it looked softer, less lank and harsh.

"We didn't expect you up so early. Didn't you sleep well?" Jan pushed a stool at the breakfast bar toward Stardust.

"I slept fine. The bed's really comfortable. But I heard something and looked out the window and saw Mr. Hilliard's car and thought I'd better come down."

"You didn't have to do that," Mark protested. "And call me Mark, please. I'm not the college professor here, just an about-to-be grandpa and very happy about it."

His attitude was so warm and friendly and non-judgmental that Jan could see Stardust thawing under it. She started to hoist herself onto the tall stool, couldn't quite make it, and laughed a bit self-consciously when Mark offered her a boost.

"Sometimes I feel clumsy as a big old cow trying to go up an escalator." She looked down at her small bulge and sighed. "And I guess I'm really not all that big yet."

Jan laughed. "Wait until you're eight-and-a-half

months along, can't see your toes, and feel as if you need a football field to turn around in. Would you like to see some pictures of Tim when he was a baby?"

"That'd be great."

"Okay, I'll dig them out later, maybe this evening. Right now, breakfast is on the way."

She gave Stardust orange juice to start with, then made a vegetarian omelet, warmed the croissants, and opened a fresh jar of apricot jam. Mark's favorite. Not that she was putting it out for that reason, of course, she assured herself as she set the dish on the breakfast bar. Then she had to smile at that devious mental side step because, if she were honest with herself, the fact that apricot jam was Mark's favorite was exactly why she put it out.

Stardust shook her head when Jan offered coffee and said she'd rather have milk. "I think it's best for the baby."

"Good girl," Jan said approvingly.

Stardust ate as if it were an activity that required all her concentration. Mark made small talk about doings at Linhurst, and Jan appreciated his giving Stardust time to adjust instead of jumping in with some inquisition. Actually, it was Jan herself who asked the first question.

"I'm planning to call the doctor's office as soon as it opens. I'll have to give them your name—"

"It's really Debbie Smith." She offered the name without hesitation although she also wrinkled her nose. "But I've always hated it because it's so boring and ordinary. So I changed it to Stardust when I left home. I wanted to go somewhere else and *be* someone else, make everything different than it had been all my life."

And once more Jan was aware of how little life had offered this girl so far. "I'll tell the doctor to call you Stardust even though your real name has to be on his records."

"How old are you, Stardust?" Mark managed not to sound nosy, just friendly and interested.

"I just turned twenty-one."

Jan suspected this answer surprised Mark as much as it did her. She had been thinking, after meeting Stardust, that the girl was probably even younger than they originally estimated, perhaps only sixteen or so.

Stardust must have seen the surprise in their faces because she added, "I think maybe Tim thought I was younger."

"You're out of school, then?" Mark asked.

"I dropped out when I left home. It was a mistake, I suppose. I wanted to go to college. But the way everything was at home, I just couldn't stay there anymore. And then getting pregnant…" Her narrow shoulders slumped for a moment, but then she squared them like a soldier determinedly facing battle.

"We can arrange for a tutor or classes so you can get a GED certificate." Jan glanced at Mark. "Maybe you could even get into some classes at Mark's college."

"Really? That'd be wonderful! Although right now all I want to do is have my baby and take good care of it."

"That's what we want too," Jan assured her. "But we also want to think about the future for both of you."

Jan gathered up the dishes and put them in the dishwasher. She seldom used the dishwasher because it seemed foolish when there were only dishes for one. She occasionally ate breakfast with colleagues or clients at a restaurant, but she couldn't remember when she'd last had anyone here to share breakfast. Or eaten more than just coffee and a piece of toast. She liked the cozy, almost family feeling.

"Well, I came over to help. What can I do now that I'm here?" Mark stretched, his shirt pulling across his chest in a way that was all too distracting. When Jan pulled her attention away from her ex-husband's form, she met his gaze and felt her cheeks redden at his raised eyebrow.

"I'm...I'm sorry." Oh, good heavens! She sounded like a stammering schoolgirl. "What did you ask?"

Now both brows were raised. "What can I do? Now that I'm here? You know, to help?"

Jan nodded briskly. "Right. Well, I'd like to move some of Tim's old weightlifting and bodybuilding equipment out of Stardust's room—"

Mark groaned. "Me and my big mouth." But he was smiling even as he complained, and Jan knew he didn't object to the heavyweight job. "Maybe you and the baby would like to do a little prenatal bodybuilding and save me all this work?" he inquired of Stardust.

She looked startled, then realized he was teasing and smiled shyly. The smile did nice things for her wan face. "I'm not very athletic. But maybe I ought to walk or do something to exercise. I want to do whatever's best for my baby. But if you don't want to bother moving Tim's stuff, that's fine with me," she added with an anxious, I-don't-want-to-be-any-bother glance between the two of them.

"It's no trouble." Jan gave Mark a playful swat on the

shoulder that she knew surprised him. Surprised her, too. "Is it?"

He grinned and bent his arm to brandish an impressive bulge of muscle. "Move over Schwarzenegger, here I come."

Jan patted the bulge of muscle approvingly. "And we need the space so there'll be room to set up a nursery for the baby."

"I believe that answers one question I had," Mark said.

Yes. It had almost decided itself. Her plans definitely included offering Stardust and the baby a home for as long as they wanted it.

Mark had to take the weight machine apart to move it, resulting in enough screws, bolts, and washers to stock a small hardware store. He lugged everything down to a storage room at the end of the garage, including the barbells and various other sports equipment from the room. Tim had never been much of an athlete, but apparently he'd wanted to improve. Mark was regretfully aware of how he failed his son in yet another area because he never had much patience with Tim's awkwardness and lack of coordination.

He heard Jan on the phone several times while he was carrying everything down to the storage room. She called the office and told them she wouldn't be in today, but various business matters apparently couldn't wait. With sweet coercion—a bulldozer camouflaged as a creampuff, he thought with a smile—she also managed to arrange a rush appointment with the doctor for Stardust right after lunch.

When he left the house around ten o'clock so he'd have time to change clothes and make it to his eleven o'clock class, Jan and Stardust were just getting ready to leave for the mall. Stardust was looking out the bedroom window as he eased the Honda around the circular driveway, and she smiled and returned his wave. He was pleased because he'd been afraid he'd offended her earlier.

Stardust helped vacuum and rearrange the bedroom while Jan was on the phone. Mark tried to make friendly conversation with her while they worked, even managed to make her laugh with his exaggerated hillbilly descriptions of some of the people they'd met while searching for her, and she contributed some amusing comments about an odd woman who gave her a ride. But she clammed up when he asked more specific questions about her life in southern Oregon, her attitude cooling to near hostility.

About all he learned was that she and Tim never actually lived together, after which she added defensively, "And I never lived with any other guy, either. I just moved around working for different people or staying with friends."

He apologized, telling her he didn't mean to sound nosy, but her mood changed, and she went downstairs, leaving him to work alone.

Yet he couldn't fault her for not being more outgoing, for being a bit standoffish or moody, he decided. A reserved shyness could simply be a part of her character, a trait that might well have appealed to Tim, who was far from being a pushy person himself. And wasn't moodiness practically a by-product of pregnancy? She also didn't know any more about them than they knew about her and had no real reason to trust them. Tim hadn't turned out to be any pillar of dependability for her, and apparently other people in her life hadn't been any more reliable or supportive.

So there was no reason to feel troubled about her reticence, no reason to see similarities with other untalkative or moody people he'd encountered on the wrong side of the law when he was a lawyer. Yet the not-quite-definable uneasiness he'd been trying to quash ever since her arrival merged into one blunt question as he drove home: Was Stardust hiding something behind that silence, concealing some secret she didn't want them to know?

He frowned. What could she be hiding? The possibility that came to him was less than comforting. A criminal past, perhaps?

Like Jan, Mark wanted to do everything possible for their grandchild. Him, a grandpa! He had sweet visions of a little boy tagging behind him…*"C'n we go fishin', grandpa?"* Or a little girl bouncing on his knee, showing him her doll. He grinned. Or maybe she'd want to go fishing, too! But he desperately did not want Jan to be hurt again. Between his betrayal of their marriage vows and then Tim's death, she'd suffered enough. Now, like a gambler staking everything on one final toss of the dice, she was risking everything she'd managed to salvage emotionally from past losses, rushing into this new bond with Stardust and the baby with her heart wide open and vulnerable. If something went wrong, if Stardust let her down, what would it do to her?

Jesus, please…take care of her.

He taught his eleven o'clock class on the application and effects of the laws governing separation of church and state, forcing himself to give his students the full attention they deserved. Then he lunched at the college cafeteria and spent the time before his afternoon class working on a scholarly article about Christian aspects of some antidiscrimination laws.

He forced himself to wait until eight o'clock that evening to call Jan. He didn't want to make a pest of himself, but he did want to know how the appointment with the doctor had gone. He also had to admit he was willing to use any excuse to maintain more contact with her. By now he also pinpointed one of his reservations about Stardust. It was a certain rootlessness he sensed in her, partly from what she said about leaving home and moving around, partly from the way she simply showed up here, instantly ready to abandon her former life and start a new life with them. He had the uneasy feeling she could disappear just as quickly, that Jan might wake up some morning and Stardust would be gone, taking their unborn grandchild with her.

He got the answering machine rather than Jan herself, but she called back within twenty minutes.

"I'm sorry I didn't pick up when you called. Stardust and I were up in her room looking at some old photos, including some of me when I was pregnant. Do you remember how *huge* I was? The Goodyear blimp had nothing on me." She sounded excited and happy and a little breathless.

"I just wanted to find out how things went today, what the doctor said."

"Dr. Addington doesn't generally take new obstetric patients, but he's going to make an exception for Stardust because I've been with him for so long. He's concerned that she's somewhat underweight, and her blood pressure is a little high. He confirmed that she's definitely pregnant—not that I had any doubts!—and that she's probably about five months along."

"That would mean she didn't get pregnant until just shortly before Tim's death. His journal made it sound earlier than that."

"But it's impossible to distinguish real time from imaginary time in the journal. I often can't tell if there's a month, a week, or an hour between entries."

"True," he agreed.

"In any case, she's somewhat malnourished, and that may have affected the size of the fetus, so she could be farther along now than the doctor thinks. Besides not eating right, she's had some very bad bouts of morning sickness. And, as she said, her memory about dates just isn't very specific. So at this point, her delivery date is still indefinite. Dr. Addington said he should be able to tell more accurately from a sonogram. She should already have had one, of course, and there's a test called an AFP, which means alpha-fetoprotein, that they usually do at about fifteen weeks that she missed having—"

"I don't remember all this from when we had Tim. Does the doctor think there may be something wrong?"

"Oh, no. It's just that having a baby, like almost everything else, is much more high tech these days." She laughed, again sounding giddy and breathless. "Oh, Mark, it's all so different now! So exciting. Anyway, Dr. Addington sent her to a lab for various blood and urine tests, and we'll have the results in a few days. She has another appointment next week."

"Did he ask her about anything she might have taken?"

"Yes. She finally said she may have smoked a little marijuana before she knew she was pregnant, but nothing since then." Jan's tone hadn't turned hostile, but it was definitely defensive, as if she were afraid he might make a big issue of this. He didn't intend to, but this was another point concerning Stardust about which he had definite doubts. "Of course, Dr. Addington cautioned her not to use *anything* now. Then he asked all kinds of questions about the medical histories of both her and Tim's families. He's very careful and thorough."

"I'm glad to hear she's in good hands."

"Oh, and I also got the name of a woman to call about Lamaze classes. It's usually the husband who participates with the wife, of course, but not terribly unusual for it to be someone else."

In spite of his reservations, Mark was so pleased with Jan's excitement. He couldn't remember her chattering on at such length about anything in years. It was good to hear. "It sounds as if you get all the fun of this pregnancy and none of the…umm…unpleasant side effects."

Jan laughed. "Exactly. One of the perks of being a grandma. I haven't had so much as a twitch of morning sickness yet." Then she went on to tell him about their shopping excursion in the mall, which included everything from clothes to cosmetics to a new spread for the bed in Tim's old room.

When Jan finally ran down, he asked, "Is there anything else I can do to help?"

"Oh, I don't think so, Mark." For a moment he felt shut out, until she added, "But there is one thing—"

"Just name it."

"I think I'd like to take Stardust to church on Sunday. I don't have any special place in mind, and I thought perhaps, if it was okay with you, we could come to your church."

"Okay?" He reeled with astonishment. "It's much more than okay. Nothing would make me happier. In fact, if you don't want to bother driving, I can come over and pick you up."

"No, just give me an address and directions and we'll find it."

He did that. Then, even though that old adage about never looking a gift horse in the mouth occurred to him, he couldn't help asking, "What brings this on? Somehow I can't think it was something Stardust suggested."

"No. Actually I haven't even mentioned it to her yet, but I'm sure she'll be willing. She's such a sweet girl, Mark, so anxious to please and so concerned about doing what's best for her baby."

The thought occurred to Mark that up until this point, Stardust apparently hadn't been all that concerned about her baby. But that was unfair. Tough as things had been when Jan was pregnant with Tim, they'd still had so much more than Stardust. Their family backgrounds weren't ideal, but they were relatively stable, and they had a decent little apartment to live in and money enough to skimp by on during the pregnancy. And, most important of all, they had each other.

"But the real reason I asked," Jan went on, sounding a little self-conscious, "is because...I guess I feel I owe it to God."

"Owe it?"

"I said if he'd bring me my grandchild, then I'd believe in his love and caring. And he did it." She sounded as if that still amazed her. "So I guess I should live up to my part of the bargain."

He was delighted with her unexpected interest in attending church, in going with *him*. He'd prayed for this. But her attitude that it was part of some bargain with God was unsettling. God was in command and salvation was a free gift, but she needed a relationship with him based on yielding and commitment, not a let's-make-a-deal bartering system. Yet it was a start, he decided, and for now he'd settle for that.

"How about another bargain between you and me? You and Stardust come to church with me in the morning, and afterward I'll take you both to dinner."

He thought she'd probably turn him down, and he braced himself for polite rejection, but to his surprise she laughed. "You're slipping, Mark. You used to be a much harder bargainer. I'd expect something such as, if you let us come to church with you, then we'd owe *you* dinner. Home cooked."

True, Mark admitted, he'd once been a much shrewder bargainer. He'd kept more than one guilty client out of jail with clever plea bargaining. "I keep telling you, I'm new and improved." He also wasn't going to risk his tenuous new relationship with Jan by doing something such as demanding home-cooked food, he acknowledged wryly to himself.

"Okay, it's a bargain, then. Church first, dinner later."

This time when Mark hung up the phone, not even a boy with a frog *and* a worm in his pocket could have been as elated as he was. But, after he gave prayerful thanks for this positive turn in Jan's attitude, he made a sober vow to himself: He would do everything in his power to make this situation with Stardust and the baby work for Jan and to keep her from being hurt. Because the doubts about Stardust just wouldn't go away.

11

IT WASN'T UNTIL JAN WAS DRIVING ACROSS TOWN ON SUNDAY morning that the thought occurred to her that she may have put Mark, and herself, and Stardust as well, in an embarrassing position with her impulsive request to attend his church. He'd undoubtedly feel obligated to introduce her and Stardust to his fellow worshipers, and how did one handle the unsavory situation of an ex-wife and a dead son's pregnant girlfriend?

Even though they were a few minutes early for the service, cars already crowded the parking lot. Jan didn't immediately open the car door; she just sat there wondering if this hadn't been a big mistake. A glance across the seat told her Stardust was also ready to turn and run.

She reached over and squeezed Stardust's hand reassuringly. "I'm sure everything's going to be fine. And you do look lovely, you know."

Tim would be so pleased and proud if he could see her like this. The thought brought Jan a pang as she studied Stardust, so pretty in the new blue linen maternity outfit that matched her eyes. She hadn't voiced any objections to attending church although Jan suspected she'd rather have spent the morning at the mall.

"It looks kind of old," Stardust finally commented doubtfully. "Sometimes stuffy old places make me feel sick to my stomach."

"We can leave if you get sick, of course. But it's really quite a beautiful old building, so stately and dignified. Very…churchy."

Ivy climbed the old brick walls of the steep-roofed building, clinging to the tall spire and draping gracefully around the stained-glass windows. It looked like a place where the old hymns had been sung so many times that they were a part of the woodwork now, a place of lasting marriages and baptisms and solemn funerals. But a wheelchair ramp made a modern addition to the wide steps.

Unexpectedly, Stardust giggled. "I guess it should look churchy. It'd be weird if it looked like a bowling alley or gas station."

"Though I've heard of church services being held in such places," Jan mused.

The bell in the steeple began to ring, a sound she hadn't heard in years. She watched the shadowy movement of the half-hidden bell, the sound seeming to linger a fraction of a second behind the movement. There was something timeless and reassuring about the sonorous peal, as if it were above and beyond human trivialities. Stardust, however, in another of her moods, stopped giggling and shivered.

"Do we have to go in?" Now she reminded Jan of the deer she'd seen in the woods near Red Dog's cabin, wide-eyed, poised for instant flight. "I don't want to be stared at."

"If anyone stares at us, we'll just stick out our tongues at them," Jan declared, and that brought another giggle from Stardust.

The car door opened, and Mark leaned down to peer inside. "I've been watching for you. Everything okay?"

In a dark blue suit, pale blue shirt, and burgundy

tie, he looked as handsome and confident as if he were about to walk into a courtroom and conquer the entire judicial system. Yet there was a different air about him now, Jan thought. Something not quite definable but somehow warmer and more approachable. And definitely very appealing. Some of her apprehension lifted.

"Everything's fine." Jan slid out of the car, not needing his helping hand but not rejecting it. Mark started to go around to the opposite side to help out Stardust, but Jan touched his arm lightly. She'd planned to wait until later, but now that she felt less apprehensive, she wanted to tell him. "Mark, something happened this morning—"

"Something *is* wrong!"

He sounded so uncharacteristically panicky that Jan laughed and grabbed his hands and shook them lightly. "Oh, no, something wonderful! While we were having breakfast, Stardust felt the baby move. Not the first time for her, of course, but the first time for *me* because she let me feel it, and it was just as if the baby was...tap dancing or leading a band! So wonderfully *alive* there inside her."

His dark eyes tenderly held hers, and she wondered if he was remembering, as was she, a similar moment from so long ago. It had happened in the middle of the night, and she'd wakened him in their cheap little apartment and placed his hand on her abdomen. And together they'd lain there in the dark, and in joy and awe felt their baby's very first movements.

She saw him swallow, felt his hands tighten on hers. Because that baby they had created together was gone now, as was the marriage they had shared, and all that remained were the sweet, painful shadows of what they'd lost.

But it wasn't all gone! "We have a grandchild, Mark, and I felt him move! And I truly do want to thank God for that."

He smiled. "Then you've come to the right place. Although you don't have to be in church to talk to the Lord, you know. You can thank him or talk to him anytime, about anything."

They walked toward the open doors of the church, Jan on one side of Mark, Stardust on the other. Jan felt no trace of awkwardness or embarrassment in him, only a quiet pride as he introduced them to people still milling around and greeting each other outside the sanctuary. It was a mixed group of young and old, many of the younger people apparently were students he knew from the college. It was obvious that some people were curious, yet it was a friendly, welcoming interest, nothing that made her feel uncomfortable.

Mark took them to a middle pew, and it was only then that Jan saw the white cloth covering the table below the pulpit and realized this was Communion Sunday. She vaguely knew about Communion; she also knew she wished she'd chosen a different day for this little venture. Why hadn't Mark warned them?

The church was nicely air-conditioned and gently infused with an amber glow from sunlight flowing through the stained glass windows. And the service was definitely not stuffy. The music was upbeat and joyous, the pastor young and good-humored, and even Stardust seemed to be enjoying everything.

But a little later, a fact Jan knew but still hadn't fully absorbed was driven home. Several men went forward to pass the Communion trays among the pews, and Mark was one of them. Somehow this brought his new life into freshly sharpened focus for her. Mark wasn't just an observer here; he was truly a part of this.

When the tray of tiny squares of bread reached her, she hesitated awkwardly. The pastor had said people were not required to be members of this church to participate, that all believers were welcome at the Lord's table, and everyone else was participating. It wasn't as if she were some fanatical atheist, she rationalized as she hesitated over the tray. She'd come here to thank the Lord for what he'd done.

But she also knew she would be overstepping some spiritual bounds if she participated just because she felt self-conscious *not* participating. Finally she let the bread pass untouched and motioned to Stardust to do the same.

"What's this all about?" Stardust whispered as she peered around at all the people holding the tiny squares of bread with quiet reverence. "I went to Sunday school a few times when I was little, but I don't remember them doing this."

"It's one of the regular church ceremonies," Jan whispered back. "As the pastor said, the bread represents Jesus' broken body, and the grape juice that's coming around now represents his blood."

Stardust wrinkled her nose. "Yuk. That's creepy. I wish they'd just sing. I like that better."

Jan was quite annoyed with Mark by the time the second tray with tiny portions of dark juice reached her.

Yet when he returned to the pew, she realized with some bewilderment that much of her discomfort came not from unfamiliarity with the ceremony, but from a strange feeling that there was more to this than met the eye, that these people had participated in something with a powerful spiritual connection and significance. Something she and Stardust were missing out on.

In spite of that, she did what she had come here for, and during the prayer time tried to offer a more formal thank-you than her earlier whisper of appreciation. She still didn't feel any intimate personal connection with God. She still had secret doubts that he truly *cared*. But somehow she didn't doubt that it was his power and generosity that had brought Stardust and the baby to her.

The pastor's message titled, "A Fashion Statement for Christians," came from Colossians and was about Christians clothing themselves with compassion, kindness, humility, gentleness, and patience. Something Mark was actually trying to do in his life, Jan realized, the depth of his commitment again driven home to her.

Afterward in the car as they followed Mark to the restaurant, Stardust offered backhanded approval. "That wasn't as boring as I thought it would be."

"Me too," Jan admitted. Then impulsively added, "I didn't tell you, but there was a special reason I wanted to go. I wanted to thank God for bringing you and the baby to me." Awkwardly, she cleared her throat. "Maybe you should thank him too."

Stardust glanced at Jan, her expression startled. "God didn't have anything to do with it. I just heard you were looking and came."

"I still think it was somehow God's doing."

"My mom says the stars control everything, that it all depends on how the sun and moon and stars were lined up when you're born."

"Astrology? Do you believe in that?"

Stardust lifted a shoulder in careless dismissal. "I think it's dumb. I think that astrologer Mom goes to just makes up stuff so he can grab her money. But it's probably not any dumber than all the God and Jesus stuff," she added bluntly. "They want money too."

Jan had to admit that her own beliefs were written in something more like Jell-O than stone, but it shocked her to hear Stardust's cold statement of disbelief. "Don't you feel as if God gave you this wonderful new life growing in you?"

Another shrug. "I figure it's just nature doing what nature does, like cats having kittens. Getting pregnant just made me mad at first. I couldn't believe my bad luck, especially after...Tim died." Stardust tilted her head. "But I guess maybe it's all going to work out okay after all."

Jan reached over and squeezed her hand. "It's going to be wonderful. We'll be a real family, you, me, and the baby. And we have to start thinking about names! If Tim had been a girl, the name we planned was Alisha."

Stardust straightened in the seat, suddenly more animated. "No, I want something exciting and glamorous. I saw a movie once with a girl named Tyger in it. Spelled with a y. I think that'd be neat. Or maybe Rogue or Phoenix if it's a boy."

Jan found all the names rather startling, but she just laughed. "Well, after the ultrasound we'll know if it's a boy or girl, so I guess we can wait until then."

Jan parked her Mercedes next to Mark's Honda in the parking lot. A faint scent, rich and spicy, drifted out from the Italian restaurant. Mark opened Stardust's door and helped her out.

"This look okay to everybody?" he asked. "I haven't eaten here before, but it's supposed to have great food. Though the lasagna may not live up to yours—"

Mark looked at Stardust when he mentioned the lasagna, but she glanced at Jan. "Umm, I love lasagna. You know how to make it?"

"I think Mark was referring to the lasagna Tim said in his journal that you made for him one time. The only time I ever tried to make lasagna, it tasted like old dishrags smothered in ketchup."

Stardust hesitated. "Yeah, I guess I forgot about the time I made it for Tim." Then she laughed. "But mine probably wasn't great, either. I just saw a recipe and tried it. But I guess Tim liked it."

Inside, Stardust ordered the lasagna, Jan the chicken mascotte, and Mark the veal parmigiana, all with antipasto salads and luscious warm breadsticks. Stardust drank milk with hers. Although the sun shone brightly outside, the room was dim, and a candle flickered in a wine bottle on their table.

Jan had been afraid conversation among the three of them might lag or be stiff and awkward, but after a brief prayer, Mark entertained them with tales of a trip to Israel that he and some students had taken.

Israel was not a place she and Mark had ever even thought about visiting back in the days when their vacations were planned primarily to enhance their business or social ambitions. His account of the trip sounded as if he'd found it spiritually enriching, but there had been lighter moments, too, such as when a luggage mix up supplied him with a surprise wardrobe of slinky cocktail dresses. Stardust laughed and asked occasional questions, but Jan just listened and smiled. She wasn't surprised when Mark mentioned that he'd been baptized in the Jordan River, where Jesus was baptized.

He really has changed, she thought while he and Stardust laughed over another mishap with a goat in an outdoor bazaar.

Once she'd told him that she didn't care whether or not he'd changed, that it no longer mattered because she didn't love him anymore. But was that bottom-line true? Had her love truly withered and died, or had it only gone into hiding, lying dormant behind some barrier in her heart and mind, ready to revive and blossom again if she dared give it a chance?

But if the barrier cracked, if the love escaped into the open, who was to say he wouldn't change back and break her heart again?

She knew too many people who had jumped whole hog into something—whether religion or a diet or an exercise program—only to go back to their old ways when the new "program" proved too tedious or hard or boring. What was to guarantee her that Mark's seeming change was permanent?

She didn't realize she'd been staring off into space while the conversation flowed by her until Mark snapped his fingers in front of her nose. She blinked as she focused on Mark, handsome and laughing, eyes alight with good humor.

"Sorry. I didn't mean to send you into a glassy-eyed stupor with my verbal essay on 'how I spent my summer vacation.'" A warmth of companionship laced his smile.

Jan just sat there, feeling a little stunned, momentarily trapped between the conflicting pull of a sweet, powerful attraction for this man she had once loved and a fear of that same attraction.

Finally she whipped her scattered wits into shape and teased back, pretending indignation even as what she said was more truth than fiction, "What do you mean, glassy-eyed stupor? Can't you tell when a woman is dazzled, *mesmerized* even, by the magnificent magnetism of your words and voice and smile?"

Mark groaned and rolled his eyes, but his laughter rumbled deep and earthy. "And I thought my students were blatant about buttering me up. They're after grades, but what is it *you* want, lovely lady?"

Jan wasn't sure what she really wanted on the larger scale of life, but she improvised with something smaller at the moment. "I was just wondering if this dinner bargain included dessert. I'm drooling over that picture of chocolate cheesecake on the menu."

Mark glanced at Stardust. "Chocolate cheesecake for everyone?"

"I think I'd rather have the zabaglione."

Jan was surprised. She wouldn't have thought Stardust even knew what zabaglione was. She was further surprised as they ate the rich, creamy desserts and discussed food in general, that Stardust was fairly knowledgeable about the subject. Stardust laughed shyly when Jan commented on this.

"Oh, I've just always loved to read about fancy food

and elegant restaurants and beautiful homes, all that 'rich and famous' stuff. Of course, I've never really had a chance to eat duck pâté or lobster or the escargot I've read about, but maybe someday."

"You aren't vegetarian, then, like Tim?" Mark asked.

"Vegetarian? Well, uh…"

Jan laughed. "It's okay, we know. We heard about a disagreement the two of you had about hot dogs in a burger stand one time."

Stardust's blue eyes looked momentarily blank. Mark studied her face a moment. "Don't you remember that?"

Stardust looked down at her dish and drew a circle in the zabaglione with her spoon. "Oh, I remember, all right. I just get to feeling bad when I think about stuff like that. We should have been happy being together, not arguing about dumb stuff like hot dogs."

She surreptitiously swiped a knuckle at the corner of her eye, and Jan instantly felt guilty that after everything had been going so well, they'd now blundered into an area that upset Stardust. Yet she couldn't help saying softly, "You loved him very much, didn't you?"

Stardust nodded. She fumbled for a tissue in the new purse Jan had bought her.

Jan put her arm around the girl's shoulders and squeezed. "We loved him too. But I guess sometimes love just isn't enough."

Jan glanced up to see Mark studying them both with an odd look on his face. He was, she supposed, about to say something virtuous about the power of God's love being enough. She hurried to cut him off, but a small voice murmuring deep inside stopped her.

But maybe God's love is enough. Maybe his love isn't like human love, which sometimes falters and falls short and fails. She remembered something else from the minister's sermon, some Scripture quotation about the Lord's love being higher than the heavens, his faithfulness reaching to the skies.

Oh, no! She chewed her lip. *One morning in church, and I'm doing it too! Thinking in Biblespeak.*

Still, the small voice and half-remembered Bible verse made a powerful and appealing case. From somewhere she remembered—maybe from way back when Mark earnestly first tried to explain his newfound beliefs to her—about God's love being so great that he gave his only son for them.

Hastily she patted Stardust's shoulder. "How about a trip to the ladies' room?"

In the ladies room, Stardust wiped away the tearstains with a damp paper towel. "I'm sorry. Talking about Tim and everything that happened with him just makes me feel like I'm getting all ripped to pieces inside."

"Then we won't talk about that anymore," Jan declared. "We'll just talk about the baby and the wonderful future, okay?"

"Mr. Hilliard is really nice, but I always have the feeling he's about to make me go sit in a corner or something. Like I was one of his students, and if I don't answer a question right he'll flunk me."

Jan laughed. "He's not that bad. A pretty great guy, actually."

"You're both so honest and honorable." Stardust swallowed, as if it was suddenly difficult to get past a constriction in her throat. She scrubbed at her hands with the towel as if she'd like to scrub away some invisible contamination of the skin. "And I'm...not. I even did some shoplifting a few times. Sometimes when I was hungry, I just didn't know what else to do."

Jan didn't hesitate. She wrapped her arms around the girl. "Oh, sweetie, I understand. It doesn't matter. That's all in the past." She leaned back, then used a fingertip to lift Stardust's downturned chin so her blue eyes met Jan's. "But I appreciate your telling me."

"But if Mr. Hilliard ever finds out..."

"Don't you worry about Mark." Jan hoped she sounded more confident than she felt. "I'll take care of Mark."

12

"MARK, MAY I TALK TO YOU FOR A MINUTE?"

Mark paused, hand on the car door. Stardust was already in the Mercedes, so apparently Jan had something she wanted to discuss with him privately. "Sure."

She came around the rear of the Honda to meet him. "Thanks for a wonderful dinner. And church too."

He suspected she'd been uncomfortable with the Communion service, but she didn't mention it now. "Maybe we can do it again next Sunday?"

"We'll see. What I wanted to talk about…you saw how upset Stardust became when we started talking about Tim and their time together?"

He nodded.

"I think it would be better if we simply avoided discussing any of that when we're with her. I shouldn't even have let such talk get started today. A few days ago I made the mistake of asking her if she'd like to take some flowers to Tim's grave, and she got agitated and upset. As you may have noticed, she's a little moody and jumpy anyway."

"Not unusual with pregnancy, I suppose, especially for someone who has been in her insecure situation."

"So let's just do everything we can to keep things upbeat and focused on the present and the future when we're around her, okay? I think it would be best for both her and the baby."

He hesitated, then nodded. "Have you gone back to work yet?"

"Oh yes. But I'm keeping some time free to spend with Stardust so she can get out of the house now and then. She's pretty well stuck when I'm gone with the car."

"I have a light teaching schedule this summer, so I'm available if you need me for doctor's appointments or anything."

"That's wonderful, Mark. Thank you. And maybe we'll take you up on that offer for church next Sunday."

Mark got in his Honda and watched the larger car pull smoothly out of the parking lot. He didn't immediately turn the key after the Mercedes glided into traffic, just sat there frowning lightly and drumming the steering wheel with his fingertips.

This had been a wonderful day. They almost seemed like a family sitting there at the table, eating and laughing together, Stardust looking less like a pale ghost and more like a happy young mother-to-be. He'd felt a rising confidence that everything was going to work out fine, that she wasn't going to pick up and disappear or do something else to hurt Jan. His and Jan's eyes had met frequently, as if they were in some joyful conspiracy together. Once she even reached across the table and squeezed his hand. It gave him renewed hope.

He agreed with Jan that they shouldn't upset Stardust by discussing things that disturbed her. He could understand how she would find talking about Tim and the short time they'd shared painful. Although it also struck him as a little odd, even if it would upset her, that she didn't even want to pay Tim the respect of putting flowers on his grave. But, as Jan said, keeping Stardust's emotions on an even keel would undoubtedly be best for the baby, too.

Yet Stardust was living right there in Jan's home, just a few feet down the hallway from where Jan slept...

Didn't they have a right to know just a little more about her than her real name? If Debbie Smith *was* her real name.

One of the private investigators he'd occasionally worked with back in his legal-eagle days could no doubt confirm or contradict the genuineness of the name in short order...

He punched his thigh with his fist and turned the key decisively. *You're not a lawyer now,* he reminded himself. *So stop thinking like one.*

Yet a thought stuck in the back of his mind like a legal notice nailed to a door. They weren't going to find out any more about Stardust directly from her. Whatever secrets she had would remain hidden—she'd found an eloquently effective way to shut off all inquiry: tears.

Then he whacked that thought as if it were the old punching bag he worked out with occasionally. Stardust's past didn't matter. It might have a few blemishes she'd rather not reveal, but she wasn't some murderous spiderwoman planning to sneak into Jan's room and smother her with a pillow some night.

Jan went to the office early Monday morning to catch up on paperwork, then showed houses all afternoon, but she managed to get away early enough to take Stardust to her own hairdresser for a cut and styling. JoLei coaxed the overbleached strands into a swingy curl that flattered Stardust's slender face and emphasized her luminous eyes. There was even time for a manicure Stardust wanted to have. She chose poisonous purple again, but JoLei talked her into a nicer wine-berry color.

That evening they took an easy walk together to get started on the exercise Stardust needed, and on Tuesday she hurried home so they could have lunch together because she wanted to spend as much time with Stardust as possible.

The doctor's appointment was scheduled for Thursday, but at the last minute the nurse called to say the doctor was tied up with an emergency and the appointment had to be rescheduled for Monday. Since Jan had already arranged to take Thursday afternoon off, they went shopping again, this time going wild on baby things plus some after-pregnancy clothes that Stardust spotted on sale and a few up-to-date CDs.

Jan had thought she had enough cash in her purse for the little shopping spree. Hadn't she had five fifties in her purse, not just three? Apparently not because they weren't there. So she wound up writing several checks, at the same time noting her bank balance was definitely not at a user-friendly level. The big house and car payments were a constant drain, of course, and the car and house insurance and utility bills had just come due, plus she'd taken all that time off work to go to southern Oregon. She'd have to get busy.

Mark called that evening, and Jan filled him in on their small whirlwind of activities. Impulsively, she also invited him to dinner the following evening. "Of course, it's a working invitation," she warned. "I'll supply the steaks, but you have to barbecue them."

"Because no one else can do them to that exact stage of perfect doneness you like, right? Pink but not too pink inside, crusty but not too crusty outside."

He was right, although she wasn't about to tell him so. She simply teased, "You sound like an infomercial for a new grill."

"Can I bring anything?"

"A date, I suppose, if you want."

She heard a clatter as if he'd dropped something, then silence. Finally he said, "That's a joke, right? Paying me back for bragging about my culinary skills?"

"Well, I assume even Christians have dates occasionally." Now she wished she hadn't plunged into this because it sounded as if she were fishing for information. Which she probably was, she had to admit guiltily. And taking a thoroughly ridiculous route to do it. "Just pick up some sour cream for the baked potatoes, okay?"

"Okay." He paused, then asked cautiously, "You aren't going to have a date there, are you? I heard you were seeing some architect a while back."

Jan had to think a long moment before she could even remember the architect's name from last year. "That didn't last long."

"I suppose it's rude or insensitive to say this, but I'm glad."

"Don't you want me to be happy?"

"I'd like a second chance to make you happy."

And how did we get into all this? Jan wondered with a flurry of panic. "Just bring chives with that sour cream," she managed to say before she hung up.

He arrived with sour cream, chives, flowers for her, and a Bible for Stardust. Stardust thanked him politely for the gift, although Jan suspected she'd have preferred something such as the Calvin Klein perfume she'd dreamily sniffed at the mall.

He barbecued the steaks on the patio. Jan made a test cut in hers just after he took it off the grill and pronounced it perfect.

"So doesn't the cook deserve a kiss?" He flashed her a devastating grin, closed his eyes, and tilted his faced toward her, lips impudently puckered.

A delicious shiver crackled down her spine, and she leaned toward him. But at the last moment, she breathlessly dodged his lips and planted an appreciatively noisy smack on his cheek. "How's that?"

He pretended a frown, then grinned. "That'll do…for starters. Kind of like an appetizer before a meal." He waggled his dark brows at her.

With a sense of shock, Jan realized she *wanted* to kiss him. She was also half inclined…tempted?…to give him a kiss that would knock his socks off. But then she realized Stardust was looking at them in a what-are-you-old-folks-*doing*? way, and Jan just gave an embarrassed little laugh instead. Dumb idea anyway…

Later, well stuffed with steak and baked potatoes, they all took a saunter down a side lane to work off some of the big meal. A creek murmured gently under a small bridge there, and a jungle of ferns and vines and limbs drooped gracefully over the water, the scent lush and damp. A few pale woodland flowers peeked through the tangle, like faces shyly peering out of a crowd. Overhead the evening sky deepened to dusky orchid, and occasionally Mark's shoulder brushed hers as they stood at the bridge.

"Tim and I used to go wading in a creek," Stardust said dreamily. "Once we tried panning for gold, but we didn't get any. But we did catch some little things he called crawdads."

Jan remembered Tim mentioning both the gold panning and the crawdads in the journal. "What are crawdads anyway?" she asked, laughing. "They sound like something out of a kids' cartoon."

"They're just, you know...funny little fishy things in creeks. He said some people eat them, but we just put them back."

Mark frowned, looking at Stardust, an odd expression on his face. "'Fishy things'...?"

Stardust shrugged. "I thought they were gross."

He nodded slowly. "I think they're more properly known as crayfish. In some areas they grow quite large, but the only ones I've ever seen around here were tiny."

He glanced at Stardust, and she nodded in agreement. "Yeah. Real little."

Jan liked picturing Tim and Stardust peacefully wading together, Tim's monsters of the night vanquished by sunlight and love. Her own pain was far from gone, but it was lower on the horizon of her emotions now, and she felt more serene and hopeful than she had in months. Stardust was here and Tim's baby was coming! And having Mark around, laughing and teasing with him, feeling the brush of his shoulder and the warmth of his glance, brightened life in a way she didn't fully understand—and wasn't sure she wanted to investigate.

Later that night, after Mark had gone home, Jan showed Stardust a magazine she'd found with some easy exercises for pregnant women. They got down on the living room carpet to try them together, laughing because Jan immediately tangled herself into a pretzel shape.

"I think I made a wrong turn somewhere," Jan said, her voice muffled by her peculiar position.

Stardust studied the magazine. "I think you're supposed to put your left leg *under* the right one, then stretch forward. Here, I'll try it."

Jan untangled herself and watched Stardust, youthfully limber and flexible in spite of her pregnancy, smoothly slip into the proper position. "Then you move your legs like this—"

"Don't strain anything," Jan cautioned.

"And then your upper body like this—" Suddenly she stopped and clapped her hand over her left eye.

"Stardust, what's wrong? What happened?"

"Oh, nothing." Stardust straightened and turned over on her knees. "I just felt a contact pop out. It must be right around here somewhere…"

Jan crawled around with her, fingertips probing the deep pile for the tiny lens. "I didn't even realize you wore contacts."

"It doesn't really matter if we can't find it. I have another pair upstairs. I'll go up and put one in."

She started to get to her feet but slipped, and Jan reached to help her before she tumbled. And then they were looking into each other's eyes, and Jan was astonished to see that one of Stardust's eyes wasn't lupine blue. It was deep hazel, almost brown.

"You wear colored contacts?"

Stardust had clapped her hand over the wrong-colored eye again, but now she removed it. "I probably should have told you." She sighed. "I probably should have told Tim."

"I don't understand."

"Back in California a girlfriend and I saw this magazine ad where you could send away for contacts to make your eyes a prettier color, so we did it, and I was wearing them when I met Tim. I don't need them to correct anything with my eyesight, but he went on and on about my lupine-blue eyes, and I was afraid he'd be disappointed or mad if I told him they were just colored contacts. So I wore them all the time and never told him."

Mixed feelings surged through Jan, then she finally laughed. "I guess it isn't any different than me changing my brown hair to blond. Although it may even be gray now, if I didn't keep it tinted. But we all have our little subterfuges."

"You're not mad?"

"Oh, sweetie, of course not. But you don't have to wear them now if you don't want. Actually, that's a lovely hazel eye I see. It's a shame to hide it."

"I think I'd rather have blue anyway. It's more...stardusty."

Jan laughed. "Whatever you want."

They never found the missing blue contact, but when they went upstairs to bed, Jan felt a sweet new closeness with Stardust, as if the girl's small confession had forged an even stronger bond between them. It made her even more aware of Stardust's insecurities about herself and how deeply she'd felt about Tim and wanted his approval.

In her own room, after she showered and spent a few minutes organizing her work plans for the next day, she kept hearing a small, peculiar noise that puzzled her.

Then she realized what it was. The temperamental intercom system had apparently clicked open on its own, or Stardust had perhaps accidentally bumped one of the buttons. And what Jan was hearing was the sound of Stardust's faint, almost babylike snores, infinitely sweet and vulnerable.

Jan turned a prospective client over to another salesman so she'd have time to take Stardust to the doctor on Monday. They hadn't gone to church with Mark the previous day after all because Stardust was feeling nauseated that morning. Today they were supposed to get the results of the blood tests, but Jan had to wait impatiently in the reception room while the doctor first examined Stardust.

When the nurse finally let her in, Stardust was dressed and Dr. Addington sat perched on a corner of a small desk. His ruddy complexion made an island of color in the all-white room, and a stethoscope hung around his neck. The lab reports rustled crisply in his hands. Jan could see no reason for it, but an unexpected flutter of apprehension made her shift nervously in the hard chair. Something was not right here.

The doctor briskly summarized the results of the tests: thyroid, cholesterol, blood sugar, liver, and various other functions were all normal. Stardust had gained a pound since the last appointment, which met with his approval. Then he frowned. "There is, however, an irregularity in the protein level on the alpha fetoprotein assay test—"

"You mean there's something wrong with me or the baby?" Stardust gasped.

"Oh, no. This probably doesn't mean anything at all." He went on to say that he simply wanted to have the test rerun, along with performing several other new tests. "And an ultrasound, of course. Which will also help us determine a more accurate delivery date." He studied the papers again. "Perhaps an amniocentesis, if necessary."

Jan listened to Dr. Addington's reassurances and tried not to let the flutter of apprehension escalate into panic. He was simply being conscientious and thorough. Yet in the stark, shadowless light of the overhead fluorescent bulbs, like the interior of some icy cave, Jan couldn't help a small shiver.

"What's amnio—" Stardust eyed him—"whatever you said?"

"It's a procedure that's been in use for years. A needle is inserted into the abdomen to draw a little of the amniotic fluid—"

"No, no, I won't do that!" Stardust clutched the arms of the chair as if she were ready to hurl herself out the door.

Jan reached for her hand and rubbed it soothingly, even though she, too, was far from calm. "It's okay, sweetie. He isn't saying the amniocentesis has to be done now. And the ultrasound is nothing more than having an instrument run across your abdomen while someone studies the results on a screen." She looked at Dr. Addington. "Right?"

"Right. You can go over to the lab for the blood work now, and I'll have the nurse schedule the ultrasound and call you."

"Fine, thank you, doctor."

He left the examining room, but while Stardust was putting on her shoes, Jan hastily stepped outside and followed him.

"Could you tell me just what this irregularity in the blood test may indicate?" She kept her voice low so Stardust couldn't hear through the closed door.

"Well, as I said, at this point it doesn't necessarily mean anything." He hesitated, and Jan thought he was going to refuse any further comment, but finally he said reluctantly, "But it does suggest a possibility of Down syndrome. I'm sure you know what that is?"

Yes. She felt a constriction in her throat. "But she's so young! Isn't it older mothers who have babies with Down syndrome?"

"Not always. And this may be nothing."

"An amniocentesis could tell for certain?"

"Probably. Although even it has a small rate of error."

"And isn't there also some danger to the fetus with the test, the possibility of triggering a miscarriage?"

"It's slight, but there is a small possibility. In any case, I think it best not to mention any possibilities about Down syndrome to Stardust at this point. There's no need to alarm her unnecessarily. She seems a bit…overly emotional."

An understatement, perhaps, given Stardust's fierce outburst about the amniocentesis, but Jan instantly jumped to Stardust's defense. "Only because she's so concerned about her baby!"

The doctor smiled. "No more so than grandma, I think." He patted her shoulder lightly. "Don't worry. The ultrasound will probably tell us that everything is just fine."

The ultrasound was scheduled for Thursday afternoon. Jan worked that morning, then rushed home to get Stardust and take her to the lab. After Stardust was prepped and ready, they let Jan go in and sit with her. The room was dim. Stardust was lying down, her head slightly elevated by a pillow, her abdomen exposed between a gown and a blanket. She looked small and scared, and Jan squeezed her hand.

"Smile. You're on Candid Camera," she teased.

Jan suspected the technician had heard that one enough times to make her groan, but it brought a small smile from Stardust. The woman technician spread gel on the vulnerable-looking mound of Stardust's abdomen, and she clutched Jan's hand as if afraid the machine might suck her into its depths. The technician settled herself on a stool, turned on the equipment, and slowly moved a wandlike instrument over the mound.

Jan could see the screen, but the triangular-shaped image made no sense to her. She had expected a clearly identifiable picture of a miniature baby, rather like a snapshot they could study for details, and her initial reaction was disappointment. This was just a blurred, ghostly image of constantly changing black-and-white lines that could be almost anything.

"That's my baby?" Stardust peered at the screen.

The technician laughed. "Yes, indeed. This is the head—" Her finger hovered over a large, round object, then moved forward. "Eyes and nose here."

Jan could momentarily see the shape of the head, but because the wand was constantly moving over the abdomen and the baby moving a little as well, the image changed to a fuzzy blur of motion before she could make out the eyes or nose. Abstract shapes drifted in and out of view as if rising from a misty fog.

"Can you tell if it's a boy or girl?" Stardust asked, still sounding doubtful.

"The baby isn't in the best position for a positive determination, but I'm pretty sure it's a girl."

"A girl! Oh, Stardust, isn't that wonderful?"

Stardust tilted her head as she studied the blurry image, apparently not nearly as excited as Jan felt. "It looks more like a jellyfish or something kind of floating around. Or maybe a movie about outer space. See? There's something that looks like a planet with a ring around it! And there's a crater erupting. I don't see how you can tell anything about it."

The technician laughed again. "Oh, it just takes some practice."

She pointed out other physical features as they briefly appeared, the curve of the tiny body, arms and legs, the spine—yes, Jan could see the spine now, the vertebrae like a precious string of pearls!—and gradually it all began to take shape for her. A window on another world, a small world of creation in progress.

There, definitely a leg moving— oh, a kick, a powerful one!

"You must have felt that!" Jan cried in delight.

"What's that part right there?" Stardust lifted herself on her elbows. "The part that looks kind of like a fist, or maybe a mouth, opening and closing real fast?"

"That's the heart beating."

The heartbeat. To Jan it looked not so much like a fist or mouth as like a pulsing beacon. She felt her own heartbeat quicken, and she couldn't take her eyes off the screen. A beacon of light, she thought joyfully, a beacon flashing straight from God.

Thank you, thank you, thank you! And she had sometimes doubted God's existence and love! Not at this moment. Who but the Lord of all creation could have done this, given such a gift as this?

Yet there was something in the technician's voice, an unexpected note of reserve as she mentioned the heartbeat, that touched a button of alarm even in the midst of Jan's joy. She remembered the small irregularity on the alpha fetoprotein test and anxiously wanted to demand, *The baby's all right, isn't she? You don't see anything wrong, do you?* Yet she also remembered Dr. Addington's admonition not to alarm Stardust unnecessarily and forced herself to remain silent.

And then that worry was lost when a little hand suddenly appeared, as plain as that snapshot Jan had hoped for. Fingers, thumb, wrinkled little palm, yes, a small hand waving to them from another world, almost as if the baby knew they were out there!

Her very own grandchild! Jan watched in awe and amazement. And she fell in love. Oh, yes, giddily, sweetly, wonderfully in love! Her grandchild, right there before her eyes, with the sweetest, most perfect little hand. *Thank you, Lord!*

"Your doctor will go over everything with you," the technician added smoothly. Now her voice held cheerful reassurance, and Jan chastised herself for being a worrywart grandma reading disaster into a momentary change of voice.

After the test, Stardust complained about her feet hurting, so they stopped by the mall and found her a couple of pairs of gaily colored sandals. Afterward Jan hurried back to work, aware that she needed to earn all she could right now. Her health insurance didn't cover Stardust, and doctor and lab bills were already mounting up rapidly, with much more to come.

Thankfully, the weekend proved financially rewarding. She finally found a house that pleased the Sanderson woman and also picked up two new listings. She and Stardust had to skip church with Mark again because one of the owners insisted on Jan doing the listing paperwork on Sunday morning. But she set aside a few minutes to offer the Lord more formal thanks for the gift that she had now seen with her own eyes on the ultrasound. Mark invited Stardust to go alone with him, but she declined.

Jan had thought they'd be able to get the doctor-interpreted results of the ultrasound on Monday, but it was Thursday before the nurse called and said to come in the following morning. Jan kept reassuring herself that the delay meant nothing. This was just how busy doctors worked, and she was careful not to give Stardust any hint of her uneasiness as the nurse led them to a room. She also realized she was murmuring a small continuous prayer, *Let it be okay, Lord, please, please let it be okay.*

Here in the examining room a machine was set up so Dr. Addington could view the ultrasound with them.

A file with Stardust's name on it lay on the desk. Jan was tempted to riffle through it, but the doctor came in before the sneaky thought turned into action.

He asked a few routine questions, then turned on the machine. Again, there was the ghostly image of a baby not quite of this world. Yet it had a certain familiarity to Jan now—yes, there was the string-of-pearls backbone, there the dance of the heartbeat!—and she felt another burst of love coupled with a fierce protectiveness toward this small, unborn being.

Dr. Addington stared at the screen, a faint frown on his angular face. Then he smiled and said jovially, "Well, I suppose the first thing you want to know is, is it a boy or girl?"

That wasn't the first thing Jan wanted to know, but Stardust nodded. "The woman at the lab said a girl, but she wasn't positive."

"Girl," he said. "Quite definitely a girl."

"A girl, Stardust! Isn't that wonderful?"

"And I have a copy of the ultrasound on videotape for you. It's something mothers always like to keep."

Dr. Addington held out the videotape carton. Stardust took it, then passed it on to Jan. Jan held it with a feeling of awe. Pictures of her grandchild before birth, like some high-tech sneak preview on creation! Then Dr. Addington cleared his throat, and Jan knew without a doubt that it was a tiny delaying tactic. He picked up the file and tapped it against his thigh.

"The reason I delayed asking you to come in is that I first wanted to discuss what the tests revealed with a couple of specialists. And I've done that now."

What kind of specialists? Jan wanted to shout. *What's wrong?* But she swallowed hard and managed to say only, "And?"

He opened the file and studied the contents again. "The second alpha fetoprotein test came out basically the same as before: irregular, slightly abnormal, but inconclusive. I'd hoped the ultrasound would give more definitive answers, but it too—"

"What are you talking about?" Stardust demanded, panic rising in her voice. "Answers about what? Is there something wrong with her?"

The doctor hesitated, and Jan remembered his earlier comment about not alarming Stardust unduly. Apparently he'd now decided that whatever was in the ultrasound had to be discussed. Her own alarm thundered upward.

"The alpha fetoprotein test indicates a possibility, only a very *slight* possibility," he added forcefully, "that the baby may have Down syndrome—"

Stardust's gasp cut him off. The sudden tears in the girl's eyes and the repulsion on her young face, startled Jan. "My girlfriend's aunt had a baby with that! They called it a—a Mongoloid idiot! It looked weird, with funny, slanty eyes, and they said it was retarded and would never grow up normal—"

"Stardust, stop it!" Jan was appalled at Stardust's nearly hysterical reaction and her ugly, almost viciously stereotyped description of Down syndrome. To the doctor she added, "But the ultrasound test shows—?"

"The ultrasound is also inconclusive. The thigh bones are just slightly shorter than normal, which is a possible indication of Down syndrome." His forefinger hovered an inch over the screen, pointing out the area he was discussing. Two plus signs with a dotted line between them showed where a measurement had been taken. "But there is no evidence of the thicker folds of skin on the neck, which is a correlating sign of Down syndrome. So at this point we cannot make a definite diagnosis of Down syndrome, but neither can it be ruled out."

The silence in the room was like another presence, a hovering, ominous presence, an invisible predator waiting to strike.

"Unfortunately, the ultrasound shows something else. There is a definite abnormality of the heart. At this point, we haven't determined the exact nature of the problem, but there definitely is one."

No, that can't be! Jan could see the little bleeping flash, the little beacon from God. There couldn't be anything wrong!

"So, what we'll do now is schedule an amniocentesis to try to make a more accurate determination about Down syndrome. But on the heart abnormality, we'll have to wait until—"

"No! I'm not going to wait for anything." Stardust's voice was hard and determined.

Both Jan and the doctor turned to look at her.

"I'm going to have an abortion." She gave them a look both hostile and defiant. "And you can't stop me."

13

Jan gasped. "Stardust, you can't mean that!"

"I don't do abortions." Dr. Addington sounded taken aback by Stardust's harsh statement. "And at this point, I surely don't think you should even consider—"

Stardust cut him off. "I'm getting an abortion."

"Then you'll have to go elsewhere." For a moment Jan thought he was going to stalk out of the room. Instead, he leaned forward, the formal stiffness of his voice changing to a personal plea filled with urgency. "Stardust, you're right at twenty-five weeks—"

Stardust glared at both of them. "I don't care what either of you think or how far along I am. I want an abortion. I can't raise a baby that's all weird looking and retarded."

"Stardust, even if there are some problems, you won't be raising the baby alone! We'll do it together. I'll be right with you."

"No. I'm not going to have a baby that people stare at and make fun of."

Jan's mind raced frantically, searching for any delaying tactic. "At least have the amniocentesis to tell for certain about the Down syndrome."

"No. It doesn't matter. Even if it doesn't have that, there's something wrong with its heart. And I don't want it if it's like that. I want a baby that's beautiful and healthy."

With a sinking heart Jan realized that Stardust, in little more than a handful of heartbeats, had degraded the baby to an impersonal, disposable "it."

"You don't need to look at me like I'm some kind of monster," Stardust snapped. "Millions of women have abortions. It's no big deal."

But those millions, Jan wept silently, weren't carrying her grandchild! "Stardust, you can't do this, you just can't. It doesn't matter if she isn't perfect—"

"It matters to me. And I *can* do this. I'm going to get an abortion." Stardust targeted the doctor with her newly hardened gaze. "All I want is for you to tell me where to go."

Jan just stared at her, feeling helpless and puzzled and appalled, unable to connect this ugly, callous attitude with the sweet girl so concerned about her baby just a few days ago. Had she instantly changed? Or had that sweet girl been an illusion, someone who never really existed?

"I seriously recommend that you think about this for a few days," Dr. Addington said, his stiffness returning. "I'd also suggest counseling. I can give you the name—"

"I don't need counseling," Stardust said scornfully. "I know what I want. An abortion."

"I'll have the nurse give you some names, then."

By the time they were back in the car, the day had turned overcast and dreary, and an unseasonably chilly rain blurred the windshield. On the way home, waves of arguments raced through Jan's head as she frantically searched for the words that would persuade Stardust to change her mind. But at the house before she had a chance to say anything, Stardust marched to the phone book and started searching the pages for the organizations and offices Dr. Addington's nurse had reluctantly named for her. When she reached for the cordless phone, Jan jumped up and grabbed the instrument before Stardust could reach it.

"Please, Stardust, let's think about this. Talk about it. Work on it. Children with Down syndrome can be wonderfully sweet and loving. They can learn and do things and live good lives. The neighbors had a little girl with Down syndrome when I was in high school, and she brought great joy to her parents. She loved to swim, and I used to take her sometimes, and we had fun together. She wasn't weird or strange! And you and the baby will always have a home here with me—"

Stardust glanced up the broad stairs, the luxurious bedroom and all the things Jan had bought for her, or might yet provide, apparently holding a tempting appeal. But not enough to counterbalance the baby she no longer wanted. She shook her head.

"Stardust, you're already six months along! It's a real baby inside you, with arms and legs and fingers and toes. Let's look at the ultrasound again, right now, and you'll see!" Jan whirled, snatched up the videotape, and headed for the VCR.

"No! I don't want to see any videotape!" Stardust stared at the carton in Jan's hand as if it were tainted, a carrier of some terrible contamination.

"What if your mother had aborted *you,* instead of giving you life?" Jan challenged.

Stardust shrugged. "Maybe we both would've been better off."

Jan paced the room in frustration with Stardust's detached and hostile attitude. "But this is a *life,* Stardust, a life God entrusted to you! His *gift* to you. When you get right down to it, abortion is *murder.*"

"No it isn't. Murder's illegal. Abortion isn't. Besides, if God wanted to give me a baby, why didn't he make it a pretty one, a nice, healthy one? I want to make something of my life." She glanced around the family room, through the arched opening to the expensive white leather furniture in the living room.

"I want a house and furniture like this, like the ones I see in magazines. I want to travel and do things. Go to Paris and Rome and the Caribbean and Tahiti. Eat in fancy restaurants and fly in the Concorde. I want good clothes and a nice car and a husband who's somebody. I want some real *stardust* in my life!" Stardust listed all her wants with a fierce passion, then added scornfully, "And I'm not going to get any of that dragging an illegitimate, retarded kid along with me."

"You're willing to trade a baby's life for the possibility of a *nice house* and *a trip to Paris?*"

Stardust shrugged again, her face sullen and set after the passionate outburst.

Jan didn't hesitate. It was almost as if the words had been there all along, just waiting to burst forth. "You don't have to raise the baby. You can be totally free of her. I'll take her and raise her myself."

Stardust met her eyes for the first time since they'd come home. "You don't care if she's retarded and has something wrong with her heart and everything? You still want her?" She sounded amazed yet suspicious, as if she suspected this were some trap Jan was laying to ensnare her.

"This is my grandchild, Stardust. Tim's flesh and blood. I love him, and I love his child, too. We'll make it a legal adoption, so you can be sure you'll never be burdened with her."

Stardust just sat there, riffling the pages of the phone book. She tilted her head, a slight frown creasing her forehead. *Please Lord.* The plea coming as naturally as if Jan had been praying all her life. *You brought this baby to me. Don't take her away now. I don't care if she isn't perfect. It doesn't matter. Just make Stardust say yes. Please!*

For a few moments she thought she'd won. Stardust absentmindedly rubbed her abdomen. Surely she couldn't kill the life right there beneath her hand! The tiny heart beating, the precious hand that had seemed to wave to them, an innocent being totally unaware that her life hung in the balance.

Stardust looked down at her abdomen. "But then I'd be stuck like this for three more months. Getting bigger and bigger. I probably wouldn't have any figure left by the time it's born. And it wouldn't be you giving birth, it'd be *me*. And everybody knows how awful childbirth is and how much it hurts. Why should I go through all that?"

"It isn't awful!" Jan cried, frustrated and appalled with the selfishness of Stardust's single-minded me-me-me thinking. "It's marvelous and wonderful, and in just a little while you forget all about the pain. Can't you do this for your baby, Stardust? For me? For Tim?"

"I don't see anything in it for *me*." Stardust headed for the stairs.

Jan realized she was still clutching the cordless phone, and almost frantically she turned it over and punched in Mark's number. In frustration she heard the impersonal message of his answering machine come on.

At the beep, she left a message of her own. "Mark, this is Jan. Please call me here at home as soon as you can. Something's happened, and I have to talk to you immediately!"

Then she just sat there, hands trapped between her clamped knees, feeling lost and alone and helpless. She'd never really thought much about whether abortion was right or wrong. It had never been anything that affected her personally, and she'd simply skimmed over it. But now it was very personal, and she shivered at the unwanted images of how it was done. This was her *granddaughter*—no, no, no!

Mark arrived, plunging through the back door into the kitchen where Jan was going through the motions of cooking dinner. Until then, she hadn't realized that in her distracted state of mind she hadn't even lowered the garage doors. "I started over here as soon as I heard your message. You sounded so upset."

Brokenly she explained what the doctor had said about the baby, and Stardust's reaction. Yet even as she saw her own shock and dismay reflected on his face, she knew it was the word *abortion* that affected him more than the news of the baby's heart problem or the possibility of Down syndrome. They could cope with those problems of life, but abortion would end all life, all hope, all future.

"Mark, I don't know what to do! I've talked to her, pleaded with her, but it's like talking to a closed door."

Mark wrapped his arms around her, his jaw pressed against her temple, and she clung to him, desperately trying to draw strength and reassurance from him.

"I failed Tim." Her voice quivered. "I vowed I wouldn't fail his child. But I am! I'm failing her, too. She's going to die, Mark, die before she ever has a chance to live. And I don't know what to do to keep it from happening!"

The tears that had been trapped inside her fell then, coming in raw sobs torn from her heart and soul, burning her cheeks as they flooded her face. "I'm so afraid, Mark. Afraid for the baby…"

He didn't murmur false assurances. He simply gave her the shelter of his strength. And even in her pain and despair, she felt the enveloping tenderness of his love. She dipped her head and burrowed into his chest, turning the crisp texture of his shirt damp with her tears.

"I d-don't…know what to do."

"I'll talk to her." The soft brushing of his fingers had a calming effect as they stroked her back.

For a moment Jan rested in his strength, then leaned back. She managed a shadow of a smile through the tears. "Use some of those famous Hilliard powers of persuasion that always worked with a judge and jury?"

"I'll try." His fingers grazed her cheek tenderly. "Should I just go up and knock?"

With a sigh she forced herself to pull away from his gentle touch. "I'll call her on the intercom first."

Jan went to the seldom used intercom box on the family room wall, but a small sound from it told her the line was already open. Had Stardust been listening to them, coldly calculating her defenses?

"Stardust, are you there?"

The hostile voice came back instantly. "What do you want?"

"Mark and I are coming up to talk to you." She purposely did not make it a request.

"I'm not dressed."

Anger at the girl and her sullen, resentful tone suddenly exploded like fireworks in Jan's brain. "Then *get* dressed because we're coming up!"

Mark held Jan's hand as they climbed the stairs, pausing halfway to turn and face her. "I think we should ask for God's help."

Jan hesitated, briefly wondering about God's hand in all this. She'd been so certain he'd brought Stardust and the baby to her. But maybe she was so undeserving, he'd changed his mind.... She could almost understand that. She hadn't been a good mother to Tim, not like she should have been! Yet even if God wanted to punish her, how could he do this to an innocent, unborn child? Burden her with the possibility of one birth defect, the certainty of another, and add to all that, the threat of death from her very own mother?

Yet even in the midst of her confusion, she nodded to Mark and bowed her head.

"Dear Lord, we pray that you'll help and guide us as we talk to Stardust. Put in our hearts and mouths what we should say to persuade her not to do this terrible thing. Open Stardust's heart to hear us and soften her heart toward this innocent child. And please help us not to fail this child as we—" he paused, a catch in his voice, then swallowed before he went on—"as we failed the son you gave us. Help us not to fail *you.*"

As they proceeded up the stairs, sound suddenly blasted from her bedroom, as if Stardust had deliberately turned on one of the new CDs full force. Mark knocked on the closed door. He waited, knocked again, but when no response came he simply thrust open the door.

Stardust lay on the bed, the heartbeat of the music filling the room. Mark walked over and turned it off, but the savage beat lingered, as if it had permanently altered the structure of the air surrounding it.

"Are you feeling okay?" There was so much concern, so much care in his voice, and Jan knew he really felt that way in spite of the circumstances. She also knew he cared about Stardust's soul as well as her body, but at the moment, all Jan could truly care about was the baby.

"I guess. Considering what I've got inside me." Stardust eyed him defiantly, as if challenging him to argue with that. "And don't try to give me all that garbage about a baby being a gift from God. Not when it's a monster like this."

"Stardust, the baby's not a monster!" Jan gasped. "She's a tiny human being, worthy of our love and care, no matter what."

Stardust ignored Jan and turned her attention back to Mark. "So what do *you* want?" she sneered. "You come to tell me I'm going straight to hell if I have an abortion? Or maybe God is going to strike me down with a lightning bolt? Well, forget it. Because I'm not going to listen to any of that Jesus and sin and salvation garbage."

Jan could see the harsh, spiteful words hit Mark like a whiplash. With a painful stab of insight she now recognized how some of her own jabs about his faith must have stung him. And with fresh understanding and new appreciation, she also remembered how he had held his tongue and temper under her assaults, how his reactions proved his commitment to the Lord. It took a man of strength and authority over himself not to return those zingers she shot at him about his faith, his Bible, and his Lord. She was ashamed of herself and those verbal darts. Now, as he once was with her, his response to Stardust was gentle and thoughtful.

"He could, of course, send lightning bolts, though I doubt that he will. But I think you should consider that even if an abortion seems an appropriate action now, the knowledge that you've taken the life of your very own child is something you'll have to live with for the rest of *your* life. Many women have found this far more troubling and long lasting than they ever thought they would."

"I can live with it," Stardust said with insolent assurance.

"If you don't want the baby, Jan wants—" He paused, glanced at Jan, and deliberately changed the wording. "*We* want to adopt and raise her."

"Not just *want*," Jan interrupted fiercely. "I'm e*ager* to adopt her. Enthusiastic about raising her. It is the deepest desire of my heart."

For a moment Jan thought her passionate words had perhaps impressed Stardust, but then the girl deliberately yawned.

Mark ignored the insolent yawn. "You'll have the best medical care and pleasant surroundings to live in until the baby arrives," he pointed out to her. "You'll also have the assurance that your baby will have a secure, loved future even as you're free to pursue whatever future you want for yourself."

He went on, speaking calmly and persuasively, and Jan didn't see how anyone with a heart or an ounce of charity or caring could have stood against his quiet eloquence. Tears streamed down her cheeks again, silent tears now, falling as steadily as the summer rain outside the window.

Yet, with a feeling like a giant fist squeezing her heart, she also knew it wasn't working. Stardust reached over to the nightstand and selected one of the decadently rich and wickedly expensive chocolate truffles she'd talked Jan into buying for her at the mall. She gazed out the window and let the chocolate melt in her mouth with eyes-closed appreciation, as if Jan and Mark weren't even in the room.

One part of Jan wanted Mark to abandon this tactic of gentle persuasion. She wanted him to rage and threaten and intimidate Stardust, smash her ugly plan with some brilliant courtroom tactic.

She also knew rage and fury would do no good because this was no courtroom, and here Stardust had all the control, all the power of judge, jury, and executioner over this baby's life.

Clenching her fists to keep from saying or doing something that would make things even worse, if they could get any worse, Jan crossed to the window and leaned against the sill. Her gaze wandered the room as she kept her eyes away from the girl arrogantly lounging on the bed.

Jan's roving glance lit on the new shoes and clothes in the closet, most of them fairly expensive. The new

CDs piled on the shelf of the entertainment center. The piles of baby things, many of them lovely but frivolously useless. The luxurious bedspread and chocolates. With shocking insight seeping into her desperation, she also considered Stardust's surprising knowledge of good food and restaurants, her ambitions for house and car and important husband. And then there were the times Jan had been puzzled because she didn't seem to have as much money in her purse as she'd thought she had, which she was now certain was due not to her own forgetfulness but to Stardust's light-fingered expertise. Was this really why Stardust had come, to use Tim's baby to live the life she coveted and acquire the luxuries she craved? But now she'd decided even luxuries weren't worth the penalty of having to raise "an illegitimate, retarded kid."

Jan crossed the room and interrupted with a hand on Mark's shoulder. No, they couldn't *stop* her from having an abortion, but— "What would it take for you to go through with this pregnancy?" she demanded bluntly of Stardust. "How could we make it worth your while?"

Stardust sat up in the bed, the first hint of interest she'd shown so far in this conversation. "What do you mean?"

"I mean, what could we give you to persuade you not to have an abortion, to carry the baby to full term and then let us adopt it?" Jan paused, hearing herself say "let *us* adopt it," then rushed on. "What's your price?"

Mark looked up at her, his eyes troubled. "Jan, I don't think—"

Jan squeezed his shoulder until her fingers bit into

the flesh, urging him to silence. A sly, crafty look came over Stardust's pale face. Jan could almost hear the greedy wheels turning.

"A car."

"A car?" Mark repeated with the same astonishment Jan felt. Somehow she'd thought even greedy Stardust might go for something more lofty or meaningful, a college education perhaps, something to give her a jump-start on the glittering future she wanted. But no, a *car.*

"You get me a brand new car, one I pick out, all paid for, and I'll have the baby. Then I'm outta here. It's all your responsibility then, no matter what's wrong with it. With guarantees that you'll never tell her anything to help her find me."

Jan swallowed, trying to conceal her dismay that Stardust could truly be this greedy and self-centered and so clearly uncaring about the baby. Yet this was bargaining time, and she didn't waste time regretting how wrong she'd been about this girl.

"And you'll follow whatever advice the doctor gives about your pregnancy, do whatever he says is best for the baby, take whatever tests or procedures he deems necessary?"

"Everything except that amnio thing. I'm not going to have some big needle stuck in my stomach."

Now Jan knew the truth there also. She'd naively thought Stardust didn't want the test because she was concerned about possible danger to the baby, as Jan was; instead, she was only concerned about herself. Yet Jan also knew the amniocentesis was irrelevant to her own decision. Whatever it showed, she still wanted this baby,

Tim's child, her and Mark's grandchild. So she didn't care if the test was never made.

"It's a deal, then," Jan said, as crisply as if she were finalizing a difficult sale on a house. "The car of your choice for a full-term pregnancy and signing adoption papers afterward."

Stardust got in the last word, her voice satisfied and triumphant. "And no amnio thing."

Outside, beyond the closed door, Mark shook his head. "Jan, I'm not sure this is the proper way—"

"Maybe not, but it worked," she cut in. "And nothing else was working."

"I didn't have anything to do with adoption cases in my legal practice, but I suspect this could be construed as baby selling. Baby *buying*. And that's not exactly on the up-and-up. If it ever got into court—"

Jan stopped on the carpeted stairs. "Why would it ever get into court?"

"Because sometimes time changes things. Mothers have regrets and change their minds. You read the newspapers. There have been a few cases where several years after an adoption, a birth parent decides he or she wants a child back, or the other parent shows up, and in some cases they've gotten the child even when the adoption was apparently final. And in this case a sharp lawyer could dig up all kinds of ammunition in Stardust's favor. The baby-buying thing for one. Decision made under duress. Mental anguish. Maybe even coercion. Who knows?"

"Surely a court wouldn't condemn us for doing whatever was necessary to save the baby's life!"

"You can never tell what a court will do until you're right there facing a judge."

Apprehension rippled a cold chill across Jan's back, but she determinedly ignored it. "Right now, all I'm concerned about is saving our granddaughter's life. Maybe you don't care that much, but I'll do whatever it takes to save her." She saw a flare of anger or hurt cross his face at the accusation, and she guiltily knew it wasn't true. "Mark, you prayed for the right words to say to Stardust to keep her from having the abortion. And these words worked."

"I care about the baby just as much as you do. All the time I was talking to Stardust I had to keep asking the Lord for patience and control. And grit my teeth and clench my fists because I wanted to take that smirk off her face with...unacceptable means. But I see possible problems lying in wait for us, legal potholes—"

"Do you want to worry about 'legal potholes' or save our granddaughter?"

He looked at her, eyes dark and troubled. "That's the bottom line, isn't it?" And, after a brief hesitation, there were no more arguments. He simply nodded. "Okay, no more lawyer talk from me. But there is something else I think we should talk about."

Jan knew from the look in his eyes what that was. Her "let *us* adopt" statement, an echo of his own words about adoption a few moments earlier, hadn't gone unnoticed after all.

She touched her fingers to his lips, gently asking him for silence, asking him not to rush her to talk about something that was still unclear in her own mind.

Us.

Why had she said *us*? Two people living separate lives in separate houses, as they were, did not make an *us* to adopt and raise a baby.

He kissed the fingers. "But soon," he whispered.

14

THAT SATURDAY THE THREE OF THEM WENT CAR SHOPPING. Under different circumstances, Mark thought as they wandered the colorful rows of gleaming cars, it might have been fun. The summer day was hot and bright, an abrupt change from last week's rain. The atmosphere at several of the car lots was almost like a carnival. Big tents for shade, fluttering strings of pennants and balloons, scents of free hot dogs and buttered popcorn. Stardust, not letting the bulge of her pregnancy slow her down, dashed around like a giddy child turned loose with a pocket of quarters in a video arcade.

"Oh, look at that red Mustang! Isn't that red fantastic?" Or, hand caressing another hot metallic hood, "Oh, I love convertibles! I've always wanted a convertible!" And, kicking a tire on a sports utility vehicle, "Maybe I should get one of these four-wheel drives. I could go anywhere and have lots of fun with that."

As it was, however, the thought that dominated his mind was the sad truth that a car and "fun" mattered more to Stardust than her own baby, a thought he knew also haunted Jan's mind.

Jan wasn't saying much today although they'd talked for a long time after leaving Stardust's room the other day. He stayed away from actually proposing to her, knowing she wasn't ready for that yet, but he made sure she knew how eager he was to raise their grand-daughter, no matter what the baby's physical or mental problems might be. She ran the videotape of the ultrasound test for him, and he felt truly awed by it, almost as if he were peering over God's shoulder, watching him create this wonderful new life. They held hands as they watched, thoughts and emotions linked by this physical continuation of their love.

They agreed to pay for Stardust's car together. He could tap into his retirement fund, and Jan, without explaining how, said she could come up with her half. This morning when he arrived at the house, he was astonished to learn how she did it. The expensive Mercedes, the luxury car that had been one of her goals ever since they started to climb the ladder of financial success, was gone. She financed payments on a two-year-old, considerably less expensive Toyota and got cash out of the Mercedes to pay for Stardust's car. At first he thought she'd surely be upset about giving up the Mercedes, but she read his mind and smiled slightly.

"Stardust's focus on the exchange of a car for a baby helped me put things in perspective," she said simply.

Finally about midafternoon, Stardust settled on what she wanted. The sporty, high-powered Firebird was hardly, in Mark's opinion, a practical choice, and it wasn't cheap. But it wasn't, price-wise, as outrageous as the Ferrari or Jaguar he'd suspected she might demand.

They went into the office to finalize the deal. The salesman filling out the papers asked what name should go on the title. Stardust whipped out her driver's license and shoved it at him.

"Deborah Smith."

So the name is genuine. Mark remembered his earlier doubt, and Jan's story about Stardust's deception with the colored contacts. Jan didn't doubt Stardust's explanation, and he had no real reason to doubt it either. Yet there was that little peculiarity about, of all things, crawdads. Stardust had said she and Tim caught them in a creek, but from her description of crawdads as "little fishy things," he was reasonably certain she had no idea they were a shelled creature that looked rather like a cross between an insect and a miniature lobster. Which meant…what? Maybe nothing.

Maybe everything.

Mark reached over and pushed the license back to her. "No, I don't think so," he said pleasantly. "For now, the title will be in Jan's and my names. Later, at the…umm…proper time, we'll sign it over to you."

Stardust's small chin shot up, and Jan touched his arm apprehensively, but he counted on Stardust's greed and hunger for instant gratification to win out. He was right.

"But I get the car right now, even if it's not in my name?"

He nodded, and she slumped back in the chair and impatiently watched the salesman finish filling out the papers. When the salesman dangled the keys, she grabbed them and disappeared out the door with neither thanks nor good-bye.

She drove the red Firebird off the lot, tires squealing, as if afraid someone might snatch it away from her, when Mark and Jan went back outside.

"She'd have done it, wouldn't she?" Jan sounded down and discouraged and a little incredulous. She had always been one to think the best of people. Him included, he thought regretfully, as he remembered with well-worn guilt how his clever deceptions had used that trust to betray her. "If you hadn't outsmarted her about the name on the title, she'd have taken the car and run off and had the abortion anyway."

He didn't want to linger on this dismal subject. "How about going somewhere cool for a glass of lemonade or iced tea?" Dizzying waves of heat shimmered just above the asphalt of the car lot.

"The house is the coolest place I can think of," she said. "Why don't we just go back there?"

"My place is closer."

Mark's house was blessedly cool; the air-conditioning was on and the drapes on the west side were pulled. Jan heard the chink of ice cubes from the kitchen.

"Make yourself comfortable," he called. "Use the bathroom off the master bedroom, if you'd like. I have to give the faucet in the other bathroom an overhaul. It's sticking."

"Since when did you take up home repair?"

He came out of the kitchen holding two glasses. "Some guys at church formed a group that helps needy seniors with repairs, and I've learned a few things about faulty faucets, leaky roofs, and broken windows from working with them. Leaky water heaters, too," he added with a smile.

The new and improved Mark Hilliard, Jan thought, surprised once more. She made her way through his bedroom to the bath. The bedroom was done in masculine tones of brown and green, with a muted plaid bedspread, and a painting of a mountain scene on the wall. It was neat but lived-in looking, with jogging sweats flung over a chair, ties draped over the mirror, and slippers overturned by the bed. But different from the old days—no oversized TV loomed at the foot of the bed, and on the nightstand were a Bible, a Billy Graham devotional guide, and two books of Christian fiction.

In the bathroom she sloshed cold water on her face and dried it on a husky green towel. The counter was uncluttered—shaving gear, toothbrush and toothpaste, deodorant, mouthwash, aftershave lotion. Soap-on-a-rope hung in the shower, a bottle of shampoo on the floor. Now she knew why, despite the feminine clutter of her bathroom at home, sometimes it felt so strangely empty. Because it was missing these simple little male things. Mark's things.

Which was not reason enough, she thought wryly, to take him up on what she suspected was coming soon—a proposal that they remarry. That they become an "us." She was deeply attracted to him, both on a physical level and a new attraction to the changed man she saw shining through the outer covering. And Alisha—yes, she'd already named the baby!—was Mark's grandchild, too, and he had as much right to raise her as she did. Yet jumping back into marriage was such a huge step, a step that still sent tremors of old heartbreak and apprehension through her.

He handed her one of the icy glasses of lemonade when she went back to the living room. She took it, kicked off her sandals, and sat on the sofa, one leg tucked under her.

"Is there one in every room?" She nodded toward the Bible on the coffee table.

He smiled. "I hadn't thought about it, but I suppose there is."

Jan leaned over and riffled the pages, Jesus' words in red, flashing by like threads of scarlet. "Doesn't knowing the baby may have serious physical and mental defects make you wonder about God? Doubt that he really does care?"

"Wonder why he lets a child come into the world physically or mentally less than whole?" Mark nodded slowly. "Yes, I suppose I do wonder. But doubt him? No. Each child has a soul that is precious to him, whatever the outward flaws."

"For a while, when I was so thankful to God for bringing Stardust and the baby to me, I was almost ready to believe and trust him. But now..." Jan shook her head.

"Aren't you still thankful and grateful?"

She looked a little surprised, then nodded. "Yes, of course I am. It isn't that. I guess it's just that I can't help wondering about loving and trusting a God who will burden a baby with all our granddaughter is facing."

"He cares, Jan, no matter how things may sometimes appear. And even if he doesn't handle situations exactly as we'd prefer, he's always in control."

She traced a trickling bead of sweat on the glass with her fingertip. "What made you become a Christian, Mark? What made you give up everything you'd worked for in your career?" He'd talked with her about being a Christian, how it had changed him, but never about what had caused him to turn his life over to God.

He leaned back against the sofa. "About six or seven years ago, the law firm had a client named Lex Adler. A difficult client, with a temper that exploded like a bomb when things didn't go his way, but he did a considerable amount of extremely lucrative business with us. I didn't usually deal with him because most of his legal work dealt with land development projects. But then he got in trouble over a traffic accident, which in reality was no accident. He'd gone into one of his rages when a car cut too close in front of him and used his own heavyweight vehicle as a battering ram to force the other car off the road. The car hit a tree, and the driver was badly injured. It was assault, deliberate assault with a vehicle, and Adler should have been convicted for it." Mark's clenched fist pounded his thigh. Jan had seen it many times before, knew it was an unconscious sign of Mark's frustration. "But the firm wanted me to get him off, so I shrugged my shoulders at right and wrong and guilt and innocence, dug up some unsavory facts about the other driver's record, plus a technicality about how the investigating officer handled the case. We got Adler off with a small settlement, and the case never went to trial. It didn't even make a splash in the newspapers."

"But you said that was six or seven years ago, which would have been while we were still married." She certainly hadn't seen him rushing off to church then.

He nodded. "Not long afterward Adler left the state, and I never gave him another thought. My Teflon conscience let it slide right on by. But then a year or so after the divorce, sometime after that fiasco when I tried to get you to remarry me, I quite by accident heard—" He paused and smiled a little grimly. "No, there was nothing accidental about it. As always, the Lord was in control and made sure I heard. Anyway, what I found out was that Adler's temper had exploded again. In a disagreement with renters in an apartment building he owned where he lived in Texas, he went into another rage and badly injured a woman. He shot her in the chest and face with a shotgun. And killed her husband."

"*Murder?*" Jan was appalled. "And he got off again?"

"No, not this time. He's in prison. But if I hadn't helped thwart justice and Adler had been convicted here as he should have been, maybe that man in Texas would still be alive."

"Oh, Mark—"

"A hardworking man with a wife and three kids—" Mark shook his head, his fist still slowly hammering his thigh. "It all came down on me like an avalanche roaring down a mountain. *I'd helped kill that man!*"

Suddenly she knew the answer to the puzzle of what had happened to his personal assets that seemed to have vanished after the divorce. "And you helped the family financially."

"The mother was desperate. She needed half a dozen surgeries to repair the damage Adler did, plus help and training because she lost much of her eyesight. And a place to live and someone to help care for her children so she wouldn't lose them to foster homes until she could get back on her feet. I flew down there several times. And she was the one who led me to Christ and changed my whole life."

"Did she recover?"

"Her eyesight is considerably restricted." Mark still sounded troubled, but the fist finally gave his thigh a rest and he smiled. "Although she's doing great otherwise, and she's remarried now. The kids call me Uncle Mark."

"You did a wonderful thing for that woman, Mark. And for her children."

"Yet I failed my own son."

Jan jiggled her empty glass, the sound of the clinking ice cubes magnified by the silence that suddenly fell between them, the failure they both had to live with. "Do you ever miss the excitement of legal work, the challenge of convincing a jury, the thrill of victory?"

He looked off toward an old-fashioned pendulum clock on the far wall, his gaze unfocused as he considered her question. "Whatever its flaws, I still believe in the judicial process. I still believe in the right of every accused man or woman to good legal representation. I still believe a competent lawyer can do good in this world and help right some wrongs." He hesitated and smiled a little reluctantly. "So, yeah, I do miss it sometimes."

With neither arrogance nor false modesty he added, "I'm a good professor, but I was a better lawyer."

"And you'd like to go back to it someday?"

"I want to do what the Lord wants me to do."

So maybe he would go back someday. And perhaps that wasn't all he'd go back to. If, like some others she'd known, his religious conversion didn't stick...

She changed the subject. "I'm going to need good legal representation with the adoption."

She suspected he noticed that she said "I," not "we," but he didn't comment. All he said was, "I'll find the best person available to handle it."

"I'd appreciate that."

Mark jumped up, giving her a little bounce on the sofa. "How about a refill?"

Jan stood up too. "I probably should be getting home—"

"I don't think you need to rush home on Stardust's account. She's going to be out putting miles on her new car, not hurrying back to the house." Jan agreed silently with his wry comment.

"Stay." He took her hand and pulled her toward the sliding doors to the patio. "We'll barbecue some hamburgers. I don't have a pool, but I'll turn on the sprinkler and you can run through it. I might even run with you."

Jan laughed. When Mark turned on the charm, he could make hamburgers and a run through a sprinkler sound more appealing than lobster and a rose-scented pool. Well…why not? Staying here with him sounded a lot better than going back to the empty house.

By that time shade from an old maple tree covered the backyard, and cool shadows dappled the vine draped patio. Jan didn't run through the sprinkler, but while Mark got the barbecue going, she did wander the yard in her bare feet, enjoying the contrast between the lingering warmth of the concrete patio and the cool, green dampness of the lawn. There was grass back home, too, but somehow its formality didn't invite the familiarity of bare feet.

Soon the hamburgers gave off a savory scent. A neighbor came over to borrow Mark's Weed-Eater. A friendly orange cat showed up to twine around Jan's legs, a couple of students called, and two pint-sized boys stopped by to ask Mark if he wanted to shoot some baskets at the playground.

"Not right now, kids. But maybe next time, okay?"

He gave them each a grape Popsicle, and they got on their bicycles and rode off.

Jan put everything on her hamburger bun, including onions, and nibbled a fiery Jalapeño pepper on the side. She washed it all down with more lemonade and listened to the squeaky music of some child practicing on a clarinet a few backyards away. She had the dreamy feeling she'd wandered into one of those old Norman Rockwell paintings, where an old man might have weathered wrinkles on his face and a little boy had a hole in his shoe, where gentle goodness and kindness and generosity reigned.

They relaxed in lounge chairs on the patio as blue dusk settled over the yard, and the suburban sounds of the afternoon faded into quiet evening.

Jan put her hands behind her head and watched a neighborhood squirrel dart across the grass, then pause to stare at her impudently. She should go home. She had a contract to go over, a sales ad to write. Stardust might be home by now. But the thought lacked urgency, and she made no move to rise. She didn't *want* to go.

She glanced over at Mark, dozing in the lounge chair just a few inches from hers. His shirt was open, his body tan now, his bare feet pointed outward in a relaxed V. There was a sweet intimacy to watching him sleep, the rise and fall of his chest, a faint twitch of his hand. He looked vulnerable in his sleep, yet he lost nothing in aura of masculine strength. Carefully, not wanting to wake him, she edged her own bare foot across the space between the chairs until it snuggled against his. The contact was innocent, and yet it made her feel a little wicked, a little bold.

Did she really have to go home?

The thought of staying drifted enticingly in her mind. Slipping into an old shirt of his for the night, sharing the familiarity of the getting-ready-for-bed intimacy in the bathroom, and then—

"Hey, lady, are you playing footsies with me?" Mark's voice, almost in her ear, was husky and intimate.

It brought Jan's little fantasy about not going home to an abrupt halt. What was she *thinking?*

She jumped up, heart thudding with apprehension. She scrambled to find her shoes, then looked for her purse. She realized that Mark was watching her with what appeared to be amusement.

"I really have to get home now!"

"I'll walk you out to your car."

At her not-so-new Toyota, Mark crossed his arms on the window frame. "In spite of everything, I've enjoyed today, Jan. Have you?"

"Yes."

He leaned through the car and kissed her. She knew he was going to, and for a moment she tensed. And then she leaned forward to meet him. The warm pressure of his mouth blended with old memories, the taste of lemonade with the sweet fire of their first kiss of long ago. The pressure of his hand cradling her neck stirred memories of the embrace at their wedding. And the hunger of his yearning blended with her own and brought back the long-ago anticipation of their wedding night.

Maybe she didn't have to go home after all…

15

HE BROKE THE KISS, GRINNED, AND CLUTCHED THE WINDOW frame with both hands in a white-knuckled grip. She could see the pulse throbbing in his throat, the quick rise and fall of his breathing and the smoky haze in his blue eyes, but all he said was, "Church tomorrow?"

"Holding out for marriage?" she countered lightly. Her own breathing was fast and shallow too, and the back of her neck still tingled where he'd cradled it.

He grinned again. "Yeah, I guess I am."

"I'll think about it."

"Marriage or church?"

She smiled. "Both."

She had to admit that she was a little disappointed that he hadn't tried to persuade her to stay, but she also saw him with new respect. This stand was another powerful indication of how much he'd changed. The Lord was definitely in control where Mark was concerned.

The Firebird was in the driveway when Jan got home from work late one evening, and upstairs in Stardust's room lights flared and music blasted. The music was also blasting through the intercom system. Jan was appalled. Were those shouted lyrics really saying what she thought they said? This was what she'd blithely bought at the mall?

Jan punched and slammed various buttons, but the intercom system stubbornly resisted all attempts to silence it. Finally she draped a doubled towel over the speaker, which helped, although the sound still boomed down the stairs.

She knew this was deliberate challenge and defiance on Stardust's part. A continuation of her deliberate abrasiveness over the last few weeks. Two more months until Stardust was out of her life, she thought grimly. Two more months until the baby was safe from Stardust's self-centered greed. Could she make it, she wondered as she stood there with the raw beat and ugly words of the music hammering her?

Yes! Whatever it took for Alisha, whatever it took to save her, she could do it.

Then she determinedly shut her mind to the sound and squeezed a fresh pitcher of orange juice for tomorrow's breakfast. For Alisha's sake, Stardust needed her vitamins.

The following evening, when Stardust had gone somewhere with the Firebird, Jan cut roses from a bush Tim had planted in the backyard, huge blooms the flamboyant color of a summer sunset. The rose no doubt had a name, and Tim had undoubtedly known it. But she hadn't asked him when she had the chance, and even Alfredo didn't know it, so now she just called it Tim's Rose.

She drove to the cemetery and parked on the lane overlooking Tim's grave. It was only one of many set in the gently rolling sea of green grass, but she could have found it on the darkest night. At the grave she removed the damp newspaper she'd wrapped around the roses, carried water from a nearby faucet to fill the metal container set in the ground below the headstone, and arranged the roses in it.

Only then did she step back and look at the rose granite headstone set flat in the ground. Timothy Vale Hilliard, with the years of his birth and death. Entwined vines and flowers framed the lettering, a sad memorial to what he had loved in life.

Oh, Tim, I'm so very sorry. She thought of him again as a little boy, full of life and fun and mischief. Thought of him in later years, turned quiet and distant. Thought of the breakdown chronicled in his journal and his final wild, despairing words.

I'm sorry it all went wrong, Tim. Sorry it turned out this way, sorry we failed you. Oh, how I wish we could have a second chance to do things differently! But life doesn't give second chances—

But God did! she thought with a sense of wonderment. God was always in control, just as Mark had assured her. He had given them a second chance with Tim's daughter, showed them a glorious preview in that ultrasound! She clasped her hands together, amazed that she hadn't seen it this plainly before. She still didn't understand clearly about the baby's potential problems, but she saw *this* as bright and clearly as a mountain glowing at sunrise. A second chance!

Oh, Tim, I wish you could have stayed around long enough to know your daughter. Maybe she'd have changed your life, as I think she's already changing mine. And I swear, Tim, I swear to you with all my heart that I won't fail her as I have failed you.

She knelt beside the grave then, unmindful of the dampness of the freshly watered grass seeping through *to her knees. Help me to do what I've promised him, Lord. Even though I don't really know you yet, even though I'm sometimes angry at you and fail to understand your ways and doings, please help me to fulfill this promise, please help me not to fail with this second chance you've provided.*

Stardust lived up to her bargain to eat right and take care of herself, but she didn't always do it graciously, and a tenuous balance of power slipped back and forth between them. When Jan was carefully preparing healthful meals, Stardust took a perverse pleasure in taunting her.

"What good do you think all this good-for-you stuff is going to do? The baby's already defective."

"I love her, and I will never see her as 'defective,' no matter what difficulties she has to face," Jan said matter-of-factly. "Right now I just want to be sure she has the best nourishment possible."

Yet Stardust desperately wanted that car so she didn't push too far. She grumbled, but she ate right. She balked at exercise until Jan carefully planted, and let her find for herself, a magazine piece by a well-known model who warned that failure to exercise during pregnancy could mean figure problems later. The model herself looked fantastic both during and after pregnancy, and Stardust's interest in walking and doing other light exercise revived.

She had no interest in naming the baby now, of course, and she flatly rejected the Lamaze classes. As it turned out, however, that refusal was irrelevant. After the next ultrasound test, during which Stardust stared at the ceiling instead of the screen, the doctor informed them that because of the baby's heart condition and the still uncertain situation about Down syndrome, the birth would have to be by cesarean.

Jan's gaze immediately darted to Stardust, who was still perched on the examining table in her paper gown. If she feared a needle in her abdomen, what about a knife? Would she panic, refuse, turn hysterical?

Stardust hesitated, but after a moment's thought, she appeared more uninterested than distressed. "They put you out, don't they, so you don't even know what's going on?"

"Cesareans are usually done with an epidural, which numbs nerves in the spine, rather than a general anesthetic. You'll be awake, but you won't feel anything."

Now he had Stardust's full attention. "No! I want to be all the way out! I don't want to feel anything or even know it's happening."

At that point Dr. Addington also informed them that he was referring them to a different doctor who specialized in obstetrics and had extensive experience with cesareans, which he, in his family practice, did not. "So you can discuss your preferences about the C-section with Dr. Osborne," he said coolly.

"I never liked that old grouch anyway," Stardust muttered when they left the office. "I'm glad I'm going to have a different doctor."

Stardust spent a lot of time away from the house, chasing around in the Firebird, although Jan never knew where she went. Money frequently vanished from Jan's purse. After a couple of weeks, Jan simply gave her a handful of cash at the beginning of each week.

"I'd rather do this than have you steal it from me," she told Stardust unemotionally. Stardust didn't admit she'd been taking the money, but neither did she deny it. Without thanks, she just grabbed the bills Jan held out as if they were something she was entitled to.

Jan was beginning to feel the pinch, money-wise. Her car payments were much lower now, but she still had the huge house payments and yard upkeep and growing medical expenses. She also knew that after Alisha was born, she'd want to give her all the time and attention possible, which would mean cutting back on her work hours. She saw only one possible solution.

She told Mark what that solution was a few days later. He'd called and asked if she was free for lunch, then picked her up at the office. She assumed he had some special reason for the invitation, but when he just chatted, she finally asked why they were having lunch.

"Do I have to have a reason to ask the woman I'm in love with to lunch?" he teased indignantly. "I just haven't seen much of you lately, and I miss you."

She carefully didn't show any outward response to his casual declaration of love, although inwardly she felt a small explosion of fireworks. "That's it?"

He grinned. "That's it."

"I've been putting in a lot of extra time working." Which seemed an appropriate lead-in to what she had to tell him.

They were at a pleasant, nautically themed restaurant overlooking the broad sweep of the Columbia River.

A tugboat industriously churned behind a big barge, pushing it upriver, the scene through a porthole shaped window, like a painting in slow motion. Mark's forkful of salmon stopped halfway to his mouth when she gave him her news.

"You're going to sell the house?" His eyebrows shot up.

She explained her reasons. "You don't object, do you?" She smiled lightly. "Or does the house hold some sentimental value for you that I'm unaware of?"

"No, no sentimental value. The times I like to remember, the happy times, were before we got the house."

Jan tilted her head thoughtfully as she watched a seagull land on the railing outside the window. "Sometimes I think I held on to the house after the divorce just to prove to you that I could do it." Her smile turned rueful. "An I'll-show-*him* kind of pride, I suppose."

He nodded as if he well understood the problems pride could cause. "Actually, I think selling the house is a great idea." He grinned. "Now you can marry me, and we'll fix up the bedroom next to ours as a nursery for the baby."

Jan reared back in the chair. "Whoa, there! Planning marriage and bedroom arrangements is just a bit…premature, I think. My intention is to put the house on the market, look for a much smaller place, and hope the timing works out so I can move right out of one and into the other."

"If you need a place to stay in between moves, my door is always open." He smiled wryly. "No strings attached."

She didn't back away from that offer. She knew he meant just what he said. "Thanks, Mark. I appreciate that."

The killer hot summer, uncharacteristic of Portland, dragged on. Stardust often complained of the heat, but between the air-conditioned car and the house, she was seldom actually in it. She did, in fact, bloom physically with her advancing pregnancy: thin arms and face filling out attractively, hair growing as fast as wild grass, pale skin glowing radiantly. Sometimes, knowing how uncaring and hostile Stardust felt toward the baby within her, the bloom seemed unfair to Jan. Stardust saw only her growing bulk and awkwardness, and her complaints came frequently and bitterly. Once she even asked Dr. Osborne if he could move the cesarean up by a couple of weeks so she could be done with this quicker. His answer was a shocked and adamant no.

Stardust looked and sounded just as shocked when Jan planted one of her real estate firm's For Sale signs in the front yard of the house. She demanded to know why, and Jan told her about cutting expenses and work time after the baby came.

"You're willing to give up all *this*," Stardust said, the sweep of her arm taking in everything from the comfortable family room to the formal living room and landscaped grounds beyond, "for a baby that isn't even *normal?*"

"I'd live in a one-room shack if it meant saving my grandchild's life," Jan said, and Stardust just shook her head incredulously.

Jan put in long hours at work, knowing she was going to need every cent for the coming medical expenses for both Stardust and the baby. The doctor was now saying that the baby would likely need heart surgery soon after birth, this reported to her by Mark.

Now that she had the Firebird, Stardust could have gone to the doctor alone, but Jan didn't trust her to keep the appointments, and Mark had offered to accompany her. He always took Stardust to lunch the same day, but Stardust didn't appreciate having a chaperone. "Sooner or later," she grumbled, "he always gets around to the religious stuff."

Mark regularly invited Jan to come to church with him, and she went a couple of times. Once she even went to a midweek Bible study, and each time she went, she felt a strange and powerful sense of the Lord's pull. He *wanted* her in his fold, she realized with a certain sense of awe and amazement. But more often, in spite of those heartfelt tugs, she let daily problems and busyness get in the way.

Another area of resistance was that her feelings toward God were still a grab bag of conflicts, the why of Tim's death and the baby's looming disabilities clashing with her need to seek the Lord in prayer. But doubt about God's powerful existence was no longer part of her thinking, nor did she doubt that he was indeed in control. He'd created this new life in Stardust, unerringly brought Stardust into her home, moved in Mark's life through far-off events in Texas. He apparently had a plan and pathway for their lives. Although at the moment, she thought wryly, from her viewpoint that plan more often looked like a first grader's wandering trail than a precise road map.

Her spirits were down one Tuesday evening when she didn't get home from writing up an offer on a house until after eight o'clock, although it was not the long day that made her feel so blue. She had, in fact, been grateful that this particular day was so long and hectic, filled with mind-challenging problems to solve. However, it hadn't been hectic enough to blot out the pain she was feeling. Nothing could.

Stardust was eating a sandwich at the breakfast bar when Jan walked into the kitchen after she finally got off work. The phone rang and Stardust picked it up. She said hello, then passed the cordless instrument to Jan with a grimace. "Mark."

For all Mark's goodness to her, Stardust usually treated him like a TV program she'd like to turn off. With anyone else Jan might have thought guilt was involved in the unfriendly attitude, but guilt did not appear to be a part of Stardust's character makeup.

"Hi, Jan." The hi started out cheerful enough, but then his tone stumbled downhill. "I just thought I'd call and…make sure you're okay."

She knew why he'd worry about her this day. She'd wondered about him, too.

Jan slipped off her shoes. "It's been a difficult day. I knew it would be hard, but I didn't realize just how hard. I know it's been just as difficult for you."

"Is there anything I can do? Would you like me to come over?"

Jan hesitated, momentarily sandwiched between

emotions. He shared the long-ago joy of this day with her as no one else in the world had. In the same way, he shared the devastating loss of which this day was an aching reminder. Yes, his being here would be a comfort...

But she wasn't sure she deserved comfort.

"I don't think so, Mark," she finally said gently. "Thanks anyway."

"What's wrong?" Stardust asked when Jan put down the phone. Stardust was not a person who made a pretense of not listening to a private conversation occurring in her presence. Neither was she one to care much about anyone's problems but her own. But apparently she did have a certain reluctant curiosity, and she'd stopped eating to listen.

"Today is Tim's birthday."

"Oh." Stardust returned to her sandwich.

The single word held a so-what's-all-the-fuss-about inflection that angered Jan. "You didn't know that?"

"I guess it was already after his birthday when I met him last year."

"It's the hardest day of the year for a mother who's ever lost a child." Briefly she felt a powerful rush of desire to make Stardust understand. "There are so many memories of his life starting. Sweet, wonderful memories. The first time I saw him, moments after he was born." She closed her eyes, the joy of that moment when the doctor placed her new son on her stomach, red and squalling and beautiful, rushing back now as pain. "And then all the sadness and pain and guilt, the lost hopes, the what-might-have-beens..."

"I guess I would've thought the anniversary of the

day he died would be the hardest."

"Maybe it is," Jan agreed heavily. "I haven't gotten there yet, so I don't know. But knowing that Tim's baby is on the way, that a part of him still exists, helps on this day. And every day."

"I guess."

With deep sadness, Jan knew that Stardust, who didn't even want Tim's child, who would have destroyed his child, couldn't understand that, either.

Jan put in a difficult Friday morning showing houses to an out-of-town couple who couldn't tell her what they wanted in a house and wanted to look at everything because "we'll know it when we see it." By midafternoon, suspecting they were simply using her as a free tour guide and feeling nauseated from something she'd had at lunch, she begged off and went home early.

She was surprised to see the Firebird in the driveway when she arrived, even more surprised to see an old blue pickup with a brown hood parked beside it. She couldn't get to the garage with the cars in front of the doors, so she parked off to the side of the driveway and let herself in through the seldom used front door. She immediately heard voices in the kitchen.

Stardust's back was to her, and part of a squatting figure showed around the open refrigerator door. "You'd think she could at least keep a beer in here," a male voice grumbled.

"There's lemonade—" Stardust apparently sensed or heard something and turned, catching the breakfast bar to steady herself when she saw Jan. "You're home early!"

A fact that obviously dismayed Stardust.

She wiped a hand on her maternity smock, as if her palms were suddenly sweaty.

The male figure stepped out from behind the refrigerator door. He'd shaved off the red beard, and now wore old khaki shorts instead of bib overalls, but Jan recognized him immediately.

"Red Dog!"

"Howdy, Mrs. Hilliard," Red Dog said with a good-ol'-country-boy heartiness that implied they were old friends. "Me 'n' Bonnie were worried about Stardust, so I thought I'd just drop in and check up on her."

Jan wondered how he'd found her home address, but all she said was, "I see."

Stardust turned back to Red Dog. "Well, it was nice of you to stop by." Her voice held definite good-bye tones. "As you can see, I'm fine, so—"

Red Dog's river-green eyes shifted lazily to the ceramic owl clock on the wall. "Oh, I'm in no big hurry. Maybe we should go up to your room so's we could visit without bothering Mrs. Hilliard."

Jan dropped her car keys and briefcase on the breakfast bar. She was almost certain Stardust didn't want to go upstairs with Red Dog. At this point she wasn't terribly concerned about what Stardust wanted, but neither was she eager to have Red Dog roaming the house. "Visit right here. You won't bother me," she assured him. "Bonnie isn't with you?"

"She couldn't make it."

"Be sure to tell her hi for me," Stardust said, the good-bye tone now almost a shove toward the door.

Red Dog didn't budge. "Well, I reckon we can talk

right here, if you'd rather," he said to Stardust in that same good-ol'-boy voice, although it now had a meaningful edge that puzzled Jan. He planted himself on a stool at the breakfast bar and smiled. His teeth were a surprising, dazzling array of caps.

"Oh, I guess we can talk upstairs." Now it was Stardust who suddenly seemed anxious to move the conversation elsewhere. "Come on. I'll show you some motorcycle posters Tim had."

Red Dog followed her toward the stairs. "You been taking real good care of her, Mrs. Hilliard. Tim would be real pleased."

Jan watched until they disappeared at the top of the stairs and the door to Stardust's room opened and closed. Should she have stopped them, she wondered uneasily, perhaps even demanded that Red Dog leave? He hadn't said or done anything threatening, yet somehow he frightened her. She headed for the phone. She'd call Mark—

No. Mark wouldn't be home now. He had a three o'clock class on Monday, Wednesday, and Friday, so she couldn't reach him for at least another hour. She decided to go upstairs and change clothes. She was careful not to let her footsteps slow as she passed Stardust's door; she wouldn't want them to think she was eavesdropping. Yet the instant she stepped into the bedroom and pulled off her sandals, she *was* eavesdropping. The temperamental intercom system carried their voices as plainly as an open phone line.

Well, she was not some snoop who listened in on private conversations, even ones that self-broadcast into her privacy. Briskly she picked up a pillow and started to put it over the speaker, only to be stopped flat by Red Dog's voice, no longer good-ol'-boy friendly. "You owe me, Deb, you owe me big time."

"I don't owe you anything!"

Jan backed away from the speaker, but Red Dog's next words magnetically drew her closer until she crouched only inches away.

"Oh, no? Who clued you in on this sweet deal? Fancy Firebird, expensive clothes, living like a little princess. All that and she's even gonna take the little retard off your hands after it's born."

"Don't call my baby that!" Stardust said, even though she'd called the baby as bad or worse herself. Even in her confusion about what Red Dog was saying, Jan felt a surge of hope at the fiercely protective tone in Stardust's voice.

"You wouldn't have any of this if I hadn't suggested the role of Stardust was wide open and you might as well play it."

"I still don't owe you. Maybe you suggested it, but *I'm* the one who pulled it off and convinced them I'm Stardust! And it hasn't been easy. Watching every word I say. Reading that creepy journal of Tim's over and over so I won't make a mistake and say something wrong. He sounds so weird. I'm glad I never knew him! And you never said anything about wanting something for yourself when you told me they were looking for his pregnant girlfriend," she added accusingly.

Jan sank to the floor beside the intercom, pillow clutched to her chest, stunned and shocked. *Role of Stardust? Glad she never met Tim?*

"It didn't occur to me until later that you oughta be

kinda grateful to me for helpin' you out," Red Dog said.
"A lot more grateful than you're acting."

"Is Bonnie in on this?"

"Bonnie split. She was mad about the whole deal
with me suggesting you pretend to be Stardust." His
voice held a shrug. "Good riddance."

"Did you know her, the real Stardust?"

Jan clutched the pillow tighter, so tight the muscles
in her arms corded and ached. *The real Stardust.*

"I don't know. I don't remember anyone by that
name. I never could see why, but girls were always
hangin' around Tim. Maybe one of 'em was Stardust. If
there even was a real Stardust. Tim was so wacko there
near the end, I couldn't tell what was real and what was
his Godzilla imagination. But the Hilliards sure enough
believed in her after they read Tim's journal." He suddenly sounded gleeful, as if this were some big joke.
"Really got 'em revved up from what I heard about how
they were running all over the county telling everybody
about some pregnant girl with 'lupine-blue eyes.' And it
was *me* who told you to get colored contacts to clinch
the deal, remember?"

"A lot of good they did! One popped out and Jan
saw my eye, and right there I had to make up a story
about having them on when I met Tim, and—"

"Well, good thing you're real clever at thinking on
your feet. And you'd better do some fast thinkin' now
because it would be a real shame, wouldn't it, if I had to
disillusion them and tell them this was all just a big
phony act? They'd probably be real interested to hear
that the guy who really got you pregnant was that jerk
who got drunk and tangled himself and his car around

a tree like a big metal pretzel."

"He loved me! We'd of gotten married if he hadn't gotten killed in that accident."

"And where'd you be now if I hadn't showed you how to cash in on this cherry deal? You owe me."

"What do you want?" Stardust's voice trembled, whether with fear or anger or loathing, Jan couldn't tell. Probably all three. She couldn't think any further than that at the moment. Her mind felt stalled. The shocking facts about Stardust and the baby floated on the surface, and she felt as if she were peering up at them through a layer of murky water.

"Money. Just a little plain ol' money, honey, that's all I want."

"I have a couple hundred dollars. You can have that—"

"Two hundred? Oh, no. I'm not the greedy type," he proclaimed magnanimously, "but two hundred is just a little on the skimpy side. But you cough up, oh, say, a measly two *thousand* bucks, and I won't say a word to dear ol' Grandma and Grandpa Hilliard about their precious 'grandchild' not being any more related to them than I am. But if I do tell them—Boom! You can bet you'll find yourself bounced out on the street, no car, no nothin'. Who's goin' to want a retard kid that isn't even theirs?"

Jan shuddered at the cruel scorn with which Red Dog spoke of the baby. She fought a wild impulse to yell back at him through the intercom.

"I can't get two thousand dollars!"

"Sure you can. You already told me the abortion threat worked magic with the car. It'll work again. Just tell 'em you want the money, and you want it *now*, or you'll get the abortion anyway, that the car isn't enough. You're not workin' these people for near what you could get out of them if you tried."

"They're good people." Jan heard grudging respect in Stardust's voice. "Jan takes good care of me and worries about the baby, and Mark is always trying to save my soul."

A malicious guffaw erupted from Red Dog. "Well, he has his work cut out for him there, doesn't he?"

"I hate you. I *hate* you!"

Then silence, silence so complete that Jan thought perhaps the intercom had closed off. One part of her wanted to rush down the hall and confront them with what she'd heard. Another part wanted to push it off into some dark corner and forget she'd ever heard it. Then Red Dog's voice came back on, sneering and cold and impatient.

"That really breaks my heart, Debbie dear, you hating me and all, but at the moment I got bigger worries. So, what's it gonna be, babe, a few bucks for me, or a dose of truth serum for the Hilliards?"

16

JAN WAITED, HOPING, DESPERATELY HOPING, YET HARDLY
knowing what she hoped for. That Stardust would refuse
to be blackmailed and kick Red Dog out? Defiantly tell
him to go ahead and do his dirty work, that she didn't
care how the Hilliards reacted because she wanted the
baby herself?

Or maybe what she really wished was the truly
impossible, that Stardust would declare it all a lie, that
this really was Tim's baby.

Instead, what she heard was Stardust—no, not really
Stardust—say with a tremor in her voice, "Okay, I'll see if
I can get the money. You want me to call you?"

"No, I'll hang around town for a few days and contact you again. But make it quick. If you don't have the
money when I come back, the Hilliards are gonna get an
earful."

The sound of the door didn't reach through the
intercom, but a few moments later Red Dog's old pickup
roared and backfired out front. Jan just sat there on the
floor, trying to sort through her thoughts, clutching the
pillow as if it were some life preserver to keep her from
sinking.

Lies, all lies. And if the Stardust they knew wasn't
real, was there another Stardust, alone and defenseless,
out there somewhere with their grandchild?

She was still sitting there a few minutes later when
a knock came on the door. She wanted to shout, "Go
away! I don't want to see you! Don't bring me any more

of your lies and threats!" But instead she stumbled to her feet, braced herself against the edge of the bed, and, in a croaky voice said, "Come in."

"Hi. I went downstairs looking for you...then I figured you must be in here. I hope you don't mind Red Dog coming to see me. He and Bonnie are old friends of mine." Stardust smiled appealingly, wrapping herself in the old cloak of eager-to-please vulnerability.

But Jan saw it for the disguise it now was. She said nothing, just waited, clutching her pillow, apprehensive yet reluctantly curious how Stardust would tackle her problem. Oddly, even though she now knew that the real "Stardust" was someone else entirely, she couldn't think of this girl by any other name.

"But he brought me some...uh...bad news."

Indeed he did.

"Some people I worked for last fall think I stole some jewelry and stuff from them when I left. I didn't. I swear I didn't! In fact, when I left they still owed me two weeks' wages. They stole from me! But now they're saying if I don't pay for the stuff—two thousand dollars!— they're going to turn me in and get the cops after me. They'll put me in jail, I know they will, because of the shoplifting I did before. And I don't want my baby born in jail..." Tears glittered at the corners of her eyes, phony tears in phony lupine-blue eyes, and her mouth wobbled with phony pleading.

It was a convincing performance, Jan thought dispassionately. She'd surely believe the story if she didn't know it had been concocted within the last five minutes. She also noted that Stardust hadn't upped the ante and tried to squeeze something for herself above what Red

Dog demanded; perhaps she figured there were limits on Jan's willingness to be bled. She was almost tempted to ask sympathetic-sounding questions just to see how far Stardust would go with her story.

But suddenly Jan was just too sick and weary to go through with it. She shook her head slowly, her eyes never leaving Stardust's blue contacts. "I know," she said softly. "*I know.*"

"You know what?" Familiar defiance glossed the surface of Stardust's words, but a darting shift in her gaze revealed a crack in the foundation of her self-assurance.

"I know that you're not the real Stardust, that the baby isn't Tim's, that you didn't even know Tim."

"You were *listening?*" Stardust showed no spark of guilt or regret for her deception and lies, only fury at what Jan had done. "How—" Her gaze flicked to the intercom with sudden understanding, and in instant rage she picked up a lamp from the nightstand and flung it at the intercom on the wall.

The lamp shattered as if wired with explosives when it hit, but the broken pieces slid to the lush carpet in a rainfall of silence.

"You deceived me." Jan's voice was still soft. She felt oddly dazed now. She tried to raise her voice, but no more than a hoarse whisper came out. "This isn't my grandchild—"

Stardust abruptly abandoned deceit. "No, it isn't! And things look a whole lot different now, don't they?" Her sneer was as vicious as Red Dog's. "Not so ready to give up your big house and live in a one-room shack for it now that it isn't *your* darling grandchild, right? And all the stuff that's wrong with it is not something you can ignore now that it isn't *your* precious grandchild."

"Was anything you told us true? Anything at all?"

Stardust hesitated before finally saying reluctantly, "Some. All the stuff about my mother and what one of my stepfathers tried to do to me is true. And so is how much I wanted to get away from everything in the past and be someone different and make my whole life different. Not that *you* care!" Stardust kicked a shard of lamp that had fallen at her feet, and in spite of her bulk whirled with surprising agility. She grabbed for the car keys she always kept in the pocket of her maternity smock.

Jan jumped up, startled. "Where are you going?"

"To get the abortion I should have gotten a long time ago! I was just about to get an abortion before Red Dog told me you were looking for a girl called Stardust. I should have gone ahead and done it instead of listening to him! Now I'm going to do it."

Jan followed her out the bedroom door. "Stardust, no, you can't do that! You mustn't even consider it. You're over eight months along!"

Stardust paused at the head of the stairs and looked back at her. "So?"

Nausea churned in Jan's stomach, mental visions so terrible they sickened her. Abortion at any time would have been an abomination but *now*— "It's a real *baby*, Stardust. Babies born this early can live!"

"Not this one," Stardust retorted grimly.

Jan reeled at the callous response. She grasped for any argument. "At eight months no doctor will—"

"Wanna bet? I'll find one. Just watch me." Her flying hair disappeared down the stairs.

Unmindful of her bare feet, Jan raced after the girl. She caught up with her at the front door, but with angry strength Stardust wrenched free, shoved Jan to the floor, and ran to the car. Jan stumbled to her feet and caught up again just as Stardust flung herself clumsily into the front seat. Jan hammered the door, but Stardust rammed the car in gear, and Jan had to jump sideways to keep from being knocked down.

The car screeched around the circular driveway and into the street. Jan ran to her own car, but her keys—her keys weren't in it! She raced back to the house, only peripherally conscious of the blazing concrete driveway burning her bare feet. Inside the house, she picked up the car keys where she'd dropped them on the breakfast bar and ran back to the car.

But by the time she reached the street, the Firebird had long vanished. She knew which direction it had turned out of the driveway, but twenty minutes of searching revealed no sign of the flashy red car. In defeat she turned to go home, then changed her mind and headed for Mark's place instead. Mark always knew what to do.

She rang the doorbell, but when there was no answer her control snapped and she pounded the door wildly. His car was here. He had to be here! Finally the door opened. Mark stood there shirtless, barefoot, in jeans, dark hair damp and tousled, towel in hand.

"I was in the shower—" His gaze took in her disheveled appearance, bare feet and tear-streaked face. "Jan, what is it? What's wrong?" He dropped the towel and grabbed her by the shoulders as she babbled hysterically. "Calm down and tell me."

He led her inside and sat her on the sofa. She gasped out a barely coherent version of all that had happened. "And I couldn't catch her, Mark! She got away, and now she is going to have an abortion!"

He gripped her by the shoulders and shook her lightly. "Okay, now, don't panic. We have time. Even if she runs into a clinic somewhere and demands an abortion, they aren't going to give it to her on the spot. It'll probably take at least several days for her to make the arrangements. But we have to find her. Does she know anyone? Has she made any friends?"

Jan shook her head helplessly. "I have no idea."

He drummed his fingers on his jeans-clad leg, eyes narrowed in concentration. "My guess is that she'll return to the house eventually."

Jan swallowed, throat dry, even the question of where Stardust had gone momentarily dimming. "Why did he do this, Mark? I don't understand."

"He?" Mark's dark eyebrows lifted. "You mean Red Dog?"

"No. I mean *God*. He brought Stardust to us and let us think the baby was our grandchild, and I was so happy. Even when I found out she isn't going to be perfect, and I was angry and bewildered, it was still okay because she was a part of Tim, a part of us, and I was so grateful to God for that. But he deceived us—"

"*Stardust* deceived us, with some help from Red Dog. It was their scheme, their con."

"But God let it happen. He betrayed us. Where is the real Stardust? Where is our grandchild?"

"I don't know the answer to that. But God isn't a betrayer, and I think it's possible for him to use even misguided human schemes for his own purposes in some plan we don't yet understand. His way of thinking is very different from ours, and so are his ways of doing things. The Bible even says that's the case right in Isaiah. 'As the heavens are higher than the earth, so are my ways higher than your ways and my thoughts than your thoughts.' We can't always understand what God is doing, and I know how difficult that often makes things—"

He stopped, and with a fingertip wiped away a tear trickling down her cheek. She caught his hand against her cheek and closed her eyes.

"All I know is that we can't let her do this. Even if the baby isn't our grandchild, it's a *baby*, and we've got to stop her." She jumped up from the sofa with sudden urgency. "Let's go back to the house. You're right. She will come back there! I doubt she keeps her money in the car, and she'll come back for it. And her clothes and other things too. But we've got to get there before she comes back and runs off again...and has the abortion!"

They took both cars. There was no Firebird in the driveway when they reached the house. Upstairs, Jan hesitated at the door of Stardust's room. She'd never infringed on the girl's privacy, but she had to know if they were too late.

She opened the door. The room was scrupulously neat. Stardust liked things *nice*. All the clothes still hung in the closet; all the shoes stood in a precise row below them. CDs stacked neatly in the vertical cabinet, a tiny flacon of Eternity, the expensive perfume Stardust loved, sitting on the nightstand. Yes, she'd be back. But would she come back *before*, or would she find someone actually willing to do an eight-months' abortion and return only after it was too late?

They settled down to wait. Jan took a quick shower and put on fresh clothes but left her sore feet bare when she went downstairs. Mark instantly noted how gingerly she was walking. He went to the kitchen and returned with the jar of hand cream she always kept in a drawer.

"Sit." He pointed to the sofa in the family room.

Jan protested, but she sat, and he knelt in front of her while he tenderly massaged the cream into her sore feet, rubbing soles and heels and instep with gentle strokes that soothed her feet and touched her heart. And confusingly brought tears to her eyes and made her smile at the same time. When he was done she leaned over and kissed him on the top of his head.

"That was wonderful." She sighed.

"I could be available on a permanent basis, you know." He smiled, but didn't push the issue, for which Jan was grateful.

She fixed sandwiches, and they picked at them. She got several business calls about an advertised house, one about her own house. She answered them mechanically. They tried to watch the news on TV, but for Jan, the words were no more than meaningless static.

Finally, when she got up to peer out the window for at least the tenth time, Mark said gently, "Will you pray with me, Jan?"

She knew he had been praying already. She had, too, she realized, wordlessly crying out to the Lord even in her bewilderment at this turn of events. She nodded, and they joined hands, and she added her own stumbling but fervent prayer to his.

And then she sat with her hands tightly clasped as images and thoughts of the baby engulfed her. In the last ultrasound, she had seen fingers and toes, delicately curved head, sweet bump of nose, bleep of beating heart. The doctor saw imperfections. He still couldn't say for certain about the Down syndrome, but he was definite about a heart problem. Jan acknowledged the possibility of physical or mental imperfections. But all she'd felt then, as she watched the ultrasound—all she felt now—was love, protective, all-encompassing, unreserved love.

Please, Lord. She squeezed her eyes and fists shut hard, as if the intensity of that effort might convince the Lord of her desperation and sincerity. *Keep the baby safe. Keep Stardust safe too. Make her realize how wrong this is!*

Yet why, she wondered, as her wrists dropped limply between her knees, should the Lord answer any prayer from her? She'd been to church a few times; she acknowledged his existence and power and how he changed Mark. But even though she acknowledged his pull on her own mind and heart, she hadn't given herself to him, as Mark had. She hadn't talked to him about her sins or asked his forgiveness. And suddenly she felt such a great, empty aloneness…

She opened her eyes. "You quoted a verse to me once. It was about being saved—" She broke off when she realized the foolish enormity of the statement. If she weren't so desperate, she might smile at it. The Bible was *full* of verses about salvation!

"The one from Romans? 'That if you confess with your mouth, "Jesus is Lord," and believe in your heart that God raised him from the dead, you will be saved.

For it is with your heart that you believe and are justified, and it is with your mouth that you confess and are saved.'"

She nodded. Somehow he had come up with the verse she had in mind, the one she needed.

He gave her a warm smile. "That's one of my favorites. So clear and comforting. And it goes hand in hand with another verse, too. 'If we confess our sins, he is faithful and just and will forgive us our sins and purify us from all unrighteousness.' Do you want to do that, Jan?" His gaze on her was so gentle, she wanted to weep. She felt his love reaching out to her, surrounding her. "Do you want the salvation Jesus offers? He wants you."

Again she felt the Lord's pull on her heart. Did he really want *her* in his fold? Hope mingled with a sense of wonder that it might be true. She felt something within her slowly opening and turning, like a flower seeking the sun. She thought about what Mark had told her, so many days ago, on the lonely trail to the cabin…how it was a daily miracle to him that the Lord knew and cared about each individual he'd created. Was it true? Did God, at this very moment, care about her?…and Mark and Stardust and the unborn baby, too?

Before she could formulate either an answer to Mark's question—or, for that matter, her own questions—they heard the door between the garage and kitchen open. Both Jan and Mark jerked, turning to stare. Usually Stardust entered the driveway with a roar and squeal, but this time they hadn't heard a sound. They exchanged quick glances but didn't move. Stardust stopped short beside the breakfast bar when she saw them. Her face looked sullen and tear-streaked…but she was still beautifully, *gloriously* pregnant.

Oh yes, the Lord cared!

Jan rose and went to her. "Are you all right?"

Stardust's tired movement was half nod, half shrug.

"Have you had anything to eat? Are you hungry?"

"I'm just tired. I'm going up to bed."

Questions flashed through Jan's mind. *Have you found someone who'll do the abortion? Is it already planned and scheduled? Or maybe...oh, please...you've changed your mind?* But what she said was, "Can you give us a few minutes? We'd like to talk to you."

Stardust's head jerked up from its tired droop. "If you're going to give me some big lecture—"

"No lecture. I just want to beg you not to get the abortion."

"What do you care? It's not *your* precious grand-child."

"But it *is* a precious child." And God had brought this baby, one of the most helpless and vulnerable of his little ones, to *her.* She was still thinking about that other Stardust out there, wondering if that Stardust had their grandchild, but what mattered at the moment was this here-and-now baby. This baby who was in desperate danger. "I love her. I want to adopt her and make her my own."

Mark came up beside her. She knew they hadn't discussed this, couldn't blame him if he pulled her up short with an objection...but his support and agreement were immediate. "*We* still want the baby," he added firmly as he put a supporting arm around Jan's shoulders.

"Even though you know it isn't Tim's? Even though it's got things wrong with it?"

"No matter what," Jan assured her. "It doesn't matter whose child she is. She's God's creation, a wonderful gift from him. And, with all our hearts, we want her."

If Jan thought Stardust's mind and heart would suddenly soften and open like some budding flower, she was mistaken. The girl eyed her as if looking down from some superior height.

"What'd you do, go all religious too?" she demanded scornfully.

The question was a sneering challenge, not a request for information, but Jan considered the implications thoughtfully. Finally she glanced at Mark, then nodded.

"Yes. That's exactly what I've done. Gone 'all religious.'"

Stardust eyed her as if she might be going to bombard her with questions, but after a few moments she simply shrugged. "I'll think about it."

Stardust stepped around them, and they both turned to watch her climb the stairs. Then Mark turned to Jan. "Did you mean it?"

She stood there, staring up the stairs. She considered the anger she'd sometimes felt toward God, the resentment and frustration and bewilderment, even that feeling of betrayal. Yet she also thought of her search for information about what happened to Tim, the search for Stardust and the baby, and she knew that another search had been going on within her for a much longer time, a search she never even recognized, much less acknowledged. A search for the filling of an emptiness within her, the same emptiness Mark had once had.

They both tried for a long time to fill it the wrong way, with success and houses and cars and all those other glittering things. But Mark found the right way, and she wanted that way, too. She nodded. "I mean it."

Softly, gently, as he knelt on the floor beside the sofa where she sat, Jan watched in awe as her ex-husband took her hand in his, and with a reverence she'd never seen before, led her through the simple steps of confession of sins and acceptance of the saving grace of Jesus' death and resurrection.

Then she offered her first halting prayer as a new Christian, happiness blooming within her in spite of the desperate situation, and afterward she smiled at Mark through her tears.

"Do you suppose this was God's plan all along?" She cleared her throat in an effort to steady her voice. "A home and love for a baby who desperately needs it? A coming to Jesus' salvation for me?"

"Could be. The Lord is capable of making good come out of grief."

Jan looked up into his eyes, and another question hung unspoken between them: Was bringing the two of them back together also part of the Lord's plan?

17

JAN DIDN'T GO TO THE OFFICE THE NEXT MORNING ALTHOUGH she nervously conducted some business by phone while waiting for Stardust to come downstairs and announce her decision. Yet when Stardust did pad barefoot into the kitchen, she was silent and withdrawn. Finally, after they'd eaten cantaloupe and toast and scrambled eggs, Jan could wait no longer.

"What have you decided?"

"About the abortion?" Stardust answered as carelessly as if this were some minor item buried under more important matters to be considered. "I'm still thinking about it."

Pleadings and arguments rose to Jan's lips, but she determinedly did not speak them. At this point, it was time to leave it to God. Yet she had to ask one thing.

"Will you promise me you won't simply go have the abortion without telling me?"

Stardust picked up her glass and took a swallow of milk. A faint mustache of white curved over her upper lip. Jan looked away before the little-girl vulnerability of that mustache made her cry.

Yet there was nothing vulnerable about Stardust's answer, only defiant stubbornness in the lift of her head. "No. Like I told you, I'm thinking about it."

How can you even consider this? It's a mere month out of your life, but it's all of this baby's life! But again, Jan stilled herself. *Let God handle it.*

Mark came over that evening and Jan made dinner,

but Stardust didn't eat with them. Over the intercom she said she wasn't feeling well and asked Jan to bring her something on a tray. When Jan took up the meal, Stardust had one of the CDs in the player although this time the sound was down to a normal level. She offered Jan no thanks for the meal.

Jan went to church with Mark on Sunday. She saw the service with different eyes now, with a new heart. The songs weren't just nice music, they were praises to God. The Scripture verses weren't merely archaic sayings, they were freshly revealed truths. And the message, with the jaunty title *What Your Favorite TV Sitcom Never Tells You,* built around 1 Corinthians 1:18: "For the message of the cross is foolishness to those who are perishing, but to us who are being saved it is the power of God" seemed aimed straight at her new heart. She'd crossed an invisible line, and there was a whole new view, a whole new eternity on this side!

On Monday evening, while Jan was at her desk in the family room, checking to see that all the paperwork was complete on a sale, the doorbell rang. She jumped up eagerly, but it was not Mark who stood at the door when she opened it.

"Howdy, Mrs. Hilliard," Red Dog said with a toothy smile that was apparently meant to be engaging. He removed his cap politely, giving no sign that he was a blackmailer here to collect on his demands. "I just thought I'd stop by to see Stardust again for a minute before I headed home."

"I'll tell her you're here." Jan went to the intercom,

but this time the temperamental system refused to work at all. Red Dog offered to run upstairs, but Jan firmly motioned him to a chair in the living room. "No. You wait here."

Upstairs, Stardust answered Jan's knock. "What do you want?"

"Red Dog is here."

Long silence. Stardust's voice sounded muffled when she finally spoke. "I'll get dressed."

Jan went back downstairs. She took a chair opposite the sofa. She did not offer refreshments or chatty conversation. She simply sat there and let Red Dog make one-sided small talk. He exuded confidence until Stardust suddenly appeared in the archway between the rooms. Then the brick red eyebrows drew together as if he realized things were perhaps not going according to plan. Raw hope suddenly rushed through Jan.

Red Dog nodded to Stardust. He repeated his suggestion of the last visit. "We could talk in your room and not bother Mrs. Hilliard—"

"No, Jan can hear whatever you have to say. So why don't you just go ahead and tell her everything."

"Everything?"

"Yes, everything. About how my baby isn't really Tim's, and its real father got killed in a car accident, and my coming here was your idea, and you told me to get blue contacts to help fool them. And now you want two thousand dollars not to tell the Hilliards all that."

Those few sentences collapsed Red Dog's confident bluff. His mouth dropped open as if he couldn't believe what he was hearing.

"And none of it matters because we love and want

the baby anyway," Jan added pleasantly.

Red Dog muttered a curse under his breath. Then he simply stalked across the room, his only good-bye an angry slam of his fist on the door as he went out. A minute later his rattletrap pickup roared out of the driveway.

Jan turned to Stardust, proud and grateful. Yet if she expected this to mean the start of some warm new relationship between them, she was again mistaken.

"Do I still get the car, even if this isn't Tim's baby, if I don't get an abortion?"

Jan's heart sank at this proof of the unchanging hard-heartedness of Stardust's self-centered attitude, but she didn't hesitate. "Yes."

"Okay, I'll have the baby," Stardust agreed sullenly. "But then I'm gone. You get all the arrangements for the adoption made ahead of time. I don't want to be stuck waiting around to get it done afterward, and I want that car title signed over to me before I sign anything. And I still don't want to be called anything except Stardust," she added, as if she suspected Jan would now deny her the name, "even if I'm not the Stardust you wish I were."

Three days later, Jan sold the house, a quick, clean deal with a comfortably affluent doctor as the buyer. The value of the house had increased to several times what Jan and Mark had paid for it, and she would come out with enough cash to buy a smaller house, take care of the mounting bills, and still have a financial cushion for after the baby was born. She had to be out in forty-five days.

Yet after two weeks of frantic searching, she still

hadn't found anything suitable. Like clients who sometimes frustrated her, she found fatal flaws with every
place. The street was too busy, the carpet too strange, the
rooms too scrunched up. Inadequate heating system,
depressing foyer, oddly placed windows. She was now
sitting in her car, studying her book of listings, and not
finding anything that appealed to her. *This is ridiculous.*
She was a real estate professional; she had access to
every listing in the city. She wasn't looking for anything
unusual. So why couldn't she find anything? In fact,
what was wrong with this place she'd just looked at?

She leaned over and peered through the window
to look at it again. A modest place, an older but well-
maintained, three-bedroom, bath-and-a-half, ranch-
style house on a quiet suburban street. Nice fenced yard,
two-car garage, reasonably priced. But the kitchen was
rather awkwardly arranged and the appliances old…

There, she was doing it again. Sitting there, she had
to laugh at herself because she was suddenly almost certain what the problem was. It was her subconscious,
sneakily picking out flaws because it had a totally different plan in mind. A plan centered around Mark.

She'd been seeing him regularly. In preparation for
the move, he helped her sort through their old half-
forgotten belongings, setting some items out for the
garbage truck, hauling others to the Salvation Army
thrift store. He helped guide her in her newfound interest in Bible study. Together they also read about Down
syndrome, preparing themselves to help the baby in
every way possible. He found a sympathetic lawyer to
handle the adoption. Laws wouldn't allow Stardust to
sign away her parental rights before the baby was born,

but everything was in readiness for her signature immediately afterward. They went to lunch and dinner and midweek church services together, plus a wonderful contemporary gospel music fest at another church.

Yet, now that she thought about it, the references to marriage and the semiproposals Mark had earlier tossed out hadn't been coming lately. She sat there in the car parked at the curb, puzzling over this. Was she mistaken? She thought back over the last couple of weeks. No. It had definitely been some time now since he'd made any reference to their remarrying.

Yet he hadn't acted withdrawn or disinterested. He was always sweet and loving, considerate and helpful. She knew her coming to the Lord was an answer to prayer for him, and they often prayed together for Stardust's physical and spiritual well-being. Yet he definitely wasn't making little references to marriage anymore.

He invited both her and Stardust over for dinner that evening. A friend had given him a nice chunk of ocean salmon, and he was going to try baking it for them. Stardust rejected the invitation, but at the last minute, while Jan was making a salad to take along, she slouched downstairs and said she'd go.

"It couldn't be any more boring than sitting around here," she grumbled with her usual ungracious attitude. "I don't see why the doctor can't hurry this up." The cesarean was scheduled for two weeks from Monday.

Giving her heart to the Lord hadn't magically turned Jan into the all-patient, all-wise woman she'd like to be, but it had enabled her to deal with Stardust with less anger and resentment. She managed to ignore the complaint and say cheerfully, "Okay, great! I'm glad you're coming. Mark will be, too."

Mark had the foil-encased fish already out of the oven when Jan and Stardust arrived, and he served it on the patio a few minutes later. He was pleased with his cooking efforts, and the new honey-mustard dressing Jan had made for the salad was great. They talked about a new class he was scheduled to teach this semester, and Jan mentioned that the house buyers had also made her an offer on the furniture. Stardust, who hadn't said anything up to this point, suddenly announced that the buyers couldn't have the CD player, VCR, or television in her room because she was taking them. Mark knew she had no right to them, but Jan didn't argue. He knew both money and possessions had a much lower priority for her these days.

Inside, he scraped the dishes and Jan arranged them in the dishwasher. While Jan went to the bathroom to freshen her lipstick, Mark picked up a book in his bedroom that he wanted to give her. When he came out, she was peering into the small bedroom he used as a catchall room. She looked a little flustered, as if she felt she'd been caught snooping, but he was embarrassed about the room's messiness.

"Don't stand too close," he warned ruefully. "I'm afraid it's a junk avalanche waiting to happen."

"Actually, I was just thinking…I believe you once suggested that this room might make a good nursery."

He tried not to sound as surprised as he felt by what almost sounded like a hint. "And?"

"I think it would do just fine."

"If you haven't found a suitable house yet, you know you and the baby are welcome to stay here as long as you want."

He suddenly suspected that offer was not what she had in mind now, and her next words proved it.

"I know that, but I was thinking of a...more permanent arrangement." She smiled—and what he thought he saw in that smile made his heart pound. *Lord, can it be...?*

Her smile broadened. "Or have I been mistaken in what I thought were hints toward remarriage?" She sounded a bit mischievous now, almost playful. "Maybe even semiproposals?"

"No, you weren't mistaken." He swallowed. "Do you want us to remarry?"

"I think so."

"Why?"

She frowned at what was obviously an unexpected and unwelcome question, and the bubbles of playfulness disappeared. "Well, all sorts of reasons. I know the baby is as important to you as she is to me. We don't yet know what her physical or mental limitations may be, but it's safe to say she's desperately going to need everything we both can give her. With the Lord's help, I think I can be a better mother this time. I know you'll make a great father. Together—I think we'll make the team she needs."

"So the only reason you want to remarry is for the baby's sake?"

"No! I'm not thinking of remarriage as some big sacrifice we'll make for the baby's sake! I want it for *us*, too. We have so much going for us now. All our years together. The losses we've shared. The faith we now share. The fact that we're both 'new and improved' people."

Yes, all true. Yet the reason for their remarriage that he desperately longed to hear wasn't there.

"Mark, what's the matter with you? You've been telling me all along that you love me, and I thought that included wanting to start over in a new marriage, but now—"

He stepped forward and swiftly wrapped his arms around her. "I do love you."

"Then why do you make me feel as if I'm climbing out on a limb and proposing to some commitment-shy stranger?"

He took a moment to gather his thoughts. "Jan, the Bible speaks of faith, hope, and love in our spiritual lives, and I think these are the basis for a Christian marriage, too. Faith in each other, hope for the future together, and, the most important of all, love. But in all of this, in all the months since we've been part of each other's lives again, you've never said anything about loving me."

Jan leaned back, her gaze searching his troubled eyes.

"I don't blame you if you can't love me again." The ache in his heart was so deep, he thought it would choke him. "I can understand how my betrayal of our marriage vows could have killed your love forever—"

"I've forgiven that! I've made mistakes too."

"But forgiveness isn't the same as *love*."

"I need you!"

"Jan, I'll always be here for you and the baby. I'll be the very best father and grandpa I can be. She'll be a part of my life, and I'll be a part of hers." Then he said the words that were among the most difficult he'd ever spoken in his life. "But a second try at marriage, even with the best intentions, isn't going to work if it's built on a one-sided love."

Love. The word hung there, floating like some shimmering golden ball just out of Jan's grasp. She'd enjoyed Mark these past few months. She marveled at the changes in him and found fresh respect for him. She depended on him; she was comfortable with him. She felt old stirrings, tantalizing new awakenings. She peered at love, touched it with a mental finger, probed it with a wary emotion. For a moment, she angrily wanted to argue with him, deny his accusations.

Yet he had seen, even if she had not, that the part of her that had retreated from loving him after the divorce, the part of her that had hammered a protective barrier around that love for her own emotional survival, had not dared crash through the barrier and venture fully into the open again.

"I don't *not* love you." She knew it wasn't what he was looking for, but she felt confused by the tangle of her own emotions and his soft-spoken accusations.

He smiled ruefully. "That's something. I appreciate it. But two negatives about love don't exactly make a positive. And I'm grateful that you've forgiven me. But forgiveness of the past doesn't necessarily reinstate trust...or revive love."

"We aren't kids full of starry-eyed illusions about love! Maybe you want too much."

He nodded heavily. "Maybe I do."

Although, deep down, she doubted that he did want or expect too much. She wanted to tell him he was wrong, that she did love him just as wholly as he said he loved her, but, peering tremulously over the old barrier around her heart, she just wasn't sure. And then anger and embarrassment took over. She'd offered herself to him and he'd turned her down!

"I'm ready to go home." They both turned as Stardust yelled down the hall at them with the inevitable self-centered, me-first challenge and defiance in her voice.

"Yes, we should be going."

"I'll take her to her doctor's appointment on Monday."

"Thank you," Jan said stiffly. "I'd appreciate that. It will give me extra time to look for a suitable house."

"Do you want to talk about this some more?"

"No. I think you've said it all."

18

JAN WENT TO CHURCH ON SUNDAY, AND MARK CAME TO SIT beside her, but she kept several inches of open space between their shoulders. Afterward, when he suggested that they pick up submarine sandwiches and go somewhere on a picnic, she declined, murmuring politely that she had some "things to do."

He'd been on her mind almost continually since that scene in the hallway of his home. Couldn't he just accept what she had to offer? Had she fought against loving him for so long that her heart was trapped forever behind some indestructible barrier?

Yet after these past months, how could she get along without him? And what did the Lord want to become of this relationship?

The statement she'd made to him about things to do was more or less true. Back at the house, she changed into old denim shorts and T-shirt, intending to start sorting through the books on the shelves in the family room right after lunch. She still didn't know where she would be moving, but she'd have to move somewhere shortly. While she was making sandwiches for lunch, Stardust wandered into the kitchen.

"Why don't we put some stuff in an ice chest and go have a picnic somewhere?"

Jan was so astonished that momentarily all she could say was, "Us? You and me? A *picnic*?"

"I'm tired of sitting around here. A lady at the store was telling me that it's really pretty driving along the river out toward Hood River and The Dalles."

Stardust's tone was petulant with boredom, yet it was the first even semifriendly overture she had made in a long time, and Jan hated to respond less than enthusiastically, but— "It's fifty or sixty miles out there, and as close as we are to your due date, I'm not sure driving so far would be a good idea. But we could go to the zoo or a park here in town."

"I'm tired of this baby running my life! I'm tired of eating what's good for it and doing what's good for it or *not* doing what's good for it. And I don't want to go walk around some dumb zoo where I'm bigger than the hippopotamus! If you don't want to come—"

Jan started to laugh at the farfetched hippopotamus comparison, then stopped when she saw Stardust's angry glare and familiar grab for the car keys in her pocket.

"Wait!" The route along the river was all freeway; it wasn't as if they'd be heading out into the wilderness, and she'd have her cell phone, of course, in case of an emergency. And Stardust, ever stubborn and headstrong, was obviously going alone if Jan didn't accompany her. "Just give me a few minutes to get our picnic ready."

"I'm driving," Stardust stated, as if that were a nonnegotiable condition of doing this together, and Jan didn't argue.

Jan wrapped the tuna salad sandwiches in plastic, added carrot sticks and cherry tomatoes, and quickly filled a container with cubed melon for dessert. Briefly she thought about calling Mark and inviting him along, but she was still smarting from his rejection.

They were on their way within fifteen minutes.

Stardust could barely squeeze behind the wheel now, but she stubbornly adjusted the seat and stretched her feet to the pedals. Jan had to admit it was a glorious day for a drive as they headed east out of the city through the area known as the Columbia River Gorge. The day was calm and the sun hot, but the coming of fall hung like a delicious secret in the air. A few leaves were beginning to turn color. On their left, the broad river gleamed like an unmoving, blue satin lake, and on their right, just beyond a metallic ribbon of railroad tracks, steep, forested slopes rose to frame the formidable cliffs. Overhead, blue sky arched between the cliffs and the green mountains on the far side of the river. If heaven had a color, Jan thought a little dreamily, this spectacular blue was surely it.

Although Stardust had mentioned the scenery as a reason for driving up the river, she barely seemed to notice the spectacular beauty of the gorge. She centered her attention on weaving in and out of traffic on the busy freeway, jockeying for position and passing other cars as if this were some competitive event and she was determined to cross the finish line first.

"We have plenty of time." Jan grabbed the strap of her seat belt as Stardust whipped the Firebird around a convertible. "No need to rush."

Stardust didn't slow down. "I've been stopped, but I've never gotten a ticket," she said airily. "They look at how big I am, then, like they're afraid I may go into labor on the spot, make it just a fast warning. I guess being pregnant is good for *something*."

They passed through Hood River and stopped for lunch at a rest area high above the river. Jan carried the ice chest across the lush grass to a concrete table in the shade. A ground squirrel immediately hopped out of the nearby bushes to investigate, and Stardust enticed him closer with tossed scraps of bread. She was unexpectedly talkative today, chattering about a movie she'd seen on TV and how it might be fun to get a butterfly tattoo on her ankle.

Although she speculated about whether the squirrel had babies, never once did she mention her own coming baby or voice any concern about the heart surgery they now knew the baby was going to need soon after birth. The baby and her uncertain future were foremost in Jan's mind almost every hour of the day, but Stardust apparently shut out everything beyond the moment of birth and her own personal inconvenience with the pregnancy.

An inconvenience that she was suddenly complaining about again. Jan was watching a handful of windsurfers skimming across the river, the colorful sails like butterflies grazing the water, when Stardust gave a sharp cry. Her eyebrows contracted in a wince, and she arched her shoulders and rubbed her hand across the small of her back.

"Is something wrong?"

Stardust shoved the Styrofoam dish of red-ripe melon cubes across the picnic table. "I can't eat any more. My back feels as if someone is sticking a knife in it."

Stardust's complaints about her aches and pains were always dramatic, the epitome of suffering. A slight swelling in her ankles had her groaning that they were "puffed up like balloons," and her headaches were always "blinding." One Sunday morning, gas pains made her so sure she was going into premature labor that Jan rushed her to the hospital. She often complained that the baby's movements kept her awake most of the night, her accusing tone suggesting that the baby was deliberately disturbing her sleep. Yet in spite of her complaints, she continued to bloom in physical appearance, which tended in Jan's opinion to negate some of her cranky complaints.

And yet…the girl *did* look unnaturally pale. With a twinge of sudden concern, Jan hurriedly repacked the remains of their lunch. It was time they were heading home anyway. To the east, massive mounds of dark clouds had replaced the blue sky, and a gusty breeze tossed Jan's hair as she carried the ice chest back to the Firebird. When she slammed the trunk lid shut, she saw Stardust leaning heavily against a front fender.

"Are you okay?"

"My stomach doesn't feel good. Maybe the tuna was bad."

Jan didn't argue, although she knew the freshly opened can of tuna was fine. "Perhaps I should drive," she suggested.

Not to Jan's surprise, Stardust muttered, "No, I can do it."

So far as Jan knew, Stardust had never let anyone else get behind the wheel of the Firebird. She guarded it with a fierce possessiveness that sometimes made Jan want to scream. How could anyone care so much about a car and so little about her own baby? She watched uneasily as Stardust steadied herself with a hand on the hood while she worked her way around to the driver's side door. Once in the car, Stardust leaned her head back against the seat and closed her eyes.

Jan felt an unexpected surge of compassion. She looked so pale, so vulnerable, with wisps of baby-fine hair clinging to her sweat-damp temples. Surely she wasn't as uncaring and unfeeling as she made out! Perhaps it was all just a protective shell. A thought that evaporated only a moment later when Stardust sat upright and muttered grimly, "I will never be so glad of anything in my life as when this is all over, and I'm finally not pregnant and can get on with my life."

They had to go several miles farther upriver before they could cross over to the side of the freeway heading west, back to Portland. By then the clouds were massed overhead and thunder growled ominously. The river had changed from blue satin to a rough, whitecapped pewter, and only a couple of hardy windsurfers were still on the water. A scrap of paper whipped onto the windshield by the rising wind made Jan duck reflexively. Stardust usually drove with relaxed, one-handed casualness, but now she clutched the wheel with both white-knuckled hands. Lightning suddenly lit the interior of the car with a blue-white flash, followed by an explosive crash of thunder, and they both jumped. Stardust wiped the back of her hand across her forehead.

"I could drive," Jan suggested again.

"I told you, I can do it!"

"But if you don't feel well—"

"I feel fine!"

But a few miles farther down the freeway, just as huge raindrops splattered the hood, a strange look came over Stardust's face. "Something happened. I'm all…wet."

She tried to look down, and Jan instinctively grabbed the wheel as the car veered toward the shoulder. "Now what's wrong with me?"

Stardust asked the question more with vexed exasperation than panic, but it was near panic that instantly swept through Jan. She could see a damp stain spreading in the crotch of Stardust's maternity shorts, and she knew instantly what it was. *Oh, Lord, please, not here, not now...*

"Give me a Kleenex out of the glove compartment so I can wipe off." Stardust still sounded more annoyed than concerned.

"Pull over to the shoulder," Jan commanded.

"I told you—"

"*Pull over!* I think your water has broken."

Stardust shot her a startled glance. "But it isn't supposed to do that!" With a logic and indignation that might have made Jan smile under different conditions, she added, "It's two weeks yet until the cesarean, so it can't happen now."

"I don't think *when* the cesarean is scheduled matters if your water broke *now.*"

Realization of what might be happening finally dawned on Stardust, and she reacted with a panic that instantly surpassed Jan's. "But I can't go into labor and have a baby out here on the freeway, in the *car!*" Fear shrilled her voice. "I have to be in the hospital!"

Jan grimly knew that Stardust's terror was only for herself, and yet it was a realistic enough fear. All sorts of things could go wrong away from the hospital. But it wasn't Stardust for whom Jan's heart thudded with fear. Stardust was strong and healthy now, and she could probably survive primitive childbirth without doctors or hospital. But the baby couldn't. The new obstetrician had made that plain. With the serious heart condition, and the question of Down syndrome still hanging unsettled, the baby's life depended on the cesarean delivery and immediate intensive care. Being born out here could cost the baby's life.

Frantically, as Stardust skidded the car to a halt on the shoulder amid a sudden torrent of rain, Jan tried to figure out what to do. The instant downburst hammered the roof like gunfire, and the veil of rain shut out mountains and river, shut out everything except the blur of cars rushing by and the terror within this one. Jan reached over and flicked on the emergency blinkers, so other cars could see them better, while she tried to think.

How far were they from Portland now? Twenty-five miles? And how long did they have? When Tim was born, Jan's water had never broken naturally even when she was in heavy labor, and the doctor finally had to do it. She remembered the much different situation of a friend whose water had broken early, and she hadn't even gone into labor for several hours. And first births were usually longer than subsequent ones, so surely there was time…

One look at Stardust's face told her none of those assurances about other childbirths mattered now. Babies arrived on their own schedule, not by statistics. Her eyes were closed, her mouth contorted, her hands clenched like claws around the sides of the bucket seat. Jan struggled to keep her own panic from boiling over. Surely, Stardust was simply overreacting, overdramatizing again. She couldn't instantly jump into full-blown labor pains—

Jan reached over and placed a hand on Stardust's abdomen. It felt hard and tight, but she didn't know if that was normal, so close to term, or if this was a true contraction.

"Don't just sit there." Stardust gritted her teeth. The hammering rain almost drowned out her voice, and another roll of thunder vibrated the car. "*Call* someone. Get someone out here to help me!"

Yes! The cell phone. Of course. Jan snatched the compact phone out of her purse and frantically pawed for her list of emergency phone numbers. She had half of Dr. Osborne's number punched in before she realized the doctor wouldn't be in his office today because it was Sunday. And that didn't matter anyway, she realized a moment later, because the phone wasn't working. Jan shook the silent instrument viciously, then pounded it against her palm and tried again. Work, *work!* she demanded. But storm or location or weak battery or something had made the instrument as useless as a toy.

She slid out of the car, unmindful of the slashing rain, and dashed around to the driver's side. Passing cars swished dangerously close in the storm-dimmed light, spraying her with water from the silvery sheeting on the roadway. Crosscurrents of wind from traffic and the storm buffeted the door as she yanked it open. Stardust looked at her uncomprehendingly, as if she were a stranger trying to force her way inside.

"You'll have to slide over to the other seat so I can drive." This time Stardust didn't argue, and Jan helped her shift her bulky weight over to the other bucket seat. Rain pounded Jan's back and bare legs as she leaned into the car, soaking whatever wasn't already drenched when she ran around the car. Finally she got inside and slammed the door. Wet hair plastered her scalp, and she pushed it out of her eyes and wiped away the rivulets dribbling down her face so she could peer at Stardust sitting there with glazed-looking eyes.

"Is anything happening now?"

"I feel kind of…weird."

"Hurting?"

"Not exactly—" Stardust broke off and grabbed her abdomen. "Now it feels like a big fist grabbing me!"

That sounded like labor to Jan. Once more she tried the cell phone, then tossed it behind the seat. She checked the headlights, started the windshield wipers and turn signal, and edged into traffic. Most of the cars were moving slower now, inching carefully through the veils of wind-driven rain, but a few impatient drivers still whipped in and out of traffic. Jan, in spite of a powerful urge to floor the gas pedal and recklessly force her way through the lanes of traffic, opted for slow and careful.

The inside of the windshield steamed up, and she swiped at it with her palm. Outside, the pounding rain hitting the pavement turned the roadway into a jumping sea. Traffic slowed to a crawl around an accident blocking one lane. She pounded the steering wheel with her fist, feeling wild and frustrated. She should have grabbed the car keys away from Stardust and stopped this jaunt at home before it ever began. She should have called Mark and asked him to come along. Even with people all around her, cars jammed so closely together that she found herself peering into the eyes of a man in a window only inches away, she had never felt more alone and helpless.

Yet she wasn't alone, of course. Not since she'd taken Jesus into her heart! She took a deep breath and poured out her desperate pleas.

Lord, please, oh please keep Stardust and the baby safe until I can get them to the hospital. Don't let the baby come too soon! Take care of this small life you created. Show me the fastest way to get them to the hospital, make a way for us, please...

19

JAN PACED THE WALL OF WINDOWS OVERLOOKING THE PARKING lot. It was past seven o'clock now, sun slanting red-gold through maple leaves glinting with a hint of rusty fall color. The thunderstorm hadn't struck here and the asphalt was dry.

Mark, where are you? She'd called him three times now, each time leaving progressively more frantic messages on his answering machine. Whatever their differences, he'd want to be here, she knew, and she desperately needed him here. Needed his strength, his comfort, his wisdom, his goodness. Where *was* he? Again she lashed herself mentally for not somehow short-circuiting today's entire unwise trip.

Then she spotted him, dodging cars as he ran across the parking lot. Even from here she could see he was in old clothes, faded jeans and a denim shirt with the sleeves ripped out. Whatever he'd been doing, he'd obviously raced out of the house the instant he picked up the messages on the machine.

She pushed through the swinging doors to meet him, and his embrace swallowed her like an enveloping tornado. "What is it? What's going on?"

"Stardust is in surgery—"

"For the C-section? But it's two weeks early!"

"I'll explain." On a short elevator ride up to the waiting room where a nurse had told her they could wait, she compressed everything into a few brief sentences.

"But she and the baby are okay?" Mark put both

hands on her shoulders and held her at arm's length, searching her face. His gaze reached deep into her troubled eyes. "Are *you* okay?"

She felt something breaking inside her, a strange feeling. A cracking, a splintering, a crumbling, as she looked into his eyes and saw all the love and concern of his heart naked there. Why should it happen now, she wondered, feeling a little dazed, why here at this unlikely moment? *Was* it happening?

Oh, yes.

The barrier had been weakened for months, Mark determinedly chipping and hammering from the outside, Jan's own emotions stealthily digging and excavating from the inside. And now a wild detonation took place, taking down the last of that barrier she'd built around love, blew it so far from her heart she knew it could never rise again. And behind it stood the truth victorious—the truth Jan had for so long been afraid to face. She didn't need him just for this moment of crisis, didn't need him just for emotional support where Stardust and the baby were concerned; she needed and wanted him for *her*. For always. Because she loved him.

It was true that she didn't love him the way she once had, but it was a realization that came with exultation not regret. Because this love was so much more, a love with more depth and intensity and maturity than she'd ever thought possible.

She stood there in his arms, reveling in the sweet feeling of love pouring in from him, love flowing out from her, all doubts and reservations vanished. She loved him! And he'd been so right in holding out for more than she offered him a few days ago.

"Jan?" Mark said tentatively, when she still hadn't spoken. "You okay?"

She opened her eyes. "I love you!" This wasn't the proper time or place...but she didn't care! The words burst out again. "I love you!"

He didn't ask why now? or demand explanations. He simply said, "Praise the Lord!"

Once such words would not have impressed Jan, but at this moment they were the most beautiful words she had ever heard. Their heartfelt simplicity and sincerity meant more to her than any flowery phrase. Mark, her Mark, was praising God that her heart had finally opened to return his love...and she praised him too. She laughed, and he laughed with her, sweeping her into his arms and swinging her around, just as he had at their wedding.

When he put her down she felt disoriented and breathless and giddy with love. She tangled her arms around his neck for support. She was just about to boldly turn her earlier rejected semiproposal into a passionate plea for marriage when Mark said, "Will you marry me, Jan?"

"Oh yes!"

He lowered his head then and kissed her with all the wild enthusiasm of new love and all the experience and remembered heat of old love.

Jan finally broke away although he still didn't release her completely. She put a restraining hand on his chest. "But first—"

He nodded with instant understanding. "First Stardust and the baby. But not until I tell you I love you and hear it again from you."

"I love you!" She smiled. "How's that?"

He kissed her on the nose and repeated a teasing phrase from another time. "Okay for starters. But I expect to hear it repeated at least at hourly intervals. And you know the old saying: actions speak louder than words."

"I'll say it whenever you want." She felt herself blushing lightly. "Although the action will have to wait a while yet."

He nodded. "Okay. We'll work out the details later. Right now, back to the business at hand."

She nodded too. "Everybody's been too busy to tell me much. Stardust was definitely in labor when we got here, although not nearly as far along as I thought she was, considering her dramatics. I was also afraid it was too late for a cesarean, but they said that they could still do emergency surgery, that it wasn't unusual to do a C-section after labor had started. But Dr. Osborne is out of town and another doctor who is taking care of his patients came. They took her off to surgery and that's all I know. It seems as if it's taking an awfully long time, much longer than it should." Then the guilt hit her again. "Oh, I should never have let her get in that car and go anywhere!"

"When Stardust makes up her mind, she's a hard girl to stop."

"Then I should have called you and gotten you to come with us!"

He shook her lightly. "Nothing would have been any different if I'd been there. You did fine. You did wonderful, in fact, getting her here."

"I prayed, Mark. And God helped. The traffic was so thick, and there were accidents on the slick highway because of the storm and blocked-up culverts and water running everywhere. But a lane just seemed to open up in front of us when I prayed, and I took it. Then I could feel the Lord telling me to get off the freeway, and I did, and we got out of the jammed-up traffic and came straight to the emergency entrance. And then I started trying to call you."

"I'm sorry it took so long for me to get your message and get here. I was over at the park playing ball with some neighborhood kids. I could see the thunderheads and lightning off to the east, but we didn't get any storm at all."

They took seats side by side on a gray sofa. The lighting was soft, the sound of unseen activities a muted hum; it might have been the lobby of a tasteful hotel except for the pervasive scent that unmistakably blared *hospital.*

By unspoken agreement Mark took her hand, and they immediately prayed for Stardust and the baby and for wisdom and skill for the doctors and nurses attending her. Jan had just lifted her head when a doctor, head still covered, mask dangling beneath his chin, came toward them. His unfamiliar face revealed nothing, and Jan clutched Mark's hand.

"Hello. I'm Dr. Whitaker." The doctor put out his hand, and both Jan and Mark rose to their feet to shake it in turn. "You're the young woman's parents?"

"We're the adoptive parents of the new baby," Mark corrected.

"Oh, I see. Well, Deborah is doing fine—"

Deborah? The name left Jan blank for a moment. Then she shook her head. Of course, Stardust's real name. That was what they used on her records here at the hospital. She'd had lab work done here, and arrangements had already been made for the C-section.

"She isn't fully out from under the anesthesia yet, but you should be able to see her within an hour or so. Normally, we give an epidural for a cesarean delivery, but in this emergency situation we decided to use general anesthesia."

So, Jan thought wryly, Stardust got her wish there. No consciousness, no pain, no involvement. "The baby?"

"It's a girl, as I'm sure you already know from the ultrasound. Six pounds, one ounce." He hesitated, as if deciding how to go on, and Jan felt a tremor like a distant earthquake rumbling closer. "Dr. Osborne had already arranged for a specialist, Dr. Michaels, to examine the baby immediately after birth. He's been contacted, and I'm expecting him any minute. You were aware that a heart problem was anticipated?" He hesitated, his gaze flicking between them as if it had just occurred to him that perhaps as adoptive parents they didn't know.

"Yes, we know," Jan assured him. "It's serious?"

"I'm afraid so. Extremely serious. But she has a much better chance of survival now than she would've had a few months ago, before Dr. Michaels came here from Boston. He's in the forefront of the latest techniques for heart surgery on newborns. He'll discuss the situation with you although it may not be until morning."

"We'd also been informed of a possibility the baby could have Down syndrome," Mark said.

"Yes, I saw that in the records. At the moment, given the baby's other more urgent problems, the answer still isn't definitive. At birth, babies with Down syndrome are often what is sometimes termed 'floppy,' due to abnormal muscle tone, and this baby exhibits some of that condition. But heart problems may also cause poor muscle tone." He lifted a blond eyebrow. "However, if it's an important consideration in the adoption, I can order immediate tests to determine if the chromosomal abnormality of Down syndrome is present—"

Jan and Mark said it together. "No!"

Jan elaborated on their answer. "Unless it's important to know immediately for the baby's sake, it doesn't matter to us," she said firmly. "It will not affect the adoption."

"That's admirable." Again the doctor's glance flicked between them, and Jan couldn't tell if his glance offered approval or sympathetic compassion.

"May we see the baby?" Mark asked.

The doctor hesitated, and Jan thought he was going to say no, but after a moment he turned and led them down a hallway and around a maze of corners to another room. "You won't have much time, and you won't be able to get close or touch her," he warned before opening the door.

When they saw the baby from a short distance, Jan suspected the doctor had let them see her mostly because he wanted to warn them what they were getting into with the adoption. She was in an incubator, wires and tubes protruding from her tiny body, gowned figures hovering, machines humming and flickering nearby. Her color was not the healthy baby pink that Jan remembered when Tim was born. But what Jan saw more than abnormal color or technology keeping the baby alive was her face, sweet as a miniature angel, wisps of dark hair standing straight up, and vulnerable little arms and legs.

At the moment, she felt no fear of anything that lay ahead, only a radiant explosion of love. And all she could think was, *Please, Lord, please, please, please, please...* The fierce pressure of Mark's hand told her his thoughts and prayers were the same.

They returned to the waiting room and spent more time in prayer. There was a coffee machine in the corner, and Mark filled two Styrofoam cups. Jan couldn't sit still to drink hers. Fear and tension knotted inside her. She paced the room, sat down, flipped a magazine open, jumped up, peered down the hall. She was also, she found, unexpectedly anxious to see Stardust. Surely now that Stardust was truly a mother, now that the baby's desperate needs were out in the open, Stardust would feel differently about abandoning her!

A nurse came a few minutes later and led them to Stardust's bed in a windowless recovery room. She was awake although the focus of her eyes, hazel now without the contacts, was a little fuzzy. Jan touched her hand.

"How are you feeling?"

Stardust blinked and stared at Jan. "Okay, I guess. Except kind of stiff and sore all over." She gingerly touched her abdomen. "Did I have a C-section?"

"Yes. And you're doing fine." Jan waited, expecting Stardust to ask about the baby—how could she not ask!—but the girl just studied the identifying plastic band on her wrist as if it were some fascinating new piece of jewelry.

"We've just seen the baby," Jan offered encouragingly.

"What all's wrong with her?"

The blunt question shocked Jan, but she tried not to be judgmental. "There is a heart abnormality, as we already knew, but the doctors haven't given us any details yet. A specialist is coming to see her. But she's beautiful, a perfect little face and arms and legs—"

"What about the Down syndrome?"

"They still don't know for certain yet, but—"

"When's the lawyer coming?"

The question made Jan's head jerk back. "Lawyer?"

"So I can sign the papers."

In spite of all that had gone before, everything she knew about Stardust's greed and self-centeredness, the cold, impatient response hit Jan like another shock wave. "There's no rush. You'll be here several days. I've already told the hospital that you're to be released only when you're ready, not shoved out the way some insurance companies make them do it. I want you to have time to recover completely and—" Jan swallowed and forced herself to continue—"think everything through."

There was a barely perceptible hesitation, just long enough for Jan and Mark to exchange glances, before Stardust muttered, "I've thought everything through."

"I think you'll feel differently when you see the baby—"

"I'm not going to see her! All I want is the title to my car and the adoption papers signed, then I'm out of here."

"Stardust, there's no need for you to go! You and the baby can live with me, just as we planned. I'll help you every way I can—"

"You don't even have a house to live in," Stardust said scornfully, as if this material fact was all that really mattered. She laboriously turned on her side, dismissing them, and Jan didn't correct her about the house or the nursery in Mark's house that she was already mentally painting pink, with stencils of gold and white angels.

Mark, who had been silent all during the conversation, now spoke, a grim promise turning his tone flat and harsh. "I'll have the lawyer here first thing in the morning."

Even in her fuzzy, postanesthesia state, Stardust's solo-track mind targeted one point clearly. "I don't sign anything until I get the title to my car."

Jan arrived at the hospital shortly after nine o'clock the next morning. She had asked Mark if he'd like to stay in a spare bedroom at the house, but he declined, and now she knew why. He had things to do, and he was busy, wasting no time in carrying out that promise to Stardust. She met him, along with the lawyer and a woman the lawyer introduced as his assistant, a notary, in the hallway. The lawyer had already told them that Stardust's signature on a notarized consent form was the most crucial step in the adoption. Later would come the other steps: petitioning the court, an investigation by the state children's services division, and finally a hearing with the court. But everything hinged on first getting this consent form signed.

"You're on your way to see Stardust?" Jan asked.

"We've already seen her."

Jan's conflicting emotions collided like storm waves, one part of her hoping Stardust had signed, another part hoping Stardust's maternal instincts had somehow awakened and she'd refused to sign and claimed the baby as her own.

Mark answered her unspoken question. "Everything's taken care of. I've been here since eight o'clock. She signed the necessary papers."

Jan knew from Mark's emphasis on the timing that he was telling her that he'd gotten here first and handed over the title to the car, so there was no problem when the lawyer arrived. So now everything truly was taken care of. She felt a strange, contradictory combination of exhilaration and letdown.

The lawyer and his assistant left, and Mark touched Jan's arm, guiding her to the elevator. "I think we can see the heart specialist in a few minutes."

It was more than a few minutes, however, before they saw him. Over an hour, actually, giving Jan time to contemplate the future. A new life with Mark, a new baby in her arms! Formula, diapers, sleepless nights. It was all rather breathlessly overwhelming and intimidating, not a job she'd anticipated taking on at this time of life. But, oh, such a glorious second chance at motherhood! She closed her eyes, thanking the Lord with all her heart and asking for his blessing.

For a few moments, Jan's joy crowded out worries about the big problems they must first face, but apprehension thundered down on her as a new doctor, most likely the specialist, approached. Jan's first thought as she looked up from prayer to see him striding toward them in hospital garb was, *but he's so young!* Also husky, dark-haired, and almost too good looking.

His experience and competence came through as he talked with them, however, reminding her that good looks and powerful competence were not mutually exclusive. At the same time, he didn't offer false assurances or mince words about the seriousness of the baby's problems or the risks.

The baby had what he called a transposition of the great arteries. It occurred in approximately 25 of every 100,000 live births, although more often to male than female babies. It meant that the two main arteries leaving the heart, the pulmonary artery to the lungs and the aorta to the rest of the body, were reversed. This meant the blood pumping through the body was not supplied with the oxygen from the lungs that it required. The baby could not survive long in that condition.

"We've already done what is called a balloon atrial septostomy," he added. "This opens a passage between the two upper chambers of the heart and supplies more oxygen to the blood—"

"You mean it's all over and done with?" Jan cut in with a gasp of surprised relief.

He shook his head. "No. This is only a temporary measure. The next step is to do a full arterial switch to correct the problem permanently."

Jan's relief evaporated, but she asked hopefully, "Later, you mean, after she's older and stronger?"

Dr. Michaels's slight smile was kind. "Only if you consider three days from now 'later and older.'"

Jan couldn't help another gasp, this time not with relief. All she could think was that tiny angel of a baby, already enveloped in tubes and wires, was going under the surgeon's knife again!

"How risky an operation is it?" Mark asked.

"Early attempts at this type of surgery were not encouraging, but new techniques in the past few years have considerably raised the success rate. My own over the past year has been 91 percent." He spoke with a satisfaction of accomplishment but not arrogance and a hint of sadness when he added, "But that also means there are still some babies who don't make it."

Jan's throat closed, and she felt choked and breathless and dizzy. "Does it have to be done so soon?"

"The longer the repair is put off, the greater the chance the baby won't survive to *have* the surgery. And a successful operation means the heart can grow and develop normally right from the start."

Jan couldn't say anything, but Mark managed a thanks for the explanation and what the doctor planned to do.

"I'll be talking to you again," Dr. Michaels said reassuringly. "In the meantime…you were praying when I came, weren't you? Don't stop now." He clasped Mark's shoulder encouragingly.

Three days. Jan spent some time at the office and took clients around to view properties. She worked up a detailed comparison of similar properties for sale to help one seller price his house properly. She made a rather good duplex sale. She gave these matters the shallow end of her mind, the deep end connected to the baby. Mark taught his classes although he admitted he couldn't have said later what his lectures were about. He said he had the room they planned to use as a nursery almost cleaned out and ready for wallpaper.

They couldn't touch the baby, but they were allowed to approach her briefly twice each day, and each time Jan's heart felt close to bursting with love. Lack of a blood relationship was insignificant and irrelevant. Mark put a request for prayer for the baby on a prayer chain at church and another at the college. Jan received calls from people she didn't even know telling her they were hoping and praying. Yet her own prayers were not only for the baby; they were for Stardust too.

Jan went to see her several times. She looked good, rested and clear-eyed, her hair artfully tousled in a new style, her fingernails carefully manicured, as if she spent much of her time on studied grooming and self-improvement. She complained that her breasts were hard and painful, but when Jan inquired, she admitted her incision was fine. Jan wryly suspected she would have preferred to be able to complain about it. And she did, finally, express some curiosity about her baby.

"Does she look anything like me?"

Jan smiled, pleased with even that self-centered expression of interest. "Babies mostly just look like themselves. But I think maybe she has your nose and long, slender fingers."

"What color is her hair?"

"Dark. Almost black."

"Eyes?"

"I'm not sure. They look bluish, but I think most babies eyes look bluish at birth and develop their real color later."

Stardust twisted that identification band round and round on her wrist, and Jan wondered if she were remembering the father, remembering the color of his hair and eyes, but all Stardust said was, "What did you name her?"

They'd intended to call her Alisha, that name held

over from long ago, but from the first moment Jan saw her, another name had taken hold in her heart, and Mark had agreed. "We've named her Angel."

Jan expected some scornful reaction, some jeer about sticking a religious name on a baby, but Stardust just looked thoughtful and finally said, "That's pretty. I like it."

"The offer's still open," Jan said softly. She already thought of Angel as her own, but if Stardust could open her heart to her baby… She put her hand on Stardust's. "You don't have to give her up."

"I've already signed the papers. And Mark gave me the title to the car."

"We can tear up the papers! And you can still have the car." As much as she already loved the baby, it made her heart ache to know that Angel would never know her birth mother's love.

"You don't want her?" Stardust's hazel eyes widened in alarm.

"Of *course* we want her—!" Jan broke off as she tried to sort through her conflicting emotions, torn between wanting to hold and protect this sweet baby, guarding her from all harm, but afraid she might be putting her own desires ahead of what the Lord wanted for the baby and what was best for her. "I want her in the same way I wanted Tim when he was born. I love her. But I want *you* to love and want her too! I want you to see her worth and beauty, that any imperfections she may have don't matter. I want you to take your place as her rightful mother, and cherish and love her. She deserves that. Think about it, Stardust, please? You and the baby can still live with us. I'd be so happy being grandma—"

Stardust targeted a single phrase of Jan's plea. "Live with *us?*"

"Mark and me. We're going to remarry and live in his house."

"Well, I guess everything's all set then, isn't it?" Jan couldn't tell if Stardust was voicing sarcasm or approval. Or, more likely, that it was simply a meaningless comment because she really didn't care. Her brief flicker of interest seemed to have burned out now. She picked up an emery board Jan had brought and concentrated on correcting some minuscule imperfection on her thumbnail.

Jan tried once more. "Please, Stardust, just see her—"

"No."

"Are you afraid if you see her that you'll change your mind?"

"Just leave me alone!"

Stardust didn't see the baby, and on the morning Jan and Mark arrived to wait out Angel's surgery, they found Stardust had signed herself out of the hospital. She hadn't even waited to see the outcome of the baby's surgery. Her things were still at the house, but Jan knew they would be gone by the time she returned home; Stardust had timed her departure carefully so she could go to the house when she knew Jan would be here at the hospital. Yet somehow Jan couldn't condemn her. All she could think was, *Poor, lost Stardust, walking out on the most precious gift in her life, running off to chase the stardust dreams that were no more substantial or real than her name.*

They were in a different waiting room this time. Here the sofas were blue and the coffee machine was down the hall, but the scent was the same pervasive aura of hospital. Over and over Jan reminded herself that it was a scent of antiseptic purity, a *good* scent, but in the back of her mind hung the dark apprehension that it was also the scent of death.

Dr. Michaels had said the surgery could take several hours, but after only the first hour Jan felt as if she had spent half her life here in fear and worry. She trusted God. He had brought this baby to them. Surely he wouldn't snatch her away now! But sometimes, for reasons known only to him and not to those left grieving behind, he called his tiniest and most innocent angels home...

She paced. She stared out the window. She thought with inward terror of what the doctor had told them about the surgery, what was going on right now: a heart-lung machine keeping Angel alive while the doctor cut vital arteries and reversed and sutured, all in a heart no bigger than a silver dollar.

On one of her passes, Mark reached out and snagged her hand and pulled her down beside him. "What happens if she doesn't make it, Jan?"

"Don't say that! Don't think it. She has to make it!"

"And if she doesn't make it, neither do we?"

She looked at him wonderingly, focusing on the troubled shadows in his eyes. "Is that what you think? That my feelings for you are all dependent on what happens to her? That it's you, me, and Angel in the nursery, or nothing?"

"That occurs to me, yes."

"Mark, I love you!" She put her hands on his temples, framing his face so she could look deep into his eyes. "It has nothing to do with the good or the bad of the past,

or with the baby, or with anything but you and me and
now. If Angel doesn't make it—" She swallowed hard. "If
Angel doesn't make it, we'll face losing her together.
Because we will be together, from now on."

"I love you, Jan."

She didn't pace anymore. She simply stayed close
beside him, finally even dropping into a restless nap
with her head on his shoulder. Once she jerked away to
look around and ask fearfully, "Hasn't the doctor come
yet?"

"Not yet, hon." Mark snuggled her head back into
the curve of his arm, and again she slept, secure that he
kept watch.

Finally he did waken her, his shake gentle, his lips
tender on her temple. "It's time, hon. He's coming."

She struggled to sit up straight, hands automatically
smoothing her wrinkled clothes and tousled hair even as
her heart jackhammered in her chest. Her gaze darted to
Mark for reassurance, and the love she saw there indeed
reassured her. Yet she also saw a reflection of the fear and
hope that buffeted her like some internal storm—the
truth that even all the love he had to give couldn't guarantee the news they hoped for.

Mark held out his hand to her, and she took it, her
eyes never leaving his. Then with hands locked in an
unbreakable bond, they stood and faced the doctor
together.

20

Blood smeared his gown and weariness slowed his steps, but triumph glowed in his eyes.

"Prayers answered," he said simply. "She made it. Her heart's pumping normally now."

Jan leaned forward. "When can we take her home?"

The doctor laughed at her impatience. "It'll probably be several weeks yet. She's going to lose weight, and she needs minute-by-minute intensive nursing care and monitoring. Infection is always a concern, and lung problems or other complications are possible."

Jan refused to let the warnings dampen her exhilaration. Their Angel had made it! "May we at least see her?"

"Probably this evening. Right now, you should both go home and get some rest." He gave them a friendly but professionally critical up-and-down appraisal. "You look as if you need it."

Mark gave Jan a sideways glance filled with love. "Actually, I think there's another little personal matter we'll take care of first."

Take care of it they did. First Mark called the coordinator of each of the prayer chains to give them the good news about Angel's surgery. Then they briefly returned to the house, where Jan found that her suspicions were correct. Stardust had been there and the bedroom stripped. She'd emptied her closet of the clothes and shoes Jan had bought her and taken all the electronic equipment, except the TV. It was abandoned in the middle of the room, perhaps because Stardust had decided it was too large to fit in the Firebird or because it was simply too heavy and awkward for her to carry down the stairs. Even the bedspread was gone. Only the boxes and bags of baby things remained. Stardust obviously had no use for them.

"You have to give her a gold star for determination," Mark said wryly as he looked around the bare room.

Jan agreed. "It couldn't have been easy doing all this with a cesarean only a few days behind her. If only she'd turned all that determination in a different direction..." Jan shook her head, still not able to comprehend Stardust's thinking or absent emotions.

Down the hall, they also discovered that she'd been in Jan's bedroom and helped herself to a half dozen pairs of earrings, a gold chain necklace, and several unopened packages of panty hose. She had not left a good-bye note.

As she stood there looking at the jumbled drawers and overturned jewelry box, Jan's feelings about Stardust were mixed, as they so often were. One part of her was relieved, even glad, that Stardust was gone. Angel was theirs! Yet another part of her sorrowed that abandoning her baby was only another in a long line of bad choices Stardust had made in her young life.

"Do you want to report the stolen items to the police?"

Jan shook her head. "I don't care about the jewelry." And the petty theft of the panty hose simply seemed a little pathetic. "It's just that..."

"I know." Mark wrapped a comforting arm around her shoulders. "You kept hoping the baby would make Stardust see things differently."

Jan nodded. "The Lord worked through the baby to bring me into his fold. But I guess it didn't work that way with Stardust."

"The Lord may not be through working on Stardust yet."

Yet even Jan's sadness about Stardust couldn't cloud the excitement of the afternoon as they took care of the "personal matter" Mark had mentioned to the doctor. Application for a marriage license, blood tests, and then a quick visit to the pastor in his office at the church to make arrangements for the simple, private ceremony they wanted. He'd already heard the good news about Angel, and he was delighted with their marriage plans. But making time for the ceremony proved difficult, especially when Mark said they wanted to do it the following week.

"That's not much notice." Pastor Doug frowned as he paged through his fully scheduled calendar. "Meetings...big wedding that's been scheduled for months now...men's prayer breakfast...dinner speaking engagement...budget committee meeting...three-day conference in Eugene. Plus all the regularly scheduled church activities, of course." He shook his head. "I'm just full up next week. But the following week—"

"No, we don't want to wait that long," Mark said firmly.

"You young people in love are all the same, always in a big rush," the pastor grumbled as he inspected his calendar again. Then he grinned, and Mark and Jan, who were obviously older than he was, grinned along.

"Well, we do have a baby on the way," Jan reminded him, and for a moment the pastor looked startled.

"Oh, you mean Angel," he said and grinned again.

"We're not fussy." Mark took Jan's hand. "Just a few minutes anytime will be fine."

Pastor Doug lifted an eyebrow, which perhaps should have been a warning that he took that statement quite literally. And perhaps as a challenge. "Anytime?" His grin broadened. "Well, in *that* case…"

Jan groaned when the alarm went off before 5:00 A.M. one morning the following week. Reminding herself that this was for a good reason, she dressed in her pale ivory suit and pinned to her lapel the orchid corsage Mark had delivered the night before. She did her makeup and brushed her hair to a sleek shine, but she still felt only minimally thrown together by the time she drove to the church. It did not help when she discovered along the way that she'd worn the wrong shoes and only one earring.

She removed the lone earring. Mark, she knew with love, wouldn't notice her shoes when he opened the car door for her at the church. She could have showed up barefoot and in blue jeans, she suspected, and he would still have looked at her as if she were gowned in satin and lace with a tiara. And she felt the same way about him, although she certainly didn't object that he looked handsome enough to wed a princess in his dark suit and dazzling white shirt. And she noted something else about him just as the parking lot lights buzzed noisily,

SEARCHING FOR STARDUST   289

turning off for the coming day.

"You cut yourself shaving." She reached up to stroke his fresh-shaven jaw with her fingertips. Mark had sometimes grumbled that only on the most important days of his life did he ever cut himself shaving. He'd gone to his first big job interview sporting a carefully trimmed scrap of tissue paper Jan had plastered to a cut under his chin, afraid if he pulled it off that he'd be spouting blood during the interview.

"Cut myself twice this morning, actually." He grimaced, then grinned. "Does that tell you something about the importance of today?"

She stretched up and tenderly kissed first one scraped spot and then the other. "Does that tell *you* something?"

He held her shoulders and looked into her eyes. "No change of mind?" he asked huskily. "No doubts?"

She smiled. "Not a one, Grandpa. Or Daddy. By the way, which one do you prefer?"

"We'll have to think about that, won't we, Grandma? Or is it Mommy?"

And a few minutes later, with the stained glass windows glowing crimson and azure and gold under a burst of dawn sunlight, they exchanged the vows that made them man and wife again. With just a deacon from the church and the pastor's wife as their witnesses, they also exchanged simple gold bands, new ones. "New rings to go with new vows," Mark had insisted almost fiercely when he took her to a jewelry store, and Jan hadn't argued, even though she still had her old one. Rings never to be removed; vows never to be broken. He kissed her with enough fervor to make her truly feel like a blushing bride, and her rainbow burst of happiness outshone even the crimson and azure of the stained glass.

Then the pastor hurried off to his conference in Eugene, and they walked outside into the rising sunshine of a new day. And Jan decided that in spite of the unorthodox hour for a wedding, it was the perfect time, after all. Dawn of a new day, dawn of a new life. All blessed by the Lord with the gift of their baby Angel.

They went out for a wedding breakfast, and then the day became even more perfect when they went to the hospital and for the first time the doctors allowed them to hold their Angel. Jan carefully snuggled the baby close, marveling at how, even after all these years, she didn't feel awkward holding a new baby, not even one as fragile and vulnerable as Angel. It felt good, familiar, and oh, so very *right*.

And to think that she had once felt doubtful about the Lord's love and caring, even for a brief time feeling betrayed by him. His love had been there all the time. His love for her, gently drawing her into his fold and bringing Mark back into her life. His love for a girl making desperate mistakes, giving her a chance, even though she had now thrown it away. His love for this baby, working circumstances in her life to give her a home and family.

Mark leaned over her, one fingertip tracing the miracle of a tiny ear. "Hey, baby Angel, this is your new mom and dad," he whispered.

Angel's eyes were still that slightly muddied blue of the newborn, but she seemed to be making a valiant effort to focus on Mark. Her tiny chest still showed the livid mark of the surgeon's knife, and her little body was not yet free of entangling wires and tubes, but she was warm and soft and her color a sweet baby pink now.

"Can you believe it?" Jan whispered. "Our baby."

She stroked a tiny, waving palm and was startled when the fingers closed around hers. Mark did the same with her other hand, and baby Angel clasped his finger just as tightly. They still didn't know about the Down syndrome, but there was nothing floppy about those lusty grips! Jan's head told her that the baby's almost fierce grip was just some reflex action, but her heart told her differently, that Angel was claiming them just as fiercely as they were claiming her.

Yet even in the joy of that moment, a shadow clouded Jan's thoughts. What if Stardust someday realized what a terrible mistake she had made and returned and wanted her baby back? How could she *not* someday realize that mistake?

No, she wouldn't even think about that possibility. Stardust had made her choice; she was gone, racing off in her bartered car to chase her tinsel dreams, out of their lives forever. Yet Jan couldn't help but feel sorrow for her, to wonder what would become of her.

Watch over her, will you, Lord? Work in her life as you did in mine, prodding and pushing, changing the circumstances of her life to guide her…nagging and pursuing, just as you did me…until she finds her way into your fold too. And I thank you so very much for all the blessings you've showered on Mark and Angel and me, bringing us together as a family. A little wistfully because she didn't even know if they really existed, she added, *And if there's another Stardust out there somewhere, the one Tim knew, would you watch over her and her baby, too?*

Their long weekend honeymoon was no more orthodox than the wedding, definitely not the luxury cruise with which Mark had once tried to entice her back into marriage. They spent it moving Jan's belongings to Mark's house, doing the last of the cleanup work, papering the nursery with pale pink paper bordered with angels around the top, and buying a new crib. But they also behaved like giddy newlyweds in the throes of young love, stopping often for kisses and hugs and laughter, and when the day's work was done, the passion they shared brought a fulfilling depth to their love that had long been missing.

Angel was just over five weeks old when she finally came home with them. Her tiny body still bore the mark of the incision, as it always would, and she'd have to go in for frequent checkups and take medication regularly for a while yet. But her heart and lungs showed no signs of weakness when she howled lustily to let Jan and Mark know she needed something.

By that time Jan had almost forgotten the earlier possibility of Down syndrome, so she was surprised when the doctor advised that they have the specific chromosome test to settle the question definitely.

Seeing her surprise, he said, "I think it's wise considering the earlier, inconclusive AFP and ultrasound tests and some small physical differences about her muscles and eyes at birth."

Jan almost said no. Months ago she'd decided that neither Down syndrome nor any other defect would change anything for her, and she still felt that way. But the doctor gently pointed out that, for Angel's sake, they *should* know now, so Jan agreed.

She didn't *not* worry during the two weeks it took to get the results of the test back. For Angel's sake, she profoundly hoped the test would show she was normal. Yet she didn't lie awake agonizing about the possibility it might be otherwise. With love and the Lord, they'd manage, no matter what the test showed.

But when the results came back showing a normal chromosome count, Jan had to admit to a glorious rush of relief. Now she truly felt as if the last hurdle had been surmounted. They were home free! *Thank you, Lord!*

It was a feeling that continued to bloom as the weeks went by. They settled comfortably into their new life together in Mark's house, at least as comfortable as life could be with a live-wire new baby in the nursery.

The problems and anxieties of new motherhood all came back to Jan now. Waking up to stumble—or let Mark stumble—groggily to the nursery for a night feeding. She'd forgotten how often babies ate! Mountains of diapers, a rash, a brief bout with colic. Anxious trips to the surgeon to be certain everything was progressing as expected. Regular visits to the pediatrician they were now seeing. Feeling drained and tired and groggy, wondering how it could take so much energy for two full-sized human beings to care for one tiny, baby-sized person.

But, oh, the joys! Baby snuggled against her shoulder while they waited for that little burp, a burp that now seemed more momentous than any client contact she'd struggled to capture in the past. The fun of bath time. "I can't tell which of you enjoys it more," Mark said once while he watched the splashy process and laughed as he dodged the spraying drops. The happiness of watching Mark holding the baby, tenderly whispering baby talk, Angel's tiny fist wrapped around his finger, her big eyes riveted on his. Seeing the amazement in Angel's eyes as she became aware of the world around her, like some small alien visitor newly arrived on a strange planet. And often, just the small miracle of sitting and rocking, holding this wonderful gift from God in her arms as the baby gently drifted off to sleep.

Yet it wasn't just the baby who brought her joy. Mark truly was a new man in Christ. He hadn't lost all sense of ambition or dedication to his work—nor his sense of fun!—but his priorities were different now, as were hers. They made time for family worship and family playtime, and sometimes Jan found herself happily humming that old song about love being better the second time around. And knowing that for her it was true…especially when the love was with the very same man.

On a Sunday not long after Christmas, Jan was baptized and joined Mark's church. She had already partaken of Communion, but the first time after her baptism was special, a time that made her heart overflow with joy and gratitude. Husband, baby, salvation!

Her real estate license remained hanging in the office, so she could go back to work anytime she wanted, and perhaps sometime she would. But for now her days were too full of husband and baby. That other life seemed as if it had belonged to someone she used to know, someone who was much too wrapped up in career and social advancement, much too involved with clothes and power lunches and making top salesperson of the year status. Neither did she miss the big, elegant house; it was more like a place she had visited temporarily than a home.

There was less money, of course. The huge medical bills swallowed up most of what Jan received for the house, and Mark's income was far below what he'd made as a high-powered attorney. But Jan didn't mind economizing; actually, she found not worrying about acquiring bigger and better and more expensive *things* a pleasant liberation. Also a nice liberation was no longer having to spend long hours in the hairdresser's chair being doused with smelly chemicals because she'd let her hair go back to its natural soft brown. With, as Mark sometimes teased lovingly when he lifted the hair behind her ear to give her a kiss on the neck, a few silvery streaks of granny gray.

Once they had a scare about Angel's heart and had to rush her to the emergency room, but a short course of medication took care of the problem. She grew and developed normally into a sweetly vivacious, curious little mischief maker, adept at early crawling and then toddling, not pleased with the confines of a playpen. Her dark hair was almost the color of Mark's, and her eyes, her eyes were lupine blue.

Sometimes those eyes made Jan think back to Tim's sad, confused journal and made her wonder if somewhere out there another Stardust existed, the Stardust they hadn't found, and another baby, their grandchild by blood. The thought troubled her. Did that grandchild need them? Was he or she safe and loved and cared for? They talked sometimes about initiating a new search, perhaps hiring a detective. Once they ran an ad in several southern Oregon newspapers, but there was no response.

As Angel's first birthday approached, Jan's thoughts more and more often turned to the Stardust who had brought this baby, their Angel, to them. Wasn't this when a mother's thoughts, even a mother such as Stardust, would surely turn to the child she had borne?

Jan knew she'd made the offer, when Angel was born, to let Stardust keep her baby. But now...if Stardust came back and took Angel away, Jan knew it would be like ripping out half her heart.

There was no danger of that happening, she always assured herself when such thoughts made her rush to the adoption papers and scrutinize each line for reassurance that everything was in order. The adoption was final. All papers properly filed, a glowing report from the children's services division after their investigation, a court hearing that wasn't nearly as frightening and intimidating as Jan had feared, the judge's signature, and finally the issuance of a new birth certificate showing Jan and Mark as parents. The adoption was gold star, solid as a government bond.

Yet Jan couldn't banish her worries. Adoptions had been challenged and broken before. Only a few weeks ago, a judge in a nationally publicized case had returned a baby to its natural father. But that situation wouldn't apply to Angel, of course. Angel's real father was dead, and the lawyer had conscientiously obtained a copy of the death certificate to present with the petition for adoption.

And there was no solid reason to think Stardust had any interest in reclaiming Angel. Never while she was pregnant had she shown any motherly inclinations; as soon as she learned the baby might not be magazine-ad perfect, she wanted to be rid of her. With all possible haste she signed the papers, grabbed her car and other possessions, and disappeared.

Yet all the arguments Jan gave herself never quite convinced her that Stardust wouldn't someday return and demand her child. Part of it came from deep inside, a raw gut feeling that at some point a mother *had* to regret giving up her baby, had to question her decision and wonder about her child. She would have! And Stardust *had* briefly shown a tentative interest, asking questions from her hospital bed, her expression vaguely pensive. Also alive in Jan's mind was the memory of those moments in the hospital when she'd earnestly asked Stardust to think things through, and there had been the barest of hesitations—oh, but a definite hesitation—before Stardust had angrily responded that she had thought everything through. And there was something else, something she hadn't discovered until they moved her things to Mark's house: that first ultrasound taken while Angel was still within Stardust's womb was missing. It had been in Jan's dresser drawer, along with the jewelry box from which Stardust had stolen the earrings and gold chain, and now it was gone. The only thing that could have happened to it was that Stardust had taken it. Why?

There was also the fact that Angel was not the "weird, retarded kid" Stardust had so cruelly rejected while she was still helpless in the womb. No Down syndrome, even the slight difference in her eyes had faded as she grew. Her heart problem was corrected. Now Angel *was* magazine-ad perfect, a beautiful little dark-haired child of light, and if Stardust ever came back and saw that…

Jan's thoughts also warily circled a potential problem between herself and the Lord. If Stardust came back and demanded her child, what would the Lord expect…and how would Jan respond? If Stardust had changed, grown more maternal and responsible, would he expect Jan and Mark to give up the child they loved, the child that was so much a part of them now? Were they, in the Lord's scheme of things, not the receivers of this gift of life but only temporary caregivers, entrusted only to keep Angel safe until her birth mother found her way?

Jan's new faith was strong and deep, but even so, she shivered. *Please, Lord, no, not that…*

21

JAN'S APPREHENSION GREW AS ANGEL'S FIRST BIRTHDAY DREW ever closer, and the worry about Stardust coming to take Angel away kept repeating itself.

Jan and Mark threw a big party for Angel on the day her birthday arrived. They invited all the neighborhood babies and children and parents too. Jan suspected that deep down she was probably thinking of safety in numbers. She decorated with balloons and streamers and made a cake with a single oversized candle. Mark barbecued hamburgers for everyone and supervised rowdy games in the backyard for the bigger children. Yet all the time, even as she was gaily leading an off-key version of the happy birthday song, acidlike apprehension lurked in Jan's stomach and jangled her nerves. She kept expecting a knock on the door or an ominous telephone call from a lawyer. Or perhaps Stardust would boldly walk into the yard with some official with power to take their baby away.

Yet nothing happened. The children went home, not surprisingly Angel got an upset stomach from too much cake and excitement, and Mark whispered as he snuggled Jan in his arms before they fell into a tired sleep, "See? Everything's fine. Nothing happened."

They hadn't talked ahead of time about ominous possibilities, but Jan knew his "nothing happened" did not refer to possible minor mishaps such as spilled juice on the carpet or scraped knees. "You were worried too."

She'd seen him, inconspicuously making rounds,

checking out every new arrival, keeping an eye on unfamiliar cars, jumping to answer the ringing phone.

"That's what dads do."

"If it happened," Jan asked reluctantly, "how would it start? A direct demand from Stardust, or a phone call from a lawyer? Or maybe a summons or official notice from a court or judge that a lawsuit had been filed?"

He hesitated before answering, as if he were perhaps trying to peer into Stardust's unpredictable thinking, then said almost roughly, "I'm not sure how it might start, but if it ever does, we'll fight it."

"I love you, Mark Hilliard," Jan said fiercely, loving him as a caring, dedicated father who'd fight for their child, but loving him even more as her husband, her mate for life that the Lord had brought back to her. And yet...

"But what if fighting it isn't what God wants us to do?" she asked in a small voice. "What if he wants us to give her up?"

Mark's arms tightened around her, his strength and love a powerful reassurance. But he had no answer for her question.

By Angel's second birthday, Mark knew that Jan was more relaxed. They even hired a baby-sitter and went out to celebrate their second wedding anniversary the week after the birthday party. One reason she was less apprehensive, he suspected, was because they were no longer living in Portland, and her subconscious perhaps viewed the distance as a safety barrier. Stardust could undoubtedly still find them in their Salem home, some fifty miles from Portland, but it would take more investigation and effort. She couldn't walk in on them on the whim of the moment.

A new opportunity had opened for Mark, and after prayerful consideration, he took it. He left his teaching job at Linhurst and went back to his first love, the legal profession.

However, he wasn't defending questionable clients often seeking to circumvent justice. Now his work was with a Christian legal association, and he handled cases such as helping a rescue mission cope with zoning laws restricting its right to expand services, defending an individual's right to give Christian witness on public property, straightening out a Christian school's problems with state accreditation. Sometimes he worked with or battled state legislators on bills concerning abortion or other legal issues of importance to Christians. He loved the work. It utilized his legal experience and expertise to the fullest, but he also had the satisfaction of knowing he was using his abilities to serve the Lord.

The headquarters of the organization was in the state capital, Salem, so they sold the Portland house and bought a two-story place in a development of newer homes on the edge of town. It was a pleasant, family-oriented area, people busy putting in new lawns and planting trees, barbecuing in backyards, having babies. They knew their neighbors. He borrowed and loaned tools, and Jan exchanged recipes and outgrown children's clothes with friends, and together once a week they led an evening Bible study. There was a small park and playground a few blocks from their house and a mini shopping center and gas station a half mile the other direction. They found a friendly community church, where he taught a junior high Sunday school class and Jan helped put out the monthly church newsletter.

She also had a high, sturdy chain-link fence installed around their big backyard and started a small day care business. It gave Angel playmates and enabled Jan to earn extra money while still being with Angel full time. They agreed Jan would probably return to real estate work after Angel was in school, but not yet; this time with Angel was too precious, she said, and he agreed. Unspoken was their sad memory that this vulnerable early age was not a time either of them had lovingly devoted to being with Tim, that they'd let ambition and material wants rob them of those irreplaceable years.

It was also the time of the Terrible Twos. Mark doubted Angel could ever be truly terrible, but by the time she was almost three, she liked to assert her independence and test her skills. She couldn't quite dress herself alone—she didn't consider the difference between front and back of an item of clothing of major importance, and shoestrings were a continuing frustration—but she was adamant about trying before she'd accept help. She delighted in building an impressive tower of blocks, delighted equally in scattering the tower with the gleeful swat of a demolition expert. She had decisive preferences in color, and red was her hands-down favorite, a fact that got her into trouble when she appropriated a tube of Jan's lipstick for some freestyle room decoration. She hadn't yet shown any exceptional musical talent but, with prompting, could get through an enthusiastic version of her best-loved song "Jesus Loves Me." Her favorite word was a wide-eyed and sometimes exasperating, "Why?" but she could also turn shy and wordless at unexpected moments.

Sometimes she reminded Mark of Tim when he was that age, so inquisitive and busy. He still lived with pain and sorrow and regret about Tim's wasted life, about his own shortcomings as a father to his son. Sometimes he even felt guilty that life was so good for them now, and Angel such a joy. It seemed more than they deserved. Sometimes, tumbling with her on the carpet or giving her a bouncy horsy ride on his back, he thought how things might have been different if they'd gone ahead with the family they once planned instead of waiting until the time was "right"...and then discovering they waited too long. And then he'd find himself tangled in a different web of thought, that if it were not for Tim's death, Angel would not even be in their lives.

He wondered, as he knew Jan also did, if their blood grandchild did exist out there somewhere, child of that ethereal, never-quite-tangible Stardust with the lupine-blue eyes of Tim's troubled journal. Did she or the child really exist? Or were they some yearning, desperate spark of Tim's imagination? Should they make another search for her, or scrape up funds to hire a detective?

He also knew that occasional uneasy thoughts about their more familiar Stardust still distressed Jan, worries that intensified about the time of Angel's birthday each year. He had worries about Stardust, too, but his and Jan's worries ran on different tracks. Jan assumed if Stardust returned that she'd make a legal assault on their right to Angel. Only a few days ago, with Angel's third birthday now approaching, he'd caught Jan studying the adoption papers usually kept tucked away in a bureau drawer, as if she were again fearful there were legal loopholes Stardust could sneak through to reclaim Angel.

His own worries, however, were that Stardust might take a much more direct route than the legal one. He had an important four-day business trip to San Francisco scheduled ten days before Angel's third birthday, but after that he wasn't going anywhere without them for a while. He, too, suspected that if Stardust ever did anything, it would be near the time of Angel's birthday, and he wasn't going to leave Angel and Jan unprotected around that significant date.

In fact, as he was driving to the airport, his apprehension inexplicably escalated, and he suddenly decided that all of them getting away from home might be preferable to a birthday party this year. He had some vacation time coming.... Yes, they could fly down and visit Rosa Martinez, the injured woman in Texas who had led him to the Lord! She was eager to meet Jan and Angel and had been inviting them to come ever since he and Jan had remarried. Jan wanted to meet Rosa, too, but so far they'd been reluctant to venture so far away from their familiar hospital and doctors with Angel. They'd check with the doctor first, of course, but now such a trip would surely be okay. Except for the scar on her chest, Angel bore little evidence that she'd started life with a cross-wired heart. Yes, they'd make it both a third birthday and a romantic third anniversary celebration. He'd discuss plans with Jan as soon as he returned from San Francisco.

Jan kicked off her shoes, plopped down on the sofa, and put her feet up for a few minutes rest while the children were napping. They wouldn't nap long, and because she had only Angel plus one little girl in day care today, she'd promised them an outing to the park. The house was quiet now, the only noises: a rototiller chattering in the Dickinson's yard down the street and the background hum of the air conditioner. Yet instead of enjoying the quiet minutes while her rambunctious twosome was asleep, she felt a little lonely. Mark had left for San Francisco only this morning, but already she missed him. Which was ridiculous, of course. Even if he were at the office here in town, he wouldn't be home until five-thirty or six o'clock tonight. Yet he'd call sometime during the day if he were at the office…

Then she had to laugh at herself. You'd think they were still love-struck newlyweds! Which was half true. They might not be newlyweds now, but they were still love struck. The experience of five years of separation made them more aware and appreciative of what they had now, that it wasn't something to be taken for granted. She'd tucked a chocolate heart and a silly little love poem in Mark's suitcase just before he left. And he'd call tonight, naturally.

She stretched out on the sofa and dozed for a few minutes, but woke instantly when the murmur of little voices drifted down the hallway from the nap room. Then a louder voice.

"Mommy? Mommy, I 'wake!"

Jan slipped on her shoes and went to the room

where the girls napped on lightweight floor mattresses arranged at right angles, their heads together. Angel had her own bedroom upstairs, next to the master bedroom, but during the day she shared the same nap room and toys as the day-care children.

Jan smiled at the two bright-eyed faces, each with tousled dark hair. They were almost the same age and looked enough alike to be sisters. "And now you're all ready to go to the park, I suppose?"

"Yes!" they chorused.

While the little girls dressed, Jan rounded up her floppy-brimmed straw hat and a plastic bottle of sunscreen. She corrected Angel's minor mistake of a backward T-shirt, then slathered both the girls and herself with the lotion. The afternoon was hot, one of those days when a crisp morning said fall was coming, but summer still had a strong grip on the afternoon. After help with shoes and prerequisite trips to the bathroom, she gave firm instructions at the front door.

"Okay now, you both hold on tight to my hands and don't let go until we get to the park, understand? No matter what, you don't let go."

Angel asked her inevitable question, the same question she'd asked when similar instructions were previously given. "Why?"

"Because that's the way we go to the park." Jan had found simple explanations worked better than complicated ones about the dangers of getting hit by cars.

Outside, she noted an unfamiliar dark blue compact car parked in front of the Henderson's house across the street. Perhaps Connie Henderson's mother-in-law had arrived for a visit, Jan thought. A visit she knew Connie was not eagerly anticipating. Also a Christian, Connie had once muttered, "I'm going to have a real hard time ever following Ella back to Arizona like Ruth followed Naomi to Judah."

They started out, girls holding on tight, although they threw in some creative wiggles and occasionally stretched Jan's arms to the limit. The street was quiet, especially during midafternoon, little traveled except by local residents. Neighbor Dorrie Rigedon drove by and tooted, and Jan waggled her head in greeting, no hand free to wave.

She heard another car behind her slow, as if perhaps someone was going to stop and ask directions. But when she looked around, the blue car abruptly zoomed away. Odd. Was it the car that had been parked in front of the Henderson's? Possibly. Jan wasn't sure.

Just before they reached the park, the same blue car, at least Jan was almost certain it was the same car, returned. This time it was headed toward her, and she noted the California license plate. Bright sunlight turned the windshield into an impenetrable glitter, hiding the driver.

California plates were a common enough sight in Oregon, both as tourists and new arrivals. Yet Jan felt a small squiggle of uneasiness when the car showed up again at the park. The girls were in swings, Jan giving them alternating easy pushes. The car pulled into the parking area about a half block away. The lone person in the car was a woman, but that was all Jan could tell.

Stardust came instantly to her mind. Stardust spying on them, Stardust trying to gather ammunition with which to challenge the adoption! Yet just as quickly when the woman started eating a sandwich and sipping a drink from a fast-foods carton, Jan realized she was probably being paranoid. The car certainly was not Stardust's flashy Firebird. Probably the woman had just chosen the park as a peaceful haven for lunch. But it wouldn't hurt to stroll a little closer just to take a better look.

Then she hesitated. She didn't want to leave the girls alone on the swings, yet neither did she want to take them closer to the car. While she was trying to decide, the car suddenly wheeled in a backward arc and squealed away. Jan got a brief glimpse of dark hair and big sunglasses as it swept past her.

She nervously let the girls play another fifteen minutes, then got a firm grip on their hands and herded them home. She didn't see the car again on the walk back to the house, and no car returned to park at the curb in front of the Henderson's. After dinner, on nervous impulse, she phoned Connie about a church potluck and casually inserted a question about her mother-in-law. Connie went into a guiltily gleeful explanation of how the visit had been canceled.

When Mark called a few minutes later, Jan debated telling him about the woman and the car, but in the end she let it go. It was probably nothing, just her nervous imagination because of the proximity to Angel's birthday, and there was no point in worrying Mark unnecessarily. He'd had a bad enough day already, with a delayed flight, a fouled-up car rental reservation and pages missing from a transcript he needed.

"But the chocolate heart and poem made everything better," Mark added on a softer, better-humored note.

"Would you like to talk to your daughter? She's right here beside me, bouncing up and down like a pogo stick." Jan heard his first words come over the line as Angel was getting the phone aligned with her ear. "Hi, Angel-puss. You taking good care of Mommy?"

Angel told her father all about going to the park and swinging, watching a Veggie Tales video, and helping Jan cook spaghetti for supper—her limited vocabulary taking some inventive turns to get her ideas across. She didn't mention the car, of course. It wasn't something a not-quite-three-year-old would notice.

Probably not something a nonparanoid mother would notice either, Jan wryly admitted to herself as she took the phone back from a none-too-willing Angel a few minutes later.

"I miss you. Everything going okay?" Mark asked.

"I miss you, too. In fact, I'm counting the hours. You'll be back about nine o'clock Friday night, right?" She glanced at the clock on the dining room wall and said in her most theatrically breathless tones, "Let's see, that's seventy-two hours and thirty-two minutes. Now it's seventy-two hours and thirty-*one* minutes—"

Mark laughed at her exaggerated countdown. "If I didn't know you loved me, I'd suspect you were putting me on with this big show of missing me."

"You sound pretty smug and sure of yourself. Maybe I am putting you on and have some wild adventure planned for tonight."

"I'm sure you do. Studying those chapters in Romans that we're working on in Bible study, reading a few pages in that Rivers novel I bought you, maybe seeing how that new polish you bought looks on your toenails—"

"You know me too well," Jan grumbled, because that was exactly how she planned to spend the evening. "I'm going to have to think up some surprises or you'll get bored."

"Never," he said, the word almost a growl.

"I love you," Jan said softly, and the words echoed right back to her in Mark's husky tones.

The next day she had her full quota of five kids, which kept her hopping. When she went out to pick up the mail from the box beside the front door, she thought she saw that same blue car turning at the end of the block. But she wasn't much into cars now, not like the old days when she saw them as vital status symbols, so she knew she could be mistaken.

She fixed lunch for the kids, cut her finger quartering apples, and was annoyed with herself for being so jittery. Then, just after she got everyone put down for naps after lunch, Connie called. Jan carried the cordless phone to the kitchen, where her voice wouldn't disturb the children.

"Hey, I forgot to mention it last night," Connie said, "but did a rather odd woman selling children's books come to your place?"

"No. But if I'm out back with the kids, I might not hear the doorbell. Actually, except for neighborhood kids selling candy or something, I didn't know there were still such people as door-to-door salespeople around these days."

"Well, that's partly what struck me as odd. She came here a couple days ago, and she looked hot and tired and walked with a bit of a limp, so I felt sorry for her and let her in. And she was about the least pushy salesperson I've ever met, almost acted as if she were in a big rush to get past showing me the books, and really couldn't care less if I bought any or not. Actually, you know what, now that I think about it? Those books looked exactly like the ninety-nine cent ones on the rack down at the drugstore. But that wouldn't make sense, would it? Anyway, she started asking about families with little kids in the neighborhood, as prospective customers she said, and then she zeroed in on you."

Panic crept up Jan's legs and into her body, moving like a cold tide about to engulf her. But she managed to say casually, "Me? What kind of questions?"

"Well, not just about you, about the whole family, actually. Did you work outside the home, and did the man of the house come home every night, and what did he do, and were you sociable or keep-to-yourselves people, and did your little girl get sick much, and a whole bunch of other stuff. Finally it occurred to me that this was just a little too nosy, a little *weird*, actually, and had nothing to do with selling books. Then I started wondering if she was up to no good, maybe casing the joint or something."

"What all did you tell her?" Jan tried to sound merely curious, as anyone would in such an odd situation. Jan and Mark had never made any secret of the fact that Angel was adopted, but neither had they told anyone the details.

"I told her more than I wish I had," Connie admitted. "Ed keeps telling me I'm way too trusting of people. Anyway, finally I did get suspicious and told her I had things to do and didn't have time to talk to her anymore, and she left."

"How old was she?"

"Oh, twenty-something, I think."

Right age. "What did she look like?"

"Long, brown hair. Medium height. Pretty. Although she kept her big sunglasses on all the time, even in the house, so it was hard to tell too much about her."

"But she did limp?"

"Just kind of a little hesitation when she took a step."

Stardust? Playing a role as a book saleslady in order to sneak around and gather information about them? Oh yes, that was possible. So was the brown hair, if she'd stopped bleaching it. But the limp? That didn't fit. Although it could be just another role, Jan thought nervously; playing for sympathy was exactly the kind of thing Stardust might craftily decide to do.

Yet the whole description, she realized, could also apply to someone who wasn't Stardust at all, some young woman with a real limp who was earnestly trying to work up some overly intimate approach to selling books.

"Did you notice what kind of car she was driving?" Jan asked.

"Something little. Blue. Not too new, I think. It was parked out in front again yesterday, and I thought she was probably out canvassing the neighborhood for customers."

Jan hung up the phone feeling unsettled and jittery. Should she call the police? And tell them what? That a young woman was in the neighborhood selling books and asking nosy questions? Nothing the woman had done was strong or intrusive enough to make a case for a stalking complaint. It wasn't even enough to worry Mark with. If Stardust was sneaking around trying to gather incriminating evidence against them as unfit adoptive parents, she surely wasn't going to find anything. Connie probably made them sound like living saints.

Of course, there was always that old baby-buying thing some judge might hold against them…

Jan shook her head impatiently. *Lord, why can't I just be happy? Why can't I just enjoy this wonderful life you've given me…?*

And yet, even as she asked the question, the dread deep within her only gained strength. What would she do if she lost Angel?

She could only pray she'd never have to find out.

22

THE NEXT DAY JAN WAS DOWN TO ONLY TWO DAY-CARE KIDS, little Julie again, plus almost-four-year-old Chrissy. The afternoon was hot, and the girls played together congenially with only minor skirmishes to monitor, so after naps Jan decided to get out the little wading pool for them to splash in.

From the patio, her gaze roved the backyard in a practiced inspection. Everything was peaceful. Julie and Chrissy were industriously digging holes in the sandbox, and Angel was trying to walk the narrow wooden edge of the sandbox, a feat that was still beyond her not-quite-three coordination and sense of balance. Although she never cried when she tumbled off. She just got up and tried again.

"I'm going inside for a minute," Jan called to the girls. "I'll be right back."

The wading pool wasn't in the laundry room where she thought she'd left it, and it took her several minutes to find it, stuffed behind the lawn mower in the garage. Then she discovered a rip in the vinyl and had to search for patch material.

"Okay, kids," she called when she finally opened the door from the garage to the backyard, dragging the floppy pool behind her. "Who wants to help patch—"

She stopped short. She certainly hadn't forgotten the blue car, but it had drifted to the background of her thoughts. But there it was, parked right at the curb next to the chain-link fence around the backyard! And the brown-haired woman in sunglasses was down on one knee, hands clutching the fence, the three girls clustered around her.

Chrissy pointed across the yard to the gate in the high fence across the back property line, as if perhaps the woman had asked some question concerning it. The woman stood up, sunlight flashing off her big sunglasses. It took Jan a shocked moment to realize that she was heading for the gate. Outrage finally broke through Jan's moment of paralysis.

"Hey! What do you think you're doing? Get away from my girls!"

The woman whirled, and she and Jan stared at each other across the yard, over the heads of the three little girls, through the metal barrier of the chain-link fence. The woman lifted something to her face—a camera!— and aimed it at the girls, and Jan dashed wildly across the grass. Then, slowed only fractionally by a slight limp, the young woman spurted around the blue car and jumped into the driver's seat. The car squealed away from the curb.

Jan stared after it, arms protectively draped around the girls. She looked down only after the car disappeared around the corner. "Are you okay? What did she want?"

"Me." Angel looked pleased, as if she'd just won some special honor.

They'd had little talks with her about being careful about strangers, and for a moment Jan's panic almost made her angry that Angel hadn't heeded the warnings. Yet neighbors walked by all the time, sometimes pausing to chat through the fence with whoever happened to be in the yard that day, so why would Angel and the other girls think this woman was any different? And the fence was there, of course, so there was no real danger. Except that this woman had targeted the lone weak point—the gate. Jan ran over and snapped the seldom-used lock. She'd never leave the gate unlocked again.

She returned to the girls. "What do you mean she wanted you?" She tried to keep her voice cheery and conversational, not pass on the panic that coursed through her with every beat of her heart.

"She said, 'which one of you is Angel?'" Chrissy, the oldest of the three, reported importantly.

"I say, me!" Angel chimed in gleefully, pointing to herself.

"What did she want?" Jan repeated.

Angel lifted her little shoulders in an exaggerated shrug. "I don't know." She spotted the pool Jan had dropped in her rush across the yard. "Swim?" She already was losing interest in the woman.

"Did she ask how to get in the yard?"

Angel nodded, her big blue eyes suddenly troubled, as if she now realized Jan was upset about something. "She take my picture."

Angel had had her picture taken enough times by doting Daddy to know what that was all about. She was always ready to ham it up for the camera.

"She took all our pictures," Chrissy corrected, as if she didn't want Angel hogging all the attention.

"What else did she say? Anything? Did she tell you what her name was? Did she give you anything, candy or anything? Did she ask you to go somewhere with her?" Jan swallowed convulsively. She tried to remember ploys that she'd heard used by child abductors. "Maybe to help her find a lost doggie or kitty?"

More big-eyed head shakes from all three girls.

"Okay, we're going inside now." Jan held out her arms, lightly herding the girls toward the house.

Angel dragged her tiny feet in protest against Jan's push and asked her usual question. "Why?"

"Because I said so!" Jan instantly regretted the sharp tone; a tone so seldom used that Angel looked startled by it. Purposely she softened her voice and tousled Angel's hair. "Maybe I'll patch the pool and you can all swim in it later. We'll see."

Inside, she let the girls each choose a toy from the treasure chest, then poured herself a glass of iced tea and sat at the breakfast bar trying to lift the shaking glass to her mouth without sloshing.

She couldn't positively identify the woman as Stardust. Physically, the brown hair, slight limp, and concealing sunglasses all combined to give a much different appearance than the Stardust she had known. Yet she had no doubt that it was Stardust—and that the girl had been snapping a photo of her beautiful daughter.

And she had no doubt about something else.

Always her worries had centered around the possibility that Stardust, if she someday returned, would try to wrest Angel away from them by legal means. She'd show up with a high-powered attorney and righteous ammunition about how she, a defenseless and vulnerable young woman, had been coerced and deceived and cheated out of her child by this rich, clever, baby-buying older couple. She'd plead with a judge to right a terrible wrong.

Now she believed Stardust may have shockingly

different plans, plans much more dangerously direct and immediate than drawn-out legal battles. In sudden panic Jan dashed down the hall to check on the girls, wild visions of an open window and a vanished child like a black hole blown in her heart. But all three girls were right where she'd left them, all looking up from their toys in mild surprise as she charged into the room like some skidding cartoon character. Jan stifled an impulse to snatch Angel into her arms and hold her so tight that there was no room for danger to slither between them.

Mark, I need you! Stardust had been planning to invade through the backyard gate and entice Angel into coming with her. Or simply snatch her and run. What other weak point in the house or yard would she discover?

Yet for the children she managed to smile and improvise another reason for her hasty appearance. "Are you girls ready for some afternoon snacks?"

"Tea party?" Angel bargained.

So they sat around the children's-size folding table and had a "tea party," with juice and slices of apple and orange and miniature oatmeal-raisin cookies. Jan conscientiously tried to use the few minutes to instill good manners and courtesy in the girls and keep the afternoon normal, even as she felt as if the small planet of her universe were plummeting out of control.

She had to talk to Mark…

Yet even after the tea party was over and she had a chance to call his hotel, she wasn't surprised when he wasn't in his room. It was only three-thirty, and he had meetings scheduled all day. All she could do was leave a message for him to call as soon as he came in.

She used up nervous energy scrubbing the bathroom. She played a game with the girls, then read to them. She picked up the quiet phone half a dozen times to make certain it was working, that Mark could get through. And at no more than five-minute intervals she dashed from window to window checking for anything out of the ordinary, such as a blue car on the street or an intruder in the backyard. Once she even imagined a shadowy face peering in the window, only to discover it was merely a late-blooming rose innocently nodding over the sill.

Get a grip!

But why didn't Mark *call?*

Julie's mother came, then Chrissy's father. Jan and Angel ate dinner, homemade veggie pizzas. At seven-thirty she read Angel a story and put her to bed. She checked all the doors and windows in the house, both upstairs and down, to be sure everything was locked. When the phone finally rang, she was in the seldom-used guest bedroom upstairs, checking the latch on the window a second time, and had to race to the master bedroom to reach the phone.

"Mark?" she said the instant she picked up.

"I'm sorry I'm so late calling. The last meeting of the day ran way over, and I just got here—" He broke off, seemingly sensitive to her vibrations of panic. "Jan, what's wrong?"

"Mark, she's here!"

He didn't ask who; he knew from the dread in her voice. "Did she come to the house? Have you talked to her?"

"No." Wildly she explained what had happened.

"Mark, she asked the girls how to get inside the yard! And Chrissy pointed out the gate for her. She could have walked right in, grabbed Angel, and run off with her! If I hadn't come out just then and scared her off—"

"Okay, I'm coming home."

It was what Jan desperately wanted, yet hearing him say the words brought her up short. This was an important meeting concerning a bill similar to Oregon's assisted-suicide law that certain groups were trying to push through in California. She tried to take a mental step backward, calm herself, and think rationally. "Mark, you can't do that. You can't leave the meeting…"

He didn't bother to argue with her. "I'm not sure how soon I can get a flight out, but I'll call you again the minute I know."

Hastily she backtracked. "Wait, Mark—Maybe I'm just imagining things. Maybe it isn't even Stardust, just some woman who really is trying to sell books. She looks different than I remember Stardust. And you know how jumpy I get around Angel's birthday—"

"I don't think you're imagining things. If you think it's Stardust, I'm sure it is."

Suddenly, Jan understood. "You've always been afraid of this, haven't you? I worried about legal problems, but you worried she might just walk in and grab Angel."

"I've been thinking we'd go down and visit Rosa in Texas when I got home from this trip so we wouldn't be home on Angel's birthday." The plan gave silent admission to her insight. She heard a faint *thud-thud-thud*— Mark was hitting his thigh. She closed her eyes, willing herself to stay calm as Mark went on. "I just never figured she'd show up this far ahead of Angel's birthday."

The faint noise of a car—a door slamming?—made Jan dash to the side window and peer out, but the street and sidewalk next to the backyard fence were empty. She swallowed and repositioned the phone at her ear. "I thought I heard something, but I must have imagined it."

He didn't try to reassure her out of her jumpiness. "Everything is locked up tight?"

Jan tried to make a shaky joke. "As tight as that time Angel managed to lock herself in the bathroom."

"Okay, keep it that way until I get home. Don't hesitate to call 911 if you need to, if you feel directly threatened. And remember how much I love both of you, and I'm going to get there as fast as I can. And don't panic. Stardust isn't necessarily planning a snatching. This may be a forerunner to a legal action. Or she may simply be curious."

"What if she approaches me? What if she wants to…make contact with Angel?"

He hesitated, and she knew he was thinking, as she was, what did the Lord want them to do? Protect Angel from an unknown threat, share her with this other mother,…*give her up?* Finally he said, "Tell her it's something you and I will have to consider together, that you can't do anything until I get home."

"Okay." Jan heard the shakiness in her voice, but inside she felt strengthened by Mark's calm strength. "I love you." In spite of the day's heat that had lingered into evening, she hugged her arms around herself as she tip-toed into Angel's room to check on her again. She felt an almost blinding tide of love as she looked down on the soft wisps of dark hair, the tiny hand she had first seen floating up from the mysterious depths of that window on the womb, the closed eyelashes lying in twin curves against delicate cheeks, the impudent bump of nose...

Stardust's nose.

She swallowed convulsively.

Stardust's baby.

What do you want, Lord? I want to do your will, but... She knelt beside the bed, her plea crashing like a brick into a window against another plea in her heart. *Don't make us give her up, Lord. Please! We've tried so hard to be better parents than the first time around. We love her so much. We want to raise her to know and love you as we do.*

Yet the question came back to her as it had at various times over the past three years, sometimes a barely visible cloud on a distant horizon, sometimes a monster leaping out from a closet in her mind. *Lord, did you choose us not to guide our Angel to adulthood but only as temporary caretakers, guardians to keep her safe until her birth mother realized her mistake? Has the time now come when you want us to give her up?*

Another sound made her tiptoe to the window and lift the curtain. This time, looking toward the front yard, she saw the source of the sound. Her heart clenched as she took in what she saw.

The blue car. Stardust standing beside the open door.

The girl had removed the sunglasses, and now, even in the dim glow of the streetlight, there was no mistaking her identity. She wore dark shorts and a light-colored blouse—inconspicuous, blend-into-the-crowd clothing. She closed the car door and, with the slight hesitation of that limp, started up the walkway to the front of the house.

Jan let the curtain drop.

I won't answer the door! Stardust can just ring until her arm is numb and the bell wears out, and I still won't answer it! Angel is ours now, you abandoned her!

The door was locked, a metal door, no way could Stardust force her way through it. *And if she doesn't go away, I'll call the police, tell them there's an intruder trying to get inside! I'll press charges—*

But with a sinking heart she knew she could do none of those things. Slowly she crossed the hallway with numb legs and went down the stairs. The living room drapes were drawn. She couldn't see out to the street, to the blue car, to the woman. But she could feel their presence.

She stood behind the closed front door, fists clenched, waiting for the ring, waiting for the moment she had dreaded for almost three years. Waiting with fear in her heart, but at the same time waiting with a strange compassion for the woman on the other side of the door. Because out there stood a woman whose heart was perhaps as desperate as her own, a woman who yearned for the return of the child she had borne and given up.

She heard a faint rustling. She steeled herself for the doorbell. Yet all she heard was the rush of blood in her own ears. The moments stretched on. Jan closed her eyes. *Please, Lord, help me to accept your will. Help me truly to want your will, not do battle against it. Help me to do your will when I open the door…*

Yet the moments crawled on, and the doorbell didn't

ring. One part of her silently screamed with impatience. *Ring! Ring and get it over with!*

Yet deeper than the impatience came the submission that she knew the Lord was waiting for as the endless moments hung suspended in time. And finally she gave it. Not a plea this time, not a frantic pleading. Just a simple promise.

Not my will, Lord, but yours.

It was almost with a sense of peace that she finally stopped waiting, unclenched her fists, and opened the door to face the Lord's will.

23

JAN LEANED FORWARD TO GLANCE AROUND, PUZZLED. THE doorstep was empty. So was the sidewalk. The blue car was almost to the corner of the block. Jan stared after the taillights in bewilderment. Had Stardust changed her mind? Lost her courage? Conceived some other devious plan?

Then she saw the white envelope stuck in the mailbox by the door, and her heart plummeted. Summons? Legal notice? Sudden anger flooded her in a red storm. Hadn't Stardust even the courage, the decency, to face her in person? She was just leaving an impersonal notice demanding their child?

A wild impulse raced through her. She didn't have to read this! She'd simply tear it up and destroy it—

No, she thought with a wrench like a fist trying to pull her heart out. She couldn't do that. She'd given her word to the Lord. *Not my will, but yours.*

Yet she couldn't still the shaking of her hand as she plucked the envelope from the mailbox. She carried it inside and started to lock the door behind her, then dully realized it didn't matter now. The danger was not out there; it was right here, in her hand.

She took the envelope to the breakfast bar, where she always opened the morning mail. She retrieved a letter opener from a high shelf, safely out of reach of the children. She slashed the flap and drew the pages out of the envelope, surprised and then bewildered again. She did not find crisp legal paper with the impressive letterhead of some attorney-at-law, just several pages of blue-lined paper torn from a notebook and covered with fine writing.

Dear Jan and Mark,

I know Mark isn't home, but this is for him too, of course. I know you've seen me hanging around, and you know why I came: to reclaim my baby, to steal her if I had to.

Maybe you saw that I limp a little now. I totaled the Firebird a few months after Angel was born. I got hurt pretty bad, and for several months I just lay in a hospital, mad and unhappy. But deep down I knew what I'd done was pretty awful, so I figured the accident was probably God's punishment for rejecting and abandoning my own baby. But a doctor told me that by rights I shouldn't even have come out of the accident alive, so I started looking at things differently. And I finally figured out that maybe the accident wasn't so much God punishing me as trying to get my attention. That maybe he was giving me a second chance.

So after I got back on my feet, I got a job in a nursing home and also got my GED. I'm not making lots of money—and you know how I used to feel about money!—but I like my job. I like working with those old folks. They really seem to need me. Next year I'm going to try to get my certificate as a licensed practical nurse. So everything's going okay.

But still I've had this big empty feeling inside,

*a big hole in my life where Angel should have been.
I guess I must've watched that videotape about a
thousand times. And I look at it and wonder, how
could I have just thrown her away, this wonderful
little baby that was inside me? How could I have
abandoned her? It gets worse around the time of her
birthday every year, as you probably know. I
remember how awful you felt on Tim's birthday. It's
the very worst time of year, isn't it?*

*Anyway, I started thinking that even if I'd done
a terrible thing, Angel was still my blood and I
should have her back. So I took some time off from
work and went to Mark's house up in Portland, and
a neighbor gave me your Salem address. So I came
here thinking maybe I'd find something that would
convince a lawyer to take my case and help me get
her back. Or maybe I'd just steal her and run.*

*But all I could find was what good people you
and Mark are, what wonderful, devoted parents.
Deep down I knew that already. From the way you
always wanted Angel, even after you knew she
wouldn't be perfect and wasn't even yours. From
the way you took me in and treated me like a
daughter. And I'm so very grateful that you kept me
from making an even more terrible mistake than
giving her up. It makes me shudder now when I
think how close I came to having an abortion.*

*She's beautiful, isn't she? But even if she
weren't, I know you'd still love her. And I would too,
now. Being perfect isn't all that important.*

*I'll probably watch that ultrasound a thousand
more times and look at that photo I snapped today,*

too. And I'll cry. But by today, I wasn't really trying to snatch Angel. I just wanted to step inside the gate and get a picture of her without the fence in the way. So I'm sorry if I scared you. Or her.

And you never have to be afraid of me again, Jan. I won't ever try to take Angel away from you, not legally or any other way. I'm not a Christian yet. But sometimes I get out that Bible Mark gave me and read it, and I found the Psalms and I like them. And there's one I memorized because it seems like it was written straight to me and gives me hope. "The Lord is compassionate and gracious, slow to anger, abounding in love. He does not treat us as our sins deserve, or repay us according to our iniquities."

Well, I bet you never figured you'd see me quoting Bible verses, right? I guess I surprise myself, too.

Jan paused, lowering the pages. How very right Stardust was. Bible verses coming from her was as great a shock as the first time Jan had heard them from Mark. What was it he had once said about Stardust? That maybe the Lord wasn't through working on her yet? Obviously it was true. She read on.

And Psalm 23. That's really something! Have you ever read it? If you haven't, you ought to!

Jan paused again, this time almost smiling at Stardust's breathless reference to the Twenty-Third Psalm. That psalm, so familiar and beloved by every

Christian, yet wonderfully new to Stardust, as if she thought she was the very first person to discover it, like some prospector uncovering hidden gold no one had ever seen before.

> Then there's "Turn my heart toward your statutes and not toward selfish gain. Turn my eyes away from worthless things." Oh, that one is really aimed at me, isn't it? All the worthless things I wanted, instead of what God offered me.
>
> Well, like I said, I'm not a Christian yet. But there's a little church not far from my apartment, and maybe I'll go there one of these days. But I've already come to know, as you kept trying to tell me, that Angel truly was a special gift from God. But I know something else, too, now. That even though I gave birth to her, she was a gift to you, Jan, a gift to you and Mark, not to me.
>
> With all my love to you and Mark, and especially Angel.

The letter was signed simply *Debbie*. Jan let out the breath she hadn't even realized she'd been holding. So Stardust was no more. Jan nodded slowly. Yes, she could think of her as Debbie now. But there was a P.S.

> I know you'll probably think you should try to find me. Because that's the kind of good people you are. But don't. The first time I gave Angel to you I did it because I was selfish and self-centered. And dumb and wrong, and every other nasty word you want to think of. But this time I'm giving her to you

because it's right and because I love her.

Maybe someday, though I don't deserve it, God will give me another gift like Angel. I hope so.

Tears pricked Jan's eyes, and she leaned her head back against the chair. *Oh, I hope so, too. Oh yes, I do hope so.* Then she felt something else in the envelope, and she dumped out the contents. It was the gold chain Debbie had taken three years ago.

The phone rang, and it was Mark, telling her he had a flight arranged. She read the letter to him, having to pause every now and then when her throat choked up.

They were both silent after she finished the post-script. Then Mark said simply, "I think we should pray for Debbie." And they did.

They didn't hear from Debbie again, no phone call nor letter, no shadowy figure watching. Jan and Mark followed her wishes and didn't try to find her, but they both knew that if Angel someday wanted to contact the woman who had given birth to her they'd do everything in their power to help her. Debbie was never out of their prayers.

And when Angel's fourth birthday came around, Jan faced it without fear and apprehension. She knew Debbie was no doubt thinking of Angel, thinking of them as they were of her, but Jan knew the promise was good; she wouldn't be back.

They made a grand celebration of the event, holding the birthday party in the evening so they could include a barbecue for the parents. They had games and horns and party hats, a birthday cake with four candles that Angel blew out in a mighty gust, afterward shouting happily, "Now I'm four years old!" as if only then was it really true.

It was well after dark before the party wound down. When everyone was finally gone, Jan dropped into a chair and surveyed the scene. Piles of paper party plates drooling melted ice cream and cake crumbs. Empty and half empty soft-drink cans, some crushed because some male was feeling macho. Bowls of leftover salad and beans from the barbecue. Peaked party hats scattered like colorful eruptions rising out of floor and furniture.

"If after-party mess is any measure of success, this was one great party," Jan observed. She felt exhausted but satisfied. And it was all on videotape. If Mark hadn't gotten every giggle, every ooh of present opening, every messy bite of cake, it certainly wasn't for lack of trying.

"A great party," Mark agreed.

"Now I'm almost five!" Angel announced importantly, in that way children have of looking forward to the mounting years, eagerly anticipating the larger numbers. She put her party hat on again, snagging the elastic band under her little chin, and grinned at them, a pixie angel with a smear of chocolate on her face.

Jan and Mark exchanged glances, and Jan knew he must be thinking as she was: *oh, but the years mount up so fast!* Already, in her lumpy scrapbook, she had three sets of birthday candles saved from years gone by; now she'd have four. She jumped up quickly, feeling a blurry gathering of sentimental tears. "I think I'll just go sit out on the patio for a few minutes before I start cleaning up."

Mark reached out and squeezed her hand as she

passed him. "I'll be out to join you in a minute, as soon as I put the camcorder away."

Outside, Jan scooted out of her sandals and sat at the edge of the covered patio. She rested her elbows on her knees, chin cupped in her hands, and let her feet luxuriate in the damp coolness of evening grass. Off toward town the glow of lights bleached the stars to dim glimmers, but overhead they shone like far-flung jewels. So many stars. Big stars and little stars, and something less clearly defined drifting among them. Drifts of stardust...

Stardust.

She'd thought of Debbie, the "Stardust" who had given birth to Angel, many times this evening. Now that other Stardust also came to mind. Jan didn't think of her often. She had never been more than a dim figure briefly brought to life on the pages of Tim's journal, and, as time passed, even that misty reality had seemed to fade. Yet sometimes she did wonder about that girl with eyes of lupine blue.

Did that Stardust really exist? Had she ever existed? Had they an unknown grandchild? Jan's face was still lifted to the stars, but she closed her eyes.

Lord, I know you care about that Stardust and our grandchild if they're out there somewhere. We won't search for her again. You've showered your blessings on us, and those blessings are sufficient. But if they are out there, will you look after them, please? Keep them safe and loved.

And maybe someday, someday if it's within your grand scheme of things, you'll send them to us.

The screen door opened behind her, and Mark draped his arm around her shoulders as he dropped down beside her. "Do you know what your darling daughter is doing?"

Jan laughed. "I'm almost afraid to ask."

"Instead of playing with her presents, she's all engrossed in taking the boxes apart. Do you suppose that suggests some future occupation as an inventor or engineer?"

"Could be. Unless she decides to become a demolition expert," Jan said, and they laughed together.

With his free hand he tucked a loose strand of hair behind her ear. "Happy?"

"Happy." She leaned her head against his shoulder, wrapped in a warm cocoon of safety and love. "I remember you telling me once that it seemed a daily miracle to you that in the midst of all God had created, all those stars out there, all the wonders here on earth, that the Lord still loved and cared for each and every one of us. And it's true, isn't it? We were lost, to him and to each other, and yet he cared about us and changed everything."

"Sometimes I think how far we've come together over the years."

Yes. Oh, yes. From despair to joy, from a collapsed marriage to a love that was stronger and sweeter and richer than she could ever have imagined. She and Mark shared a closeness now that she had never realized possible in their youthful days of starry-eyed romance. They were companions and friends, mates and lovers. And parents, second-chance parents. The Lord had given them each other, and then he had given them Angel, too.

"Do you know how much I love you?" Mark nuzzled his lips against her ear.

Jan turned and draped her arms around his neck. "Shall we argue about who loves whom the most?"

"Let's!" With tease in his voice he added, "My love for you is bigger than mountains and oceans and—"

"Small stuff. My love for you is bigger than stars and galaxies and—"

He cut off her extravagant claims with a kiss, and then those stars and galaxies were spinning inside her head. Dreamily she wondered, how many times had he kissed her over the years? Yet he could still make her feel like this. Like a young girl falling in love, just awakening to passion. Like a passionate woman, bold and eager—

And just at that moment Angel whizzed through the screen door and tumbled between them in a small explosion of arms and legs and giggles.

"Guess I surprised you, huh!" she announced with satisfaction and a delighted giggle.

"Well, yes, I believe you did surprise us," Mark agreed with a meaningful smile at Jan over Angel's head.

"This was the bestest birthday ever." Angel gave a contented sigh as she squirmed to make a nest between them, rightfully confident of her welcome there. Then, like a small toy with a battery abruptly run down, she fell asleep right in their arms.

Lovingly, Jan straightened the warm body snuggled between them like a small pretzel. *And many more, little one.* She smoothed a wisp of dark hair, still baby-fine, around a tiny curve of ear. *Thank you, Lord. Thank you for Angel, thank you for us, thank you for all you are.*

"I guess it's time to take her up to bed," Jan whispered.

Mark nodded. "But first—"

And then he leaned across their sleeping daughter and finished that interrupted kiss, and once more the stars and galaxies whirled in a dizzy spin of love and promise.

Dear Reader:

This book was difficult to write because it touches on such emotional issues. Betrayal by a loved one, collapse of a marriage, loss of a child, the question of abortion. Have you had to face any of these problems in your life? They've touched the lives of people I care about, and their struggles often came to mind as I wrote about Jan and Mark's struggles in this book.

And, if you *have* confronted such problems, you know how they sometimes have a way of coming between us and God. "Why?" we demand in anguish. "Don't you care, Lord?"

Yet even in our darkest times, even when understanding escapes us, know that the Lord is there. He doesn't abandon us, and, even though he doesn't always change the circumstances that give us despair, he will help us cope with them, help us make the right decisions and see us through to the other side.

That is why writing Jan and Mark's story was also a joy to me, in that I could show how these two people faced their problems, and perhaps, in some way, it will also help you face the troubles and tragedies in your own life.

This book is special to me, and I hope it is to you, too.

2 Thessalonians 3:16.

Lorena McCourtney

Write to Lorena McCourtney
c/o Palisades
P.O. Box 1720
Sisters, OR 97759

CONNOR WAS HARD AT WORK LATER THAT DAY, SHOVELING OUT the stalls, when he had the sensation he was being watched.

He turned, half expecting Taylor's guardian angel to be there, and found himself looking at two boys who were exact replicas of one another, from their strawberry blond hair and bright blue eyes to the smattering of freckles dancing across their noses and cheeks. One of the two stepped forward, gazing up at him with large, solemn eyes. Connor guessed him to be about ten.

"Hi." Connor smiled.

The boy returned his smile. "Hi. Are you the crazy loon Dad says has come to work with Aunt Taylor?"

"He doesn't look crazy," the second boy said, and his twin shot him a disdainful look.

"Well, course not. You can't tell someone's crazy just by looking at them." He turned back to Connor, studying his face intently. "Least, I don't think you can."

"Did your father happen to mention exactly why he thought I was crazy?"

The boy nodded vigorously. "Uh-huh. He said anyone—"

"Any *man*," his twin corrected, stepping up beside his brother.

The more talkative twin glared at his brother. "Don't innerupt, Mikey. You know it's not p'lite."

Connor had to look away to hide his sudden grin. The boy's haughty expression and tone were perfect imitations of Donelle Camus, who Connor was willing to bet was this dynamo's grandmother.

"Anyway," the boy turned back to Connor, "Dad said any man who was willing to spend every day, day in and day out, being bossed around by Aunt Taylor had to be crazy as a loon."

"An' if he wasn't, he soon would be!" Mikey piped up.

Connor bent over and whispered conspiratorially, "If I tell you a secret, can you keep it?"

Two blond heads inclined toward him; two pairs of blue eyes widened in anticipation. "Sure!" they chorused.

He looked left, then right, then whispered, "It's not that bad."

They looked at him, searching his face to determine if he was being honest, then Mikey nodded, a grin breaking out over his face. "I told you so, Mark. I told you Aunt Taylor would be fun to work for."

"Well!" Connor laughed. "I don't know that I'd go *that* far!"

"So you want some help?" Mark inquired.

Connor raised an eyebrow and nodded toward the stalls. "You'd be willing to help with this?"

"Sure, we do it all the time." Mikey went and pulled a shovel from the wall hanger. Mark followed suit.

"Right. Dad keeps tellin' us it will help prepare us for what we have to face when we're adults."

Connor's lips twitched again, but the boy's words were so serious and sincere, he kept as straight a face as he could. "I'd say you've got a pretty smart dad." He joined the boys who were already tackling adjacent stalls.

By the end of the afternoon, Connor had two devoted followers. The twins trailed after him from job to job, always willing to lend a hand, always wanting to talk about their Aunt Taylor.

Connor enjoyed listening to them, not only because they were entertaining, but because he learned more about Taylor in that one afternoon than he had the entire two weeks he'd been at Galloway Glen. As they followed Connor to the ranch house in response to the supper bell, the twins finally ran out of revelations about their aunt, so they launched into an animated recounting of the wilderness trip they'd just taken with their father and grandfather.

Connor was still listening and laughing as they entered the kitchen.

"Okay, you two, give the man a break," said a tall cowboy seated at the table.

Connor grinned. "Let me guess, the Marlboro man, right?"

The man laughed. "Only if I want to receive a sound dressing down from my mother." He cast an affectionate glance at Donelle, who sat across the table from him, then stood and extended his hand to Connor for a firm handshake. "I'm Ryan Camus. And I take it you're our new ranch hand, come to take on all the work we don't want to do."

"Something like that."

Seated next to Donelle was an older version of Ryan. He, too, stood and offered his hand to Connor.

"Hey, Grandpa!" Mark chirped, going to perch on the kitchen counter. "This is Mr. Alexander. He's not crazy at all."

"Yeah, Dad." Mikey tossed his father a superior look. "He's as normal as you are."

"Poor man," Taylor's father muttered, then introduced himself. "Holden Camus, Mr. Alexander.

Welcome to Galloway Glen."

"Thanks." Connor shook his hand. "It's been a pleasure so far."

"Uh-huh, right." Ryan's grin was broad and knowing. "I can't think of anything more pleasurable than being bossed around by Taylor—"

"As though anyone would believe you could think," came the teasing retort from behind him, and Connor glanced up to see Taylor sauntering into the room. He stared at her, taking in the picture she made, and suddenly found he was having trouble breathing. She was surrounded by her family, and happiness glowed in her eyes, giving her a radiance that seemed to shimmer around her. Her high, exotic cheekbones were tinged with pink, and her easy laughter rippled through the air. Connor found his gaze drawn to her lips, which were relaxed and smiling. She was stunning. Gorgeous.

What I wouldn't give to have a woman look like that because of me. Especially one particular woman…with emerald eyes and auburn hair…

"Are you okay, Mr. Alexander? You look like you swallowed a bug."

A moment of silence followed this concerned proclamation from Mark, then the room exploded with laughter. Connor shook his head, smiling wryly, and his eyes met Taylor's.

Sparks flew between them—a surge of awareness—and the pink on her cheeks deepened to a dusty rose. She looked away and went to hug her father while Connor moved to take a chair as Donelle got up and began setting food on the table.

The meals with Taylor and her mother had always

been enjoyable, calm affairs. Not so this particular dinner. Things started out calmly enough, with everyone holding hands and Taylor's father offering the blessing, but the moment the "Amen" was over, everyone launched into animated discussion. It quickly became clear to Connor that every member of the Camus family was blessed with a quick wit and a clever tongue. Yet underlying the teasing and jesting was a warm, deep affection. These people truly loved and respected each other.

Connor found himself struggling with a lump in his throat. His childhood had been fairly typical: hardworking parents who spent whatever time they could with their only child. But what he saw around this dinner table was something remarkable, something rare. And he was grateful he was getting to share in it.

I wonder how welcome I'd be if they knew what I'm really up to? The thought struck him, dimming his enjoyment of the nonstop chatter around him. The food, which had tasted so good only a second before, now tasted like sawdust. He took a long drink of water, then set down his fork.

"Well," he said with forced cheerfulness, "time for this working boy to get some shut-eye."

They tried to coax him to stay longer, but he just smiled, shook his head, and made his way out the door.

I hate this, Father. He walked toward his cabin. *I hate deceiving such good people.*

"Connor?"

He paused, then turned. Taylor had followed him out. She walked up to him now, concern in her green eyes.

"Are you okay? You seemed…well, you just left so

suddenly." Her cheeks flushed slightly and she shifted uncomfortably. "I don't want to pry. I was just...uh, well..." She shook her head impatiently. "Oh, never mind."

Before she could spin and hurry away, he put out his hand and caught her arm gently. She stopped, and those beautiful eyes came to rest on his face again.

"Thanks." His heart was pounding a rapid beat in his chest. "I'm fine. I just need some time alone."

Her expression softened with understanding. "They can be a bit much, I suppose."

He shook his head in quick denial. "Not at all. I think your family is amazing. I haven't enjoyed a meal that much in ages."

Her smile was quick and alive with affection—and it warmed him from head to toe. "They are pretty wonderful, aren't they?"

"They really are..." He stood there, watching her. She had no idea what a captivating picture she made...how her eyes glowed...how her hair danced in the breeze. A sudden, intense longing seized him. He wanted to reach out, take hold of her, and pull her close. Instead, he settled for lifting one hand to smooth an errant wisp of hair from her face. "And so are you."

Her gaze flew to lock with his, and he saw a multitude of emotions reflected there: surprise, awareness, pleasure. She bit her lip, and for the life of him he couldn't keep his fingers from reaching out to gently, tenderly trace the line of her jaw, her mouth...

With the whisper of a sigh, she turned her face into his hand and, closing her eyes, rested her cheek against his palm. His breath caught in his throat, and, cupping her face, he urged her toward him. He leaned down to brush a gentle kiss across her lips. *Just one, Lord, just one small kiss...*

At least, that's what he'd intended. But it seemed so right when his mouth touched hers that he moved forward, slipping his arms around her, drawing her close, cradling her against him.

She fit in his arms perfectly. Like she was made for him. And the realization sent his emotions reeling. When he finally raised his head, he felt dazed, as though he'd been spun in circles and turned upside down. He looked down at her face. From the look in her eyes, she was in much the same condition as he. And he exulted that she didn't move, didn't step away; she merely looked up at him with a faraway smile—

A sharp pang of guilt pierced him. What was he *doing?* He didn't have the right to do this!

Self-loathing filled him, and he stepped back, dropping his arms. The look of startled confusion on Taylor's face only compounded the accusing voices hammering at him from within.

"I'm sorry, Taylor." He could hardly believe the hoarse voice was his. "I—"

What could he say? *I shouldn't have kissed you because you don't really know me? I don't deserve to have you care about me because I'm not who you think I am?* How about simple and to the point. *I'm a liar. I'm only here because of the wolves. I'm using you.*

He clenched his teeth, shaking his head helplessly, and took another step away from her.

"Good night," he croaked, then he turned and walked away into the darkness.

———— ⸙ ————

I am such a fool.

The thought kept going through Taylor's mind as she got ready for bed, her movements stiff, almost mechanical. She felt like a spring that had been wound too tightly—ready to come completely, totally undone.

Tears threatened, but she refused to cry. She'd given all the tears she intended to give when her husband died. No one else was going to get them. Her heart had closed itself off the day Josh died, and she had no intention of letting it open again. No one else was getting in, no matter how tantalizing he might be.

Liar, the voice in her head mocked. *Liar. He's already there.*

"No," she whispered, startled at the agony in her voice. "No!" She swallowed a lump of painful emotions. She dropped onto the bed. Pulling her knees to her chest and circling them with her arms, she buried her face.

You believed what his eyes were saying. You wanted to believe he cared.

"No." She saw again the look in Connor's eyes as he stepped away from her after kissing her…repulsion, disgust, rejection.

You trusted him. You let him in.

"No." The hot tears coursing down her cheeks made it all too clear that she'd lost the battle with humiliation and pain. Tomorrow would be different. Tomorrow she would remember her vow, and her heart would remain safely closed.

No one—not Connor Alexander with his tantalizing smile, not Duncan MacEwen with his assurances of friendship, not even Brad Momadey with his burning, haunted eyes....

No one was going to hurt her again.

"Wylie Marsten, you're a thief of the first order."

Wylie laughed and rang up the purchase. "Maybe so, MacEwen, but since I own this general store and I'm pretty much the only game in town, I guess that means I can make the rules. Now, hand over your wallet."

Duncan grinned and did as Wylie commanded. As the older man pulled the appropriate bills from the wallet, Duncan thought again of Taylor.

He'd called her to see if she wanted to come to town with him, but she'd told him she and Connor had already been to town. To say he'd been less than pleased would be an understatement. Connor Alexander was becoming a definite nuisance.

Duncan hoisted his bag of groceries and headed for the door, only to run headlong into two small torpedoes as they burst through the door.

"Oops!" Mark Camus exclaimed, stepping back to give the Scotsman a sheepish look. "Sorry, Duncan!"

"Yeah, sorry," Mikey echoed.

"No problem, lads. It's clear you were on a mission of great importance."

Two heads nodded vigorously. "We're buying supplies for Mr. Alexander!" Mark said.

Duncan's lips thinned. *Alexander again!* "Are you, now?" He did his best to keep his tone amiable.

"Yup!" Mark turned to glance at the aisle with hand tools. "And we gotta hurry, 'cuz if we get back soon enough he's gonna show us how to build a birdhouse."

"Is he, now?" Duncan's dry tone was lost on the boys. They just beamed up at him.

"Isn't Mr. Alexander the best, Duncan?" Mikey's adoration was evident in his young eyes.

"He sure is," Mark echoed, grabbing his twin's sleeve and tugging him toward the tool shelves. "C'mon, Mikey, I don't want to be late."

They drifted away, and Duncan walked out of the store, an oddly sour taste in his mouth.

"Aye, he's just a peach of a man, I'm sure." He muttered the comment through clenched teeth. "A true gem! Why, it should be an honor that the fine Connor Alexander is tryin' to steal my woman!" He pulled open the door of his Blazer with a fierce motion, tossed his package inside, then slammed the door.

He leaned against the Blazer, thinking. Just what exactly did he know about Connor Alexander? The longer he thought, the deeper his frown grew. Realization dawned, and with a firm nod he straightened.

He didn't know much. Not much at all. And that just wasn't acceptable. Duncan had learned long ago that the only way to deal effectively with an adversary was to know all you could about him. He turned and started down the sidewalk. It was time to pay a friendly, unofficial visit to his deputy friend, Amos Erdrich.

And maybe, just maybe, he'd ask Amos to do some friendly, unofficial checking on Mr. Connor—"the best"—Alexander.

THE SUMMER STORM LIT UP THE NIGHT SKY IN A JAGGED DISPLAY of energy, lightning bouncing, streaking, fragmenting between towering thunderheads. Sara Walsh ignored the storm as best she could, determined not to let it interrupt her train of thought. The desk lamp as well as the overhead light were on in her office as she tried to prevent any shadows from forming. What she was writing was disturbing enough.

The six-year-old boy had been found. Dead.

Writing longhand on a yellow legal pad of paper, she shaped the twenty-ninth chapter of her mystery novel. Despite the dark specificity of the scene, the flow of words never faltered.

The child had died within hours of his abduction. His family, the Oklahoma law enforcement community, even his kidnapper, did not realize it. Sara did not pull back from writing the scene even though she knew it would leave a bitter taste of defeat in the mind of the reader. The impact was necessary for the rest of the book.

She frowned, crossed out the last sentence, added a new detail, then went on with her description of the farmer who had found the boy.

Thunder cracked directly overhead. Sara flinched. Her office suite on the thirty-fourth floor put her close enough to the storm she could hear the air sizzle in the split second before the boom. She would like to be in the basement parking garage right now instead of her office.

She had been writing since eight that morning. A glance at the clock on her desk showed it was almost eight in the evening. The push to finish a story always took over as she reached the final chapters. This tenth book was no exception.

Twelve hours. No wonder her back muscles were stiff. She had taken a brief break for lunch while she reviewed the mail Judy had prioritized for her. The rest of her day had been spent working on the book. She arched her back and rubbed at the knot.

This was the most difficult chapter in the book to write. It was better to get it done in one long, sustained effort. Death always squeezed her heart.

Had her brother been in town, he would have insisted she wrap it up and come home. Her life was restricted enough as it was. He refused to let her spend all her time at the office. He would come lean against the doorjamb of her office and give her that *look* along with his predictable lecture telling her all she should be doing: Putter around the house, cook, mess with the roses, do something other than sit behind that desk.

Sara smiled. She did so enjoy taking advantage of Dave's occasional absences.

Dave's flight back to Chicago from the FBI academy at Quantico had been delayed due to the storm front. When he had called her from the airport, he had cautioned her he might not be home until eleven.

It wasn't a problem, she had assured him, everything was fine. Code words. Spoken every day. So much a part of their language now that she spoke them instinctively. "Everything is fine"—all clear; "I'm fine"—I've got company; "I'm doing fine"—I'm in danger. She had lived the dance a long time. The tight security around her life was necessary. It was overpowering, obnoxious, annoying...and comforting.

Sara turned in the black leather chair and looked at the display of lightning. The rain ran down the panes of thick glass. The skyline of downtown Chicago glimmered back at her through the rain.

With every book, another fact, another detail, another intense emotion, broke through from her own past. She could literally feel the dry dirt under her hand, feel the oppressive darkness. Reliving what had happened to her twenty-five years ago was terrifying. Necessary, but terrifying.

She sat lost in thought for several minutes, idly walking her pen through her fingers. Her adversary was out there somewhere, still alive, still hunting her. Had he made the association to Chicago yet? After all these years, she was still constantly moving, still working to stay one step ahead of the threat. Her family knew only too well his threat was real.

The man would kill her. Had long ago killed her sister. The threat didn't get more basic than that. She had to trust others and ultimately God for her security. There were days her faith wavered under the intense weight of simply enduring that stress. She was learning, slowly, by necessity, how to roll with events, to trust God's ultimate sovereignty.

The notepad beside her was filled with doodled sketches of faces. One of these days her mind was finally going to stop blocking the one image she longed to sketch. She knew she had seen the man. Whatever the cost, whatever the consequences of trying to remember, they were worth paying in order to try to bring justice for her and her sister.

Sara let out a frustrated sigh. She couldn't force the

image to appear no matter how much she longed to do so. She was the only one who still believed it was possible for her to remember it. The police, the FBI, the doctors, had given up hope years ago.

She fingered a worn photo of her sister Kim that sat by a white rose on her desk. She didn't care what the others thought. Until the killer was caught, she would never give up hope.

God was just. She held on to that knowledge and the hope that the day of justice would eventually arrive. Until it did, she carried a guilt inside that remained wrapped around her heart. In losing her twin she had literally lost part of herself.

Turning her attention back to her desk, she debated for a moment if she wanted to do any more work that night. She didn't.

When it had begun to rain, she had turned off her computer, not willing to risk possible damage from a building electrical surge should lightning hit a transformer or even the building itself; something that happened with some frequency during such severe storms.

As she put her folder away, the framed picture on the corner of her desk caught her attention; it evoked a smile. Her best friend was getting married. Sara was happy for her, but also envious. The need to break free of the security blanket rose and fell with time. She could feel the sense of rebellion rising again. Ellen had freedom and a life. She was getting married to a wonderful man. Sara longed to one day have that same choice. Without freedom, it wasn't possible, and that reality hurt. A dream was being sacrificed with every passing day.

As she stepped into the outer office, the room lights

automatically turned on. Sara reached back and turned off the interior office lights.

Her suite was in the east tower of the business complex. Rising forty-five stories, the two recently built towers added to the already impressive downtown skyline. Sara liked the modern building and the shopping available on the ground floor. She struggled with the elevator ride to the thirty-fourth floor each day, for she did not like closed-in spaces, but she considered the view worth the price.

The elevator that responded tonight came from two floors below. There were two connecting walkways between the east and west towers, one on the sixth floor and another in the lobby. She chose the sixth floor concourse tonight, walking through it to the west tower with a confident but fast pace.

She was alone in the wide corridor. Travis sometimes accompanied her, but she had waved off his company tonight and told him to go get dinner. If she needed him, she would page him.

The click of her heels echoed off the marble floor. There was parking under each tower, but if she parked under the tower where she worked, she would be forced to pull out onto a one-way street no matter which exit she took. It was a pattern someone could observe and predict. Changing her route and time of day across one of the two corridors was a better compromise. She could hopefully see the danger coming.

Adam Black dropped the pen he held onto the white legal pad of paper and got up to walk over to the window, watching the lightning storm flare around the building. He felt like that inside. Storming, churning.

He had lost more than his dad—he had lost his confidant, his best friend. Trying to cope with the grief by drowning himself in work was only adding to the turmoil.

The passage in Mark chapter 4 of the storm-tossed sea and Jesus asleep in the boat crossed his mind and drew a smile. What had Jesus said? "Why are you afraid? Have you still no faith?" Appropriate for tonight.

He rubbed the back of his neck. All of his current exclusive commercial contracts expired in three months time. A feeding frenzy was forming—which ones would he be willing to renew, which new ones would he consider, what kind of money would it cost for people to get exclusive use of his name and image?

The tentative dollar figures being passed by his brother-in-law Jordan were astronomical in size.

The stack of proposals had been winnowed down, but the remaining pile still threatened to slide onto the floor.

All he needed to do was make a decision.

He couldn't remember needing God's guidance more than he did now.

Five years of his life. The decisions he made would set his schedule for the next five years of his life.

Was it that he didn't want to make a decision or that he didn't want to be tied down?

Adam knew the root of the problem had little to do with the work and everything to do with the state of his life. Grief marred his focus, certainly. It was hard to define what he wanted to accomplish. But he was also restless. He had been doing basically the same thing for three years: keeping his image in the public eye and building his business. It had become routine. He hated routine.

His dad would have laughed and told him when the work stopped being fun, it was time to find a new line of work.

They'd had eight days together between the first heart attack and his death. Eight good days despite the pain—Adam sitting at his dad's hospital bedside and talking about everything under the sun. They had both known that time was short.

"I'll be walking in glory soon, son," his dad would quip as they ended each evening, never knowing if it would be the last visit. And Adam would squeeze his hand and reply, "When you get there, you can just save me a seat."

"I'll save two," his dad would reply with a twinkle in his eye that would make Adam laugh.

It was time to go home. Time to feed his dog, if not himself.

Sara decided to take the elevator down to the west tower parking garage rather than walk the six flights. She would have preferred the stairs, but she could grit her teeth for a few flights to save time. She pushed the button to go down and watched the four elevators to see which would respond first. The one to her left, coming down from the tenth floor.

When it stopped, she reached inside, pushed the garage-floor parking button, but did not step inside.

Tonight she would take the second elevator.

Sara shifted her raincoat over her arm and moved her briefcase to her other hand. The elevator stopped and the doors slid open.

A man was in the elevator.

She froze.

He was leaning against the back of the elevator, looking like he had put in a long day at work, a briefcase in one hand and a sports magazine in the other, his blue eyes gazing back at her. She saw a brief look of admiration in his eyes.

Get in and take a risk, step back and take a risk.

She knew him. Adam Black. His face was as familiar as any sports figure in the country, even if he'd been out of the game of football for three years. His commercial endorsements and charity work had continued without pause.

Adam Black worked in this building? This was a nightmare come true. She saw photographs of him constantly in magazines, local newspapers, and occasionally on television. The last thing she needed was to be near someone who attracted media attention.

She hesitated, then stepped in, her hand tightening her hold on the briefcase handle. A glance at the board of lights showed he had already selected the parking garage.

"Working late tonight?" His voice was low, a trace of a northeastern accent still present, his smile a pleasant one.

Her answer was a noncommittal nod.

The elevator began to silently descend.

She had spent too much time in European finishing

schools to slouch. Her posture was straight, her spine relaxed, even if she was nervous. She hated elevators. She should have taken the stairs.

"Quite a storm out there tonight."

The heels of her patent leather shoes sank into the jade carpet as she shifted her weight from one foot to the other. "Yes."

Three more floors to go.

There was a slight flicker to the lights and then the elevator jolted to a halt.

"What?" Sara felt adrenaline flicker in her system like the lights.

He pushed away from the back wall. "A lightning hit must have blown a circuit."

The next second, the elevator went black.

Ten seconds clicked by. Twenty. Sara's adrenaline put her heart rate at close to two hundred. Pitch black. Closed space.

Lord, no. It's dark. Get me out of this box!

"How long before they fix it?" She did her best to keep her words level and steady. She had spent years learning control, but this was beyond something she could control.

"It may take a few minutes, but they will find the circuit breaker and the elevator will be moving again."

Sounds amplified in the closed space as he moved. He set down his briefcase? She couldn't remember if there was a phone in the elevator panel or not. How could she have ridden in these elevators for three months and not looked for something so simple?

"No phone, and what I think is the emergency pull button seems to have no effect."

Sara tried to slow down her heart rate by breathing deeply. Her cellular phone would not work inside this elevator, nor her signaling beeper.

"You're very quiet," he said eventually.

"I want out of here," she replied slowly so as to hide the fact her teeth were trying to chatter.

"There's nothing to be afraid of."

She wanted to reply, "You've never been locked in a pitch-black root cellar and left to die before," but the memories and the panic were already overwhelming her. Her coping skills were scattering to the four winds right when she needed them most. She could do this. Somehow. She had no choice. Her hand clenched in the darkness, nails digging into her palm. It was only darkness. It wasn't dangerous.

"Consider it from my viewpoint. I'm stuck in the dark with a beautiful woman. There could be worse fates."

She barely heard him. *Lord, why tonight? Please, not this.* The darkness was so bad she could feel the nausea building.

"Sorry, I didn't mean any offense with that remark."

She couldn't have answered if she wanted to. One thought held her focus fast: surviving. The memory verse she had taken such delight in that morning had scattered. Psalm 23 was a tangle. The moment she needed clarity, her mind was determined to retreat into the past instead. A cold sweat froze her hands. Not here. Not with someone else present. To suffer through a flashback when her brother was around was difficult enough. To do it with a stranger would be horrible.

Adam Black didn't understand the silence. The lady had apparently frozen in one position. "Listen, maybe it would help if we got introduced. I'm Adam Black. And you are...?"

Silence. Then a quiet, "Sara."

"Hi, Sara." He reached out a hand wondering why she was so tense. No nervous laughter, no chatter, just frozen stiffness. "Listen, since it looks like this might actually take some time, why don't we try sitting down." His hand touched hers.

She jerked back and he flinched. Her hand was like ice. This lady was not tense, she was terrified.

He instantly reviewed what he had with him. Nothing of much use. His sports coat was in his car, his team jacket still upstairs in his office. What had she been wearing when she stepped into the elevator? An elegant blue-and-white dress, that had caught his attention immediately, but there had been more...a taupe-colored coat over her arm.

First get her warm, then get her calm.

"Sara, it will be okay. Sit down, let's get you warm." He touched her hand again, grasping it in his so he could turn her toward him. Cold. Stiff.

"I'm...afraid of the dark."

No kidding.

He had to peel her fingers away from her briefcase handle. "You're safe, Sara. The elevator is not going to fall or anything like that. The lights will come back on soon."

"I know."

He could feel her fighting the hysteria. The tremors coming through her hands were growing stronger. He didn't have to be able to see her to know she was heading for deep shock. "You're safe. I'm not going anywhere. And I'm no threat to you," he added, already wondering what would make a grown woman petrified of the dark. The possibilities that came to mind all made him feel sick.

"I know that, too."

He carefully guided her down to sit with her back leaning against the elevator wall. He spread her coat out over her and was thankful when she took over and did most of it herself, tucking it up around her shoulders, burying her hands into the soft warmth of the fabric.

"Better?"

"Much."

He couldn't prevent a smile. "Don't have much practice lying, do you?"

"It sounds better than admitting I'm about to throw up across your shoes." There was almost the sound of an answering smile in her reply.

He sat down carefully, close enough so he could reach her if necessary but far enough away so she hopefully wouldn't feel any more cornered than she already did.

"Try leaning your head back and taking a few deep breaths."

"How long has it been?" she asked a few moments later.

"Maybe four, five minutes."

"That's all?"

Adam desperately wished for matches, a lighter,

anything to break this blackness for her. "We'll pass the time talking about something and the time will go by in an instant, you'll see. What would you like to talk about first, do you have a preference?"

Silence.

"Sara. Come on, work with me here."

He was reaching out to shake her shoulder when she suddenly said through teeth that were obviously chattering, "Sports. Why did you retire?"

Adam didn't talk about the details of that decision with many people, but in the present circumstances, she could have asked him practically anything and he wouldn't have minded.

"Did you see the Super Bowl we won?"

"Of course. Half this town hated you for months afterward."

He didn't have to wonder if that was a smile.

"I liked the feeling of winning. But I was tired. Too tired to do it again. It wasn't just the physical exhaustion of those last games, but the emotional drain of carrying the expectations of so many people. So I decided it was time to let the next guy in line have a chance."

"You got tired."

"I got tired," he confirmed.

"I bet you were tired the season before when you lost the Super Bowl to the Vikings."

"I was."

"Your retirement had nothing to do with being tired." She sounded quite certain about it. Her voice was also growing more steady. "You won that Super Bowl ring to prove you were capable of winning it; then you retired because the challenge was gone. You didn't play another season because you would have been bored, not tired."

"You sound quite certain about that theory."

"Maybe because I know I'm right. You're like your father. 'Do It Once—Right—Then Move On.' Wasn't that the motto he lived his life by?"

Adam's shoulder muscles tensed. "Where did you hear that?"

"You had it inscribed on his tombstone," was the gentle reply. "Sorry, I didn't mean to touch a nerve."

Adam didn't answer. When and why had this lady been to the cemetery where his father was buried? It was outside of the city quite a distance and it was an old cemetery where most plots had been bought ahead for several generations. That inscription had not been added until almost a month after the burial.

She was a reporter. The realization settled like a rock in his gut. She had executed this meeting perfectly. Setting up this "chance" encounter, paying off a building maintenance worker to throw a switch for her, giving him every reason to believe he was going to be playing the hero, keeping her calm while the lights were out. He had been buying the entire scenario, hook, line, and sinker.

"I like the quote and the philosophy of life it contains."

"Sara, could we cut the facade? What do you want? You're a writer, aren't you?"

Silence met his anger.

"What kind of writer would you like me to admit to being?" The ice in her voice was unmistakable.

"Just signal for this elevator to start moving again

and I'll consider not throttling you."

"You think I caused this?"

"Not going to try denying you're a writer?"

"I don't have much practice lying," she replied tersely, echoing his earlier words.

"Great. Then I would say we are at an impasse, wouldn't you?" He waited for a response but didn't get one. "When you get tired of sitting in the dark, just signal your cohorts that we are done talking and we'll go our separate ways. Until then, I have nothing else to say to you."

"That's fine with me."

And with that, there was nothing between them but a long, cold silence.

♥ Palisades Pure Romance

Be sure not to miss these earlier releases!

Island Breeze, Lynn Bulock
ISBN 1-57673-398-X

Ex-cop Cody North has a full life as proprietor of Island Breeze condos and as father of a teenage boy. Bree Trehearn is on the run, needing to get as far away from rural Indiana as possible. It doesn't take long for Cody to wish that she had stayed in Indiana, but then Bree disappears. It takes all of Cody's police skills and his newfound faith to find her.

Summit, Karen Rispin
ISBN 1-57673-402-1

Julie Miller's a risk taker. She loves living on the edge, savoring the beauty and majesty—and the challenge—of God's creation. Nothing brings all of that together like rock climbing. Her career as a rock-climbing guide is ascending smoothly until David Hales, an internationally recognized rock climber, shows up and gets all her jobs. Which angers Julie almost as much as the fact she can't stop thinking about the man. Then Julie uncovers a sinister plot that puts both their lives in danger. Only by trusting each other—and God—will they survive the dangers that await them.

Hi Honey, I'm Home, Linda Windsor
ISBN 1-57673-556-7

Instead of finding her party guests at her front door, Kathryn Sinclair finds herself face-to-face with her supposedly deceased husband! An obsessive journalist who put his job before everything else, Nick Egan was reportedly killed in a terrorist attack over six years ago. But now he stands there, as impressive as ever, ready to take up where they left off. Well, Kathryn isn't interested! But Nick and their precocious boys have other ideas. They're determined to prove to Kate that God has truly changed Nick's heart—no matter what it takes.